Richard Oct-1998

CHILDREN AND
SOCIAL WELFARE
IN EUROPE

For
ZOMA

CHILDREN AND SOCIAL WELFARE IN EUROPE

Keith Pringle

Open University Press
Buckingham • *Philadelphia*

Open University Press
Celtic Court
22 Ballmoor
Buckingham
MK18 1XW

and
1900 Frost Road, Suite 101
Bristol, PA 19007, USA

First Published 1998

A catalogue record of this book is available from the British Library

ISBN   0 335 19701 9 (pb)   0 335 19702 7 (hb)

Library of Congress Cataloging-in-Publication Data
Pringle. Keith. 1952–
    Children and social welfare in Europe/Keith Pringle.
        p.   cm.
    Includes bibliographical references and index.
    ISBN 0–335–19702–7.—ISBN 0–335–19701–9 (pbk.)
    1. Child welfare—Europe.   2. Family policy—Europe.   3. Public
welfare—Europe.   4. Children—Europe—Social conditions.
5. Europe—Social policy.   I. Title.
HV749.P76   1998
362.7′094—dc21   97–31569
                                                                       CIP

Typeset by Graphicraft Typesetters Ltd, Hong Kong
Printed in Great Britain by Biddles Ltd,
Guildford and King's Lynn

CONTENTS

ACKNOWLEDGEMENTS

Partly because this book is wide-ranging in scope, I have drawn upon the assistance of many people: too many to name them all. So, first, I want to express general gratitude to those whom I do not mention specifically. I would like to thank my colleagues at the University of Sunderland for their patience, particularly my friend Shahida Ali for her constant support and for suggesting one of the main themes of the book.

The other person who set me thinking about some central issues in the relationship between the United Kingdom and the remainder of Europe was Sven-Axel Mansson at the University of Goteborg. I have benefited much from our strong research links with Sven-Axel, Margareta Back-Wicklund and Lars Plantin at Goteborg. One of the inspirations for the book was an ERASMUS network (including Goteborg) coordinated by Cherrie Stubbs at the University of Sunderland: her friendship and professional support have been invaluable. Several colleagues within the network have made a particularly direct contribution to my efforts here, including Margit Harder in Denmark and my friends and teaching colleagues Petra Gieseke and Elke Jonsson in Germany.

In Britain, several professional colleagues have offered much appreciated help in one form or another, including Robert Adams, Alistair Christie, Denis Hart, Jeff Hearn, Cathy Itzin, Liz Kelly and Trefor Lloyd. This volume has its distant origins in a third-level undergraduate module and I want to thank the series of student groups who have completed it for helping me to think through many issues with them over time. My friends have shown great patience and, in addition, Dave Martin supplied an invaluable and unlimited series of newspaper cuttings, many of which have found their way into the text. My most personal and deepest gratitude is owed to the following: my companions Daisy and Tigger; my parents; and finally Zom, to whom this book is dedicated with my love.

As ever, no one except myself bears any responsibility for what is written in the pages which follow.

1

EUROPE AND SOCIAL WELFARE

The social welfare of children which is the focus of this book clearly has to be viewed as part of the broader issue of welfare across Europe more generally. In recent years a considerable literature about that wider perspective has begun to develop and tease out the complexities of the subject. What, after all, do we mean by Europe? Which elements of social welfare require comparison across Europe – and how can this be done? Above all, perhaps, why should anyone bother to compare social welfare across Europe at all? In this chapter I want to examine these complexities and to draw out from them certain parameters and central themes which will frame the survey of children and social welfare across Europe that is provided in the chapters which follow.

From this preliminary review I will demonstrate that the situation of children in Europe may provide important evidence about the efficacy of welfare systems more generally. I will also suggest that a meaningful analysis of their welfare must focus on an understanding of the range of oppressions which unfortunately figure centrally in the lives of so many children and their carers.

WHAT IS EUROPE?

Europe or European Union?

'What is Europe?' may seem rather an obtuse and unecessary question with which to start. That it is not becomes clear when we look at some of the major texts which have already been written about social welfare and Europe. A central point to be noticed in reviewing such texts is how often their use of the term Europe means, in practice, the European Union. Often this happens with little or no explanation of why that limitation has been imposed (Hantrais and Letablier 1996; Ruxton 1996). In some cases a reasonable justification is at least provided (Munday and Ely 1996).

I am not arguing that such selectivity is necessarily invalid. However, where used, such geographical limitation ought to be explicitly acknowledged and carefully justified. Moreover, I think it needs to be stated plainly that 'Europe' does not always have to be constructed as the 'European Union'. In fact, we have to be careful not to fall into the trap of making the assumption that any country outside the Union is somehow not quite as fully European as member states. Above all, we must beware of inadvertently engaging in some kind of European Union imperialism. This issue is not merely of academic interest. After all, unspoken (and sometimes spoken) assumptions about the nature of being 'European' lie at the heart of those controversial policies within the European Union that are constructing the concept of 'Fortress Europe' (Rex 1992; Allen and Macey 1994; Lewis and Schnapper 1994; Mitchell and Russell 1994).

Beyond the European Union

That there is no inevitable reason why Europe should be equated with the Union is demonstrated by several other studies which cast their definition, either explicitly or implicitly, well beyond it: for instance, to Eastern Europe (Brown and Crompton 1994; Rootes and Davis 1994). In addition there are, of course, states of considerable economic and demographic importance within Western Europe which remain outside the Union, such as Norway and Switzerland. It may be significant that on the whole far less has been written about their welfare systems than those of Union member states. We need to acknowledge that the concept of 'Europe' is socially constructed and many constructions are possible. In that context, the next task for consideration in this study is to decide which limits we wish to place on our working definition of Europe. This is not a simple question.

For example, let us consider Eastern Europe: just what constitutes this entity? In some studies it seems to include all or some of the former Soviet Union (Cornia and Sipos 1991; Einhorn 1994; Ray 1994). Standing (1996) regards the Commonwealth of Independent States (CIS) of the former Soviet Union as constituting a major part of what he describes as Eastern Europe, with countries such as Hungary and the Czech Republic being defined as Central Europe. On the other hand, some texts clearly treat the former Soviet Union and its post-1991 successors separately from Eastern Europe (Rai *et al.* 1992; Benson and Clay 1992). Such uncertainty is understandable. On the one hand some parts of the former

Soviet Union seem to profess a strong affinity with 'Europe' and/or a desire to join the European Union (*The European*, 8–14 August 1996). On the other hand, what about the Russian Federation itself? Should it be considered as Europe? Given that it stretches as far as the Pacific Ocean and the Baring Sea, are there parts that one might consider 'Europe' and other areas which one would not? What criteria would one use to determine this, and who should exercise that determination?

Similar, though perhaps less striking, dilemmas exist in other directions. For instance, to the south and east, what about Turkey, which has close economic and political links with the European Union – as well as very concrete historical and territorial connections with Europe?

Towards a pragmatic definition of Europe

These points illustrate the fact that massive uncertainties about what constitutes Europe exist on grounds that are geographic, cultural, historical, political or some combination thereof. There can be no simple, commonly agreed formulation. In deciding the parameters of the concept we therefore have considerable latitude, and in this context it seems reasonable to take into account the demands of each particular study: for instance, its projected depth and breadth in intellectual as well as geographic terms. For the purposes of the present study, several factors have influenced the parameters which I will set on the concept of Europe. First of all, there seems no overriding reason why the topic of this book has to confine itself to the European Union. On the contrary, we shall see in due time that looking beyond the Union has considerable advantages for some of our central themes. Moreover, I am keen to avoid any suggestion that some countries are more European than others simply because of their membership of a formal power bloc. Consequently, I will look beyond the Union in this study.

On the other hand, the topic of children and social welfare is itself a very broad field and one which I intend to address in some analytic depth. For that reason, it is important that I should not spread my net too widely in geographic terms. These pragmatic considerations, together with my genuine uncertainty about which parts of the former Soviet Union can be considered as at present 'European' on geographic or cultural grounds, have caused me to exclude all of that area from this study. I have therefore decided to draw upon material from the countries of continental Europe extending as far east as (but not including) the former Soviet Union. For ease, I will refer to those countries of the former Eastern bloc which are included in this study as 'Eastern Europe'. The two offshore islands of Britain and Ireland are also included in this study on grounds which are political, social, economic, cultural and historical. By contrast, but on the same grounds, I have decided not to include Turkey. In making these judgements, I want to emphasize once again that in no way do I suggest my definition is absolute. It is pragmatic, though not, I hope, simply arbitrary.

The concept of Europe is only one complexity thrown up by recent writing on European social welfare. Various other complexities centre on the idea of comparing welfare systems across Europe. The further questions I want to address in this preliminary chapter include the following. What is the purpose in engaging in such a process of comparison? Assuming that there are valid purposes, what are the problems about making such comparisons? Which frameworks have previously been used, what are their limitations and what framework or underlying principles will inform this study?

WHY COMPARE EUROPEAN SOCIAL WELFARE SYSTEMS?

There are a range of possible answers to this question, some more problematic than others. First, I would like to emphasize one which is rarely mentioned perhaps because it does not seem sufficiently 'academic' or worthy: for many people it is simply fun to find out about other countries. Most comparative texts make the point that understanding the welfare systems of states entails gaining knowledge of their wider cultures, their histories and their economic, social and political trajectories. One is therefore necessarily engaged in emotional and intellectual voyages of discovery.

Second, there are pragmatic and concrete reasons for some people comparing welfare systems in Europe. For instance, given that the British professional social work qualification is not recognized within the European Union, it may well assist British social workers to obtain jobs there if they can show they have undergone training/education on the issue of European social welfare.

Third, from the point of view of appreciating the form and content of present and future European Union social policies (see Chapter 7), it is necessary to understand the welfare contexts not only of member countries (Munday and Ely 1996) but also beyond.

Our fourth reason for comparative study takes us into broader issues. Comparing our own welfare system with those of other countries may help us to identify and then question the assumptions about social welfare which underpin our own system: comparative study helps us to deconstruct welfare systems. From a parochial British point of view this may be particularly useful given that, as we shall see, in many respects the trajectory of welfare developments in the United Kingdom differs markedly from those in other European countries.

Our fifth and final reason in favour of comparative study opens up the greatest area of controversy. It can be suggested that such study promotes avenues for reconstructing welfare systems, not merely deconstructing them. In other words, by studying how social welfare systems operate in different countries we may be able to learn from one another and thereby make suggestions about how we can improve them. This is an attractive possibility. However, as we shall now see, for a variety of reasons it has only a limited degree of validity.

How far can welfare systems really learn from each other?

First, we need to recognize that the social issues which various welfare systems address are themselves partly social constructions – or at least the relative importance attached to social issues by different societies may be to some extent a social construction. For instance, when I teach social work students in different countries I regularly ask them to tell me what social workers there would regard as major social problems. The variation from country to country is striking. One of the most important issues regularly identified by students in both Sweden and Finland is alcohol abuse. By contrast, that issue rarely figures at the top of lists from students in the United Kingdom – and vice versa as regards the subject of child abuse. Yet it would be unwise to assume that those different national judgements simply reflect the relative prevalence rates for alcohol abuse and child abuse in the various countries (see Chapter 8). It seems likely that to some extent at least we are encountering here different social constructions of social problems.

So the idea that we can simply pluck a social policy from one country and transpose it to another is already undermined by a realization that different countries have different ways of defining social issues. It is further undermined when we recognize how difficult it is to agree criteria for what constitutes a 'good' social policy in a single country, let alone between different countries. For instance, controversy rages in British public and professional circles about conflicting approaches to the issue of abortion. That same topic also elicits violently different responses between the various member states of the European Union, both publicly and constitutionally (Hantrais and Letablier 1996: 33–5).

What all these difficulties highlight is that social issues, and the ways that different countries approach them, are deeply embedded in webs of culture, history, social structure, economics and politics which are always very specific to the particular country (Cooper *et al.* 1995). Moreover, the problems of transposing a social policy from one country to another are intensified when we recognize that within European countries there exist large regional variations in social conditions, attitudes and sometimes policies (Duncan 1995). The shaping of social policies and practices occurs at sub-national levels far more in many European countries, such as Spain (Ayala 1994; Cousins 1995) and Germany (Munday 1996b), than it does in Britain. This is even more true now, since there seems to have been a trend towards further decentralization of service provision during the early 1990s in several other states, such as Italy (Saraceno and Negri 1994; Ferrara 1996), Sweden (Ruxton 1996) and many of the East European countries like Hungary (Ferge 1993). In this context, the idea of simply moving an apparently effective social policy from one country to another becomes even less credible.

In putting forward these arguments, I am not suggesting that it is pointless for countries to try to learn from one another by comparative analysis. I hope to show in the chapters which follow that such a practice can be beneficial. However, it has always to be undertaken with care and with a full appreciation that social measures can never simply be divorced from the specific and complex contexts within which they have developed.

Common challenges to social welfare?

What makes the enterprise of learning by comparison particularly pressing and, to a degree, feasible is the fact that many countries in Western Europe have been encountering similar social and economic phenomena over the past two decades, which have placed considerable strains on the provision of social welfare. There are, of course, exceptions to trends and differences in the extent and timing of economic and social pressures between countries.

Generally speaking however, the countries of Western Europe have endured a lower degree of economic growth, even though the troughs have not always coincided (Cochrane and Clarke 1993). A more marked downward trend also occurred in many of the countries of Eastern Europe after the oil crises of 1973 and 1979. This was seriously compounded in the view of many commentators by the inability of their command economies to respond sufficiently to the need for increased complexity even before the massive social, political and economic dislocations following 1989 (Cornia 1991). Slowdowns in growth in the Western countries have had a double impact on social welfare issues:

more extensive social need in terms of unemployment, poverty and the less tangible costs to people's well-being which flow from them; at the same time reduced taxable income to finance welfare and smaller numbers of people contributing to social insurance-based schemes where these play a major part in the provision of welfare (Esping-Andersen 1996a).

West European countries have also been subject to demographic pressures, again to greater or lesser extents. These pressures take two forms: lower fertility rates in most countries (especially in Germany and the states of the Mediterranean) coupled with an ageing population profile. The impact on welfare provision of these trends is twofold. On the one hand, in terms of supply, a smaller ratio of earners to non-earners implies a reduced taxable base and a less favourable balance of contributors to social insurance schemes. On the demand side, an ageing population does to an extent imply increased social need, although it is important not to overstate the connection between age and need – it is the proportion of the population who are over 80 or 85 years old which is perhaps more significant in this regard (Cochrane and Clarke 1993; Walker and Guillemand 1993).

The demographic situation in the states of Eastern Europe has been, and is, somewhat different. Under state socialism the most significant features were a tendency towards high infant mortality rates and relatively low life expectancies, partly owing to gross environmental hazards (Sipos 1991; Einhorn 1994). Now, with the difficult economic and social transitions occurring since the late 1980s in some of these countries, increasing poverty is leading to later and lowered fertility rates (Einhorn 1994). The transition process has also resulted in a dramatic added deterioration in adult mortality rates, particularly among young and middle-aged men. Stress-related illnesses are now more prominent, perhaps reflecting greater social insecurity (Standing 1996: 250).

Social welfare provision within the member states of the European Union faces yet another common pressure of variable proportions in the form of economic demands deriving from the objective of monetary union by 1999. Greece, Italy, Portugal and Spain face a particularly considerable adjustment – the same countries which contain the bulk of the European Union's less favoured regions (Begg and Nectoux 1995). What those demands might imply for some nations of Eastern Europe seeking entry to the Union at the beginning of the new millennium can be barely imagined.

In the context of these relatively common pressures, the idea that West European countries might learn from one another's experiences at some level is not implausible. As for Eastern and Western Europe as a whole, Standing (1996: 226) notes that if 'there has been a convergence, it has been towards an era of social insecurity.' However, given the great difference in the social, economic and political circumstances between Western Europe and most of the countries of Eastern Europe, the potential for direct social policy transposition is highly doubtful in most cases. On the other hand, we shall see in Chapter 6 that some interesting parallels between East and West can still be drawn (Cornia and Sipos 1991; Corrin 1992; Aslanbeigu *et al.* 1994; Einhorn 1994; McLean and Kurczewski 1994a).

HOW TO COMPARE SOCIAL WELFARE SYSTEMS

Three worlds of social welfare?

When we have decided that it is worth comparing welfare systems in Europe, the next question is how to achieve this. In the 1980s, various commentators began to develop frameworks for the study of comparative social welfare, though not necessarily confined to Europe. In 1990, Gosta Esping-Andersen published his *The Three Worlds of Welfare Capitalism* (Esping-Andersen 1990), which has provided perhaps the most influential framework, indicated by the fact that many debates about comparing welfare systems have taken his work as their starting point. I will briefly summarize his framework with reference to Western Europe. I will then examine several different critiques of his approach which have central relevance to our study. From this analysis I then develop some of the underlying principles which frame the survey in the following chapters.

Esping-Andersen (1990, 1996b) posited three different ideal-types of welfare regime:

1 *Conservative corporatist.* The state (rather than the 'market') tends to be important, but not usually in a direct fashion. Financial welfare provision relies more on the principle of social insurance than purely on taxation. Provision, strongly embracing the principle of subsidiarity, often maintains (or even reinforces) existing class, gender and status differentiation though commitment to principles of social solidarity is also accorded considerable importance. Such welfare systems are said to flourish in countries where Catholic parties are historically strong and parties of the left relatively weak – and where there has been a history of absolutism and authoritarianism. Partly because of the influence of religion in such societies, they are frequently committed to traditional family forms, with the state intervening only where it is felt that the family cannot resolve its own problems (according to the principle of subsidiarity). Entry of married women into the labour market tends not to be encouraged. Esping-Andersen

identified Austria, France, Germany and Italy as having welfare systems closest to this ideal-type. In discussions of this form of system, Germany is often used as the prime example.

2　*Liberal or neo-liberal* (as in economic, rather than political, liberalism). These welfare systems are said to depend upon market-based social insurance approaches to financial provision, with relatively low state benefits for the residual poor using means tests. Universal benefits are not favoured. Benefits are also stigmatized because they are seen as disincentives to work. Private forms of welfare provision are encouraged to take people beyond the bare minimum. Social solidarity is not an important consideration: indeed, such regimes are said to tend to high stratification. Esping-Andersen regards this as an 'Anglo-Saxon' model, with the USA, the UK and New Zealand as the prime examples in recent years, and to a lesser extent Canada and Australia.

3　*Social democratic or Scandinavian.* The dominant principles in these systems are said to be universalism, social solidarity and equality across classes. Benefits tend to be largely provided by the state using high taxation levels. Rewards tend to be high for both the middle class and the working class. This model depends more than either of the others on full employment in order to limit income support and to provide funding for benefits (though note that high employment levels are also important for successful operation in the Conservative model). Generally, many 'family' responsibilities are fulfilled by the state, so that it is said that individuals have more labour freedom, particularly women. Esping-Andersen identifies Scandinavia as offering the closest real-world examples of this kind of welfare system.

As noted above, Esping-Andersen's framework has become the starting point for most of the debates which have developed since 1990 regarding the comparative study of welfare systems. Moreover, the plan of this present study is partly based on Esping-Andersen's framework, with several chapters being devoted to his welfare system categorizations. I believe this requires comment, since it is important that readers should not assume that I thereby accept those categorizations. In fact, I believe that Esping-Andersen's framework is open to a whole series of valid and serious criticisms which I summarize below. Moreover, as we survey the situation of children and social welfare across Europe in the chapters which follow, we will have an opportunity of examining those critiques in detail.

I have chosen Esping-Andersen's categorization of welfare system models as a chapter framework purely on pragmatic grounds and not because I agree with its analysis. His schema is the most convenient baseline point for this study simply because, as I noted above, so many of the debates about social policy in Europe (including child welfare) have started from his analysis. It will become clear to readers as they progress through each chapter that in fact my approach to child welfare in Europe embraces a degree of complexity which Esping-Andersen's categorizations largely fail to acknowledge.

Some critiques of Esping-Andersen focus on gaps in his framework, while others pose more fundamental questions about the very assumptions on which it is based. We will now briefly review these critiques.

A model for the Mediterranean and Ireland?

One obvious problem, as noted by Ferrera (1996: 18), is that 'the academic debate has so far largely neglected the study of the South European welfare state.' Leibfried (1993) attempted to fill the gap in Esping-Andersen's analysis by positing a fourth welfare regime, variously designated by commentators as the 'Rudimentary', 'Latin rim' or 'Catholic corporatist' model and embracing Greece, Spain, Portugal, Italy (either as a whole or only the south) and sometimes the Republic of Ireland. All these designations, it seems to me, carry either unfairly derogatory or overly particularistic connotations. Moreover, as we shall see, debates continue about how far a discrete category along these lines is appropriate (Ferrara 1996; Katrougalas 1996). The situation of children and social welfare in those countries (including the Irish Republic) will be fully surveyed in Chapter 4.

Eastern Europe

The South was not alone in being absent from Esping-Andersen's 1990 analysis. At that time, his original framework was understandably unable to encompass the 'new democracies' just developing in Eastern Europe. I have already indicated that this study will include the countries of Eastern Europe (Chapter 6). We should note at this preliminary stage that several commentators have, in different ways and to different extents, attempted to apply Esping-Andersen's categorizations to the present situation in East Europe (Deacon 1992, 1993; Ferge 1993; Gotting 1994). In Chapter 6 I review and critique such an enterprise in the context of children's welfare.

Welfare systems in motion

Having outlined the geographical gaps in Esping-Andersen's analysis and summarized the parameters of the major debates about the trajectory of welfare systems in both Southern and Eastern Europe, let us return to a consideration of the other critiques which have emerged about Esping-Andersen's analysis, critiques which our study of children and social welfare will seek to embrace.

One important critique of his framework is its static quality. In particular, Kangas (1994) has emphasized that it is vital to analyse welfare systems as dynamic phenomena, changing form and trajectory over time. By applying that perspective to the systems in Finland, Sweden, Germany and the United Kingdom, Kangas has demonstrated that important welfare trends can be uncovered. These have relevance to policies on children and families and I incorporate such a perspective throughout this study.

Welfare systems and middle-class allegiances

Esping-Andersen's framework also fails to consider fully the impact of fiscal measures in terms of welfare outcomes (for instance, tax breaks and housing subsidies), and this forms the basis of another critique. One result of taking these factors more fully into account in such countries as the United Kingdom (1948–79), Sweden and Germany is to highlight how beneficial their welfare systems have been for many middle-class sections of the population. This in turn may help to explain why (at least until recently) the systems there enjoyed such wide public acceptance for so many years (Cochrane and Clarke 1993). As we shall see in our study, this consideration has important implications for past and future welfare developments towards families, particularly those which are most vulnerable.

For my purposes, perhaps the most telling critiques of Esping-Andersen start from the realization that his framework is based on a narrow set of quantifiable welfare data such as social security and pensions expenditure (Cochrane and Clarke 1993). Two major problems arise from this narrow perspective and both are highly relevant to the shape of my study. I will outline them at some length here. One focuses on Esping-Andersen's overconcern with those specific quantitative measures and the other on his lack of emphasis regarding dimensions of disadvantage such as gender.

What is social welfare?

The first of these two problems centres on the range of material which a full comparative analysis of welfare systems demands. There are major areas of social welfare which are not readily quantifiable or where quantifiable data are hard to subject to comparative analysis. Yet they ought to be integral to any analysis: for instance, social service or social care provision.

Recently, several studies (e.g. Alber 1995; Anttonen and Sipila 1996) have explored the problems of devising and analysing comparative data in this specific field. They have demonstrated that such analysis is feasible provided one remains aware of the limitations of the material being analysed. A more extended analysis of comparative social welfare provision in the area of families and family policy within the European Union has recently been published (Hantrais and Letablier 1996). This study draws upon a wide range of statistical data relating to such issues as day-care provision, financial supports and parental leave arrangements. These data are utilized with full critical awareness of their inherent problems. These include: lack of synchronization between countries/ institutions; the impact of national cultures on variations in data collection; diversity in concepts and definitions since the latter are always rooted in particular cultural contexts (Hantrais and Letablier 1996: 4–15). Readers need to bear these same problems in mind when they consider the quantitative data I use in this present study. The major limitation of Hantrais and Letablier's important contribution is that for the most part it still confines itself to statistical sources – although it does also make frequent and effective use of European attitude surveys. By contrast, in this volume I want to combine qualitative and quantitative material.

In fact, several comparative texts have sought to escape beyond that quantitative limitation, particularly by surveying social work and social care services. Some of these exercises tend to take the form of rather descriptive accounts of provision in different countries with a relative lack of analytical material (Davies and Sale 1989; Colton and Hellinckx 1993; Birks 1995). However, the contributions in Hill (1991), as well as the work of Cannan *et al.* (1992) and Cannan (1992), demonstrated at a relatively early stage that a more critical and analytical approach could be successfully developed. In more recent years, several important texts surveying comparative social care/social services material have adopted an even stronger analytical approach to good effect (Lorenz 1994; Cooper *et al.* 1995; Harder and Pringle 1997; Hetherington *et al.* 1997).

It is my aim in this text to achieve an analysis encompassing a range of social welfare provisions using qualitative and quantitative material. The concept of 'social welfare' is of course rather an amorphous one, so it is important for me to define what I mean by it here. In a previous publication (Pringle 1995) I attempted to summarize what I meant by 'social welfare', and I will adopt that definition again in this study:

By social welfare I refer to those systems of service provision whose ostensible aim is to promote social wellbeing and alleviate social distress. In practice that means statutory and voluntary agencies in fields such as social services/social work, health, community work, youth work, education, housing, social security, employment. Some of these fields are, of course, more central to issues of social welfare than others and therefore warrant more attention. However, they all feature at some point in this study as do agencies in other fields that can impinge on the social welfare of human beings such as the law and the police.

(Pringle 1995: 1)

I add two qualifications to this definition. First, in surveying children and social welfare across Europe it is probably more appropriate to talk about 'statutory, non-profit and for-profit' agencies rather than 'statutory and voluntary' ones. Second, we need to recognize at this preliminary stage that many concepts used in the definition above are rooted in a British context. To some extent they will have different meanings in different countries and/or not have precise equivalences: social work itself, for instance. While this is significant and needs to be addressed, I agree with Munday (1996a: 5) when he says:

Our view is that it is unwise to become bogged down in a pedantic over-concern with terminological exactitude in this uncertain field. Predictably, different terms will be used by European countries to refer to more-or-less similar activities in the social sphere and this should be accepted.

I have outlined a critique of Esping-Andersen's framework centred on the rather narrow range of social welfare data which he chose to study. It is now time to address another major critique, which focuses on the failure of Esping-Andersen's analysis to consider a range of social oppressions that are central to both the formation of social problems and the functioning of welfare systems. The issues which his analysis almost totally ignores include oppressive power relations associated with sexism, racism, heterosexism, disablism and ageism. Yet these have a crucial impact on the lives of children and their carers across Europe. In fact it is a consideration of those forms of oppression, together with the development of an anti-oppressive practice framework for welfare work with children and their carers, which provides the basis of this book. So let us now briefly consider the main contours of this critique, starting with the absence of gender as a factor in Esping-Andersen's schema.

Esping-Andersen and gender

For several reasons, the shape and operation of welfare systems are centrally linked to issues of power and oppression. First, in any welfare system both the extent of social needs and the amount of resources

available to meet them will always be crucial and sensitive matters
heavily influenced by political considerations. Moreover, in the scenario
where limited resources are directed at more extensive social needs, the
means of resource allocation and the process by which different social
groups access those resources also become deeply political questions.
Finally, within the anti-oppressive perspective which underpins my analysis in this book, a central criterion for judging the effectiveness of
a welfare system is to consider how far it embraces the needs of people
who are marginalized and oppressed within society. Therefore, a major
criticism of Esping-Andersen's approach is that it focuses too exclusively on issues related to class and neglects other major determinants
of oppressive social relationships.

Let us consider Esping-Andersen's lack of focus on gender first. To a
large extent this lacuna is a direct result of the narrow data range he
adopted for his analysis and which we discussed earlier (Cochrane 1993a:
10). It is also a product of the central issue which he pursued in his
work, as Duncan (1995: 265) makes clear:

> Esping-Andersen's starting point was to ask how far different welfare states
> erode the commodity status of labour in a capitalist system (how far people
> are independent from selling their labour) and, as a consequence, how far
> welfare states intervene in the class system.

As Cochrane notes,

> this fails to acknowledge the extent to which women already operate in a
> 'decommodified' domestic sphere and the extent to which their involvement
> in that sphere is a necessary basis for the 'commodification' of labour.
>   (Cochrane 1993a: 10)

Dominelli (1991: 9) has underlined the massive equivalent financial
values of those welfare services which women provide gratis outside the
labour market. She argues that analyses which focus on the sphere of
public welfare to the exclusion of the private ignore the contribution the
domestic economy makes to sustaining and reproducing public welfare
relationships. Furthermore, women play an absolutely central role within
the formal welfare services of all European countries, not least those
with the highest labour market participation rates for women (Sainsbury
1994; Windebank 1996). In his original formulation, Esping-Andersen
(1990) did make passing reference to the issue of women's horizontal
(and vertical) job segregation in the labour market, but it was surely
worthy of more note. It is interesting that in his later work Esping-
Andersen (1996b) does pay more attention to the topic – but it still
remains secondary to his major concern.

Various feminist and pro-feminist commentators have sought to address more effectively the issue of gender in terms of a comparative

analysis (Langan and Ostner 1991; Ginsburg 1992; Lewis 1993; Cochrane and Clark 1993; Sainsbury 1994; Windebank 1996), and many of these are well reviewed by Duncan (1995). As he notes, in several cases these attempts may represent simply an 'adding on' of issues of gender to a framework which in effect retains the central dynamic of Esping-Andersen's original categorizations. The danger, then, is that the 'explanatory dynamic remains gender blind however much gender description is added on' (Duncan 1995: 267). Moreover, the welfare regime categorizations which result from these essentially 'add-on' models seem unable to deal with the real complexities which gender throws up (Duncan 1995: 267). For instance, Leira's (1994) analysis of welfare systems and working mothers in Nordic countries has demonstrated that on some key childcare issues there is no fully coherent social democratic/Scandinavian model (Leira 1994: 96; Duncan 1995). Similarly, Anttonen and Sipila (1996) have reconfirmed a deconstruction of the conservative corporatist model as it applies (or rather fails to apply) to some forms of childcare provision.

Duncan (1995) attempts to place gender centrally and to capture the complexity by which gendered relationships are generated, partly by refocusing his analysis on sub-national processes. In a similar vein, Hantrais and Letablier's (1996) work on family policies across the European Union seeks to go beyond oversimplified categorization, while retaining a strong comparative analysis. In effect, they suggest overlapping but different categorizations of member states for different themes of family policy. Moreover, where they do make use of categorization, Hantrais and Letablier (1996: 180) always stress that overlaps between categories and complexities disrupt any spurious neatnesses of pattern.

We should also note at this point (see also Chapter 6) that a gendered analysis has central relevance to those systems of welfare developing in Eastern Europe, as is demonstrated in the work of Cornia and Sipos (1991), Rai *et al.* (1992), Ferge (1993), Aslanbeigu *et al.* (1994), Einhorn (1994), McLean and Kurczewski (1994a) and Makkai (1994).

Issues of gender are vital to any survey of child welfare such as this study provides. That in itself would be reason enough for these debates to have prime relevance to us. They are even more germane because, as I have made clear at length elsewhere (Pringle 1995: 39–77, 169–203), I regard feminist and pro-feminist perspectives to be central in any meaningful analysis of childcare policy and practice. And those perspectives will remain central to the comparative analysis offered in the chapters which follow. Moreover, I shall attempt to utilize these perspectives in ways which do justice to the complexity of lived experience, as indicated in the recent work of Duncan (1995) and of Hantrais and Letablier (1996).

Esping-Andersen and racism

Gender is not the only major dimension of power and oppressive social relationships which Esping-Andersen's framework tends to ignore. In particular, several commentators (Dominelli 1991; Ginsburg 1992; Cochrane and Clark 1993) have drawn attention to the neglected issue of 'race' and cultural diversity in comparative analyses of welfare systems. In the chapters that follow, I will seek to demonstrate, via the specific topic of children and their carers, that there are several reasons why the subjects of culural diversity, 'race' and racism must be central to any survey of welfare systems. As I have suggested, one crucial barometer of the effectiveness of a welfare system is the extent to which it addresses the needs of marginalized sections of the population – and the manner by which it does this. As one scans Europe, it is striking how consistently ethnic minority groups are marginalized in virtually all national states. Of course, there is massive variation across a number of dimensions between countries and, indeed, within them. Which ethnic minorities are marginalized? To what extent are different ethnic minorities marginalized? How is that marginalization manifested? Nevertheless, the serious marginalization of certain sections of a country's population who are socially defined as significantly different on the grounds of culture, nationality or the colour of their skin seems to be universal across Europe (Dominelli 1991; Ginsburg 1992; Rex 1992; Lewis and Schnapper 1994). And this applies to the 'new democracies' of Eastern Europe as much as anywhere else (Cornia and Sipos 1991; Ferge 1993; Einhorn 1994). How far do welfare systems seek to ameliorate these processes of marginalization and in what ways? Or do they sometimes replicate and even intensify the politics of marginalization?

Such concerns are brought into particular focus by several factors. One is the pressure on welfare systems across Europe which we have reviewed earlier: as these pressures mount, how do people marginalized on the grounds of culture and 'race' fare? Another is the massive political and economic dislocations occurring in Eastern Europe and other parts of the world, which have an impact on immigration issues in Western Europe. A third factor is the process by which the growing momentum towards a 'united Europe' will deal with the issue of citizenship and identity. These questions about social policy and marginalization apply not simply to national governments but also to the European Union (Chapter 7). It is clear that the legislative mechanisms developed by the Union over time have paid far less concrete attention to issues of 'race' than to gender (Cannan *et al.* 1992; Lorenz 1994: Chapter 7). The European Union White Paper on social policy (European Commission 1994) indicates that this trend *may* be changing. However, member states are implementing increasingly restrictive immigration and asylum policies which justify the view that a 'Fortress Europe' is indeed being constructed (Allen and Macey 1994; Mitchell and Russell 1994). This impression is enhanced by the fact that most of the Union mechanisms which address the issue of migration (for instance, the Schengen Implementation Agreement and TREVI group) place that issue within a negative, and indeed criminal, context.

As we shall see in each of Chapters 2 to 7, a survey of the specific situation of children and their carers across Europe highlights all the general issues which I have raised here about racism and cultural diversity.

Developing a broad anti-oppressive framework in analysing social welfare in Europe

From what I have said so far, there is a danger that readers may believe I am placing oppressive power relations associated with gender and 'race' in separate categories. I want to make clear that this is far from the case. Adopting a transeuropean perspective, Allen and Macey (1994: 124–5) convincingly argue that, in the context of lived experience, oppressive power relations associated with gender and 'race' (along with ethnicity, nationalism and religion) often interreact with one another in complex and sometimes contradictory ways. As they acknowledge, their approach reflects much wider debates in the social sciences not only about the relationship between different forms of oppression but also about modernity and postmodernity in the field of social enquiry (Giddens 1990; Game 1991; Marshall 1994; Assiter 1996; Penna and O'Brien 1996). In many ways the position I take in this study is close to that of Allen and Macey: a recognition of the complex interrelationships between different forms of social disadvantage, retaining the central requirement of addressing the materiality and structural aspects of oppression which a purely postmodern/poststructural perspective might dismiss.

This approach to oppressive power relations which underpins my whole analysis draws on two other sources. The first is an anti-oppressive practice (AOP) perspective which has become influential within the British social work profession (Ahmad 1990; Thompson 1993; Dalrymple and Burke 1995). The second, which is highly consistent with the first, is the model of gendered power relations developed by Bob Connell (1987, 1995). One significant point made by Connell is that a meaningful analysis of gender relations is only possible if their complex interaction with issues of 'race', sexuality, age, disability and class is recognized. In such a view, the privileging of one form of oppressive power relations over another in analysing any given social situation becomes pointless:

the overall and shifting form of those relations of power must be the focus of attention.

The particular need to go beyond gender issues when engaged in comparative social policy analyses has recently been underscored by Jean Carabine (1996). She emphasizes the absence of sexuality as an issue in many social policy debates, including those conducted by feminist scholars. Carabine (1996: 47) offers a specific critique of the analyses presented in Sainsbury (1994), based on their relative silence about not only sexuality but also issues of disability and 'race'. Clearly we need to bear this perspective in mind and, as far as the data available allows, I will attempt to address a range of oppressions in the chapters which follow.

Elsewhere I have successfully adopted such a multidimensional anti-oppressive perspective in analysing a particular aspect of the British welfare system (Pringle 1995). I shall use that perspective again throughout this study. One of my contentions is that an understanding of welfare responses to children and their carers across Europe can only be gained when the complexity of oppressive power relations which impact so massively on their lives is fully appreciated. Moreover, the same oppressive relations of power tend to structure welfare systems themselves, thereby not merely limiting their effectiveness in challenging social disadvantage but actually creating situations where they may reinforce it. Consequently, my central concern in this book is to address forms of social oppression and their complex interactions as they impact on children and their carers.

CHILDREN, ANTI-OPPRESSIVE PRACTICE AND SOCIAL WELFARE IN EUROPE

This brings me to perhaps the most important contention of the study, and the one with which I will end this chapter. I noted above that one major form of social oppression is ageism, including ageism directed towards children (Qvortrup *et al.* 1994). If, as I have already suggested, one of the most important barometers for judging the effectiveness of social welfare systems is the way they approach those sections of the population subject to marginalization and oppression, then the experience of children across Europe has to be a vital consideration. I will seek to demonstrate that for all too many children in Europe (as in the rest of the world), extensive and severe oppression is integral to their lives.

Oppression occurs in many social locations. It is probably true that for the vast majority of children the most important location is the family. I therefore do focus to a considerable extent on the family context in this study. However, it is clear that children have lives outside the family, in terms of both positive and negative experiences, and it is vital not to make an analysis of child welfare purely familial (Qvortrup 1994).

STRUCTURE OF THE STUDY

The structure of the book clearly reflects the issues which have been raised in this chapter. The following six chapters analyse child welfare across Europe and the extent to which it is also addressed by pan-European institutions. In Chapter 8 I demonstrate how to apply the analysis I have developed to specific childcare issues using one major social problem as a case study. The problem I have chosen for that case study is child sexual abuse. There are two particular reasons for my choice.

First, child sexual abuse is an issue that demonstrates particularly clearly the way in which oppressive power relations generate social problems. Second, an exploration of various welfare approaches to child sexual abuse across Europe will then further open up another central theme in my analysis. This theme is the somewhat inverse relationship which seems to exist across different countries between development of anti-oppressive welfare models on the one hand and levels of commitment to principles of social solidarity on the other.

In the final chapter I develop that major theme further. I also draw together the overall analysis built up in previous chapters to provide a discussion of the critical issues surrounding the forms of oppression which have a bearing on children and their carers in Europe. How can welfare systems effectively challenge those forms of oppression? How can they surmount the massive barriers standing in the way of such a challenge?

2

NEO-LIBERALISM AND CHILD WELFARE: THE UNITED KINGDOM?

In Esping-Andersen's recent work (1996a), he notes that over the past decade and a half the United Kingdom has moved towards being the only welfare system in the European Union which approximates to the neo-liberal type. In Chapter 1 we noted that the hallmarks of this type include provision of residual and often stigmatizing social protection, allegedly avoiding labour disincentives which are said to limit the creation of cheap labour and an efficient economic market. Even the means of social protection in this type of welfare system are said to be largely based on privatized market principles.

In this chapter I want to see how far that stereotype holds true for a broad range of child welfare support structures in the United Kingdom. In the process we will explore how far those structures challenge the many different forms of disadvantage which children face in Britain at the end of this millennium. The welfare structures that I will particularly focus on are: first, the supports available to children and their carers in terms of money, day-care provision and parental leave arrangements; second, the impact of social care services, particularly the personal social services, on the lives of children.

Many of the British welfare structures which I review in this chapter were to a considerable extent instituted by the Conservative government which held power from 1979 until 1997. That government, deeply influenced throughout by Thatcherism, was generally recognized as being largely neo-liberal in its philosophy and policies. This needs to be borne in mind as we review the shape of child welfare provision in the United Kingdom, which is highly distinctive in European terms. A Labour administration is now in power: it is too early to say how far it will want, or be able, to alter that distinctive shape.

FINANCIAL SUPPORT STRUCTURES

As Schweie (1994: 211) notes, child dependency allowances within contributory schemes now play a relatively minor part in family support, since they adhere mainly to long-term benefits such as Invalidity Benefit. Insofar as they do play a part they go mainly to fathers. In this context, as well as in the historical perspective of contributory benefits to which they are attached, they represent a portion of British social policy devoted to bolstering fatherhood rather than parenting.

Universal child allowances (child benefit) have experienced long-term erosion in economic value and currently are not indexed. Social assistance in the form of the so-called non-contributory Jobseekers Allowance, like its predecessor Income Support, is means tested and has certain features particularly relevant to child support. For instance, child allowances or other private incomes such as maintenance payments are taken into account, which reinforces the considerable tendency within the benefits system to create poverty traps, a tendency enhanced by rapid tapering against earnings (Schweie 1994: 212–13). This is especially problematic for the most economically disadvantaged lone mothers, who would often tend to enter the labour market at low levels of pay. As for married or cohabiting couples, Schweie noted that the poverty trap tendency was increased where families had to consider employment plus Family Credit or Income Support plus extra entitlements such as school meals and housing costs (Schweie 1994: 212).

Nevertheless, Hantrais and Letablier (1996: 155–6) report Eurostat data from 1994 which indicate that when expenditure on families/maternity is taken in the round as a percentage of total social protection spending, the United Kingdom comes out quite highly on a league table of Union countries. This is particularly significant, since Britain's overall social protection spending, expressed as a percentage of gross domestic product (GDP) is also quite high (Begg and Nectoux 1995: 289). Moreover, Hantrais and Letablier quote a recent French study demonstrating that in the early 1990s the United Kingdom was one of the most generous Union members (even ahead of France) in terms of average spending per child under the age of fifteen, derived from child, maternity and housing benefits (Hantrais and Letablier 1996: 169). This is also largely borne out by the data brought together by Ruxton based on 1996 data from the European Observatory on National Family Policies (Ruxton 1996: 102–12), though of course the situation varies considerably in detail, depending upon factors such as family income and number of dependent children.

This relatively positive picture partly reflects the emphasis in recent British family benefits policy on targeting of resources, thus producing a vertical redistribution effect to the benefit of the poorest families. It also reflects the fact that, along with Germany and Greece, the United Kingdom seems to have had a relatively advantageous policy on housing costs and subsidies for unemployed families (Hantrais and Letablier 1996: 162).

On the other hand, this apparently positive picture has to be seriously reassessed for several reasons. First, the structure of the benefits system has some far from liberating characteristics, not least the ease with which it holds poor families in poverty traps, as we saw above. Moreover, due to the nature of the labour market and other factors such as childcare provision (see below), poor mothers are especially vulnerable to this problem, in particular lone mothers. In saying this we need constantly to remember that in Britain issues of 'race' and racism always tend to compound disadvantage, albeit in complex ways. Cochrane (1993a) correctly points out that the econonic vulnerability of mothers in poverty will also be subject to the multiple and multiplying effects of racism on life opportunities if those women are black.

Nor are lone mothers generally assisted by another element within the financial supports structure, Child Support. In terms of financial help, Schweie (1994: 213) correctly emphasizes that:

> it is designed not to *augment* lone mothers' and children's income resources, but to *substitute* [sic] public transfers by private transfers . . . Only mothers who are economically better off may gain something from it.

However, it is not only the financial inadequacy of Child Support which militates against the welfare of many women and children. Both Laws (1994) and Millar (1994) point out that this system may reintroduce former partners into the lives of women and children where such a reintroduction is not welcomed by them. What is worse, in some cases that resistance to contact with former male partners may well be based on a history of violence of various sorts to the women, to the children or, indeed, to both (Mullender and Morley 1994). It is true that from 1995/6 certain reforms of the Child Support system adopted by the government (largely as a result of an outcry from fathers) may have ameliorated some problems in that system (Ruxton 1996: 120). However, on the whole these reforms seem directed, not surprisingly, at the interests of fathers and their 'new' families rather than mothers and their children.

We also need to qualify heavily the picture of relative financial generosity painted above in relation to British welfare supports, by placing those supports in a wider financial context. The United Kingdom may have been in the forefront of a trend in the Union towards the targeting of benefits (itself, of course, a neo-liberal feature) with vertical redistributive effects, but we need to consider whether the motivation for that drive has been social justice or a desire to limit welfare spending. The fact that less savage targeting might easily have ameliorated such problems as poverty traps and that means-tested benefits in Britain have an alarmingly low take-up rate (Ruxton 1996) suggests that social justice has not been the primary aim. Moreover, the take-up rate problems clearly point to a stigmatization of benefits which reminds us of the neo-liberal stereotype.

As Novak (1997) has pointed out, the relatively new contributory and non-contributory Jobseekers Allowances take this punitive neo-liberal approach one stage further. Moreover, he places them in a clear context:

> The Jobseekers Act of course does not stand alone. It is part of the rapidly increasing shift of state policy, evidenced in practically every area of the so-called welfare state, and running alongside unprecedented increases in poverty and inequality, to treat the poor with contempt.
>
> (Novak 1997: 109)

Nor did Novak (1997: 108), writing before the election victory of the Labour Party in May 1997, see much prospect of any future Labour government engaging in a 'substantial redirection of policy'.

Insofar as British financial family supports do have a vertical redistributive effect, it is nevertheless offset in various ways. A recent German study indicates that Britain's positive relative position is counteracted when tax relief for children and partners is included in the calculations, especially where families have two or more children (Hantrais and Letablier 1996: 156). Moreover, in surveying the available data, Hantrais and Letablier (1996: 170) conclude that when cash benefits are combined with services in kind, it is France, Luxembourg, Belgium, Sweden and Denmark which have the most generous child support packages. A further large deficit within the British system, compared to other Union member states, is the issue of school and day-care costs for young children, as based on recent European Observatory data (Ruxton 1996: 112–13). As we will see, it is not only the cost but also the availability (or lack) of childcare in Britain which presents a threat to the welfare of many children, particularly in the poorest families.

DAY-CARE PROVISION

The data on this subject across Europe are not as concrete as they sometimes appear to be in summaries. For a start, the vast majority of data available are limited to the European Union. To a large extent this reflects the fact that one of the most active European bodies coordinating data and developing policy in this field has been the European Commission Network on Childcare and other Measures to Reconcile Employment and Family Responsibilities (henceforth referred to in this study as the Childcare Network for the sake of convenience).

However, even within the Union comparative data present considerable problems of use and interpretation, as the recent review of services by the Childcare Network makes clear (European Commission 1996a: 127–8). These problems relate to such issues as lack of uniformity in data collection methods, difficulties in assessing actual degree of service volume, quality measurement and interaction of service provision with other forms of provision, such as financial subsidies or parental leave.

Having stated these provisos about the data, most commentators (including the Childcare Network themselves) are more or less united in their judgement about the state of day-care provision in the United Kingdom. The Network's own review concludes that:

> overall, publicly-funded services are most developed in Denmark and Sweden, followed by France; while, overall, publicly-funded services are least developed in Ireland, Greece, and the UK.
>
> (European Commission 1996a: 129)

Similarly Schweie (1994: 211) comments that British childcare 'facilities are inadequate, piecemeal, and scarcer than in other EU countries'. Let us now tease out some detail from these trends.

First, the United Kingdom's poor showing in terms of public day-care applies to both under-three provision and that for 3 to 6-year-olds, though it is particularly striking in the case of the former (Ruxton 1996: 156). Moreover, this state of affairs represented a deliberate policy strategy on the part of the Conservative government which was in power from 1979 until 1997 (European Commission 1996a: 130).

Much public provision is targeted on families and children assessed by social services and health as being 'in need'. As we will see later in the chapter, that process closely parallels a major theme in child protection policy of identifying allegedly 'dangerous families'. Indeed, as Cannan (1992) eloquently demonstrates, much public day-care provision has a direct regulatory function in relation to families identified as being 'dangerous'. Moreover, in comparing French and British provision, she rightly regards day-care policy as reflecting not only divisive government social policies in the United Kingdom but also more general British attitudes to the family, which are characterized by a passion for privacy and a need to pathologize and punish alleged deviants from the ideal norm. So, in Britain,

> what public daycare remains takes the most deprived and disturbed children. By contrast, professional and middle-class parents may pay for their children to attend private nurseries. There is thus a widening class and ethnic differential between the two types of provision.
>
> (Cannan 1992: 158)

Cannan goes on to demonstrate that other forms of childcare provision in Britain (such as extended family care, childminders and playgroups) are of variable quality: 'the consequence for children is that the public care system, and its relations in the private, informal and voluntary sectors, is highly variable in quality, and unstable' (Cannan 1992: 158–9).

The Conservative government sought to encourage major improvements in day-care provision by looking to employers to provide facilities either directly or via private subsidy for their employees. However, as the Childcare Network review has recently noted, employers on the whole seem reluctant to play a central role (European Commission 1996a: 120). Nor did the national voucher scheme to buy nursery places for 4-year-olds, put forward by the Conservative government towards the end of its eighteen-year-long reign, seem to offer much prospect of relief in practice (European Commission 1996a: 119; Ruxton 1996: 153). The Labour administration elected in 1997 has now rescinded the voucher scheme. Currently the overall picture for the United Kingdom remains as Windebank described it:

> in Britain, more than anywhere else, the majority of out-of-home care is undertaken on an unpaid basis by relatives, and overall, outside-home care is a minority concern, since the vast majority of childcare is managed within the couple, usually by women modifying their work schedules ... in Britain, childcare is a personal rather than a state concern.
>
> (Windebank 1996: 155–6)

This comment is important for two reasons. First, it highlights that the picture of day-care provision which I have outlined is highly consistent with what one might expect from a neo-liberal welfare system: reliance on private and privatized forms of provision; residual, stigmatized public services. Anttonen and Sipila (1996) drew heavily on child day-care service data in their attempt to identify European welfare models relating to social care. They tentatively suggest a 'British means-tested model' which seems to parallel Esping-Andersen's neo-liberal one very closely.

The second reason for the importance of Windebank's comment is that it once again draws our attention to a feature of welfare provision which Esping-Andersen's framework, crucially, said little about: the intersection of class discrimination and oppression with other forms of oppression, in particular gender and 'race'.

Gender and childcare provision

The issue of gender arises on several counts. As Windebank (1996: 160) notes in reviewing day-care provision in Sweden, France and Britain, 'in none of the forms described here has [social policy] done more than redistribute traditionally defined mothering roles amongst women.' Consequently, in the case of the United Kingdom no matter what form of day-care provision we are discussing, from private/public nursery to care by relatives, we are primarily talking about women relying on other women to take on a mothering role to give them some freedom from parenting so that they may engage in the labour market. Men do not figure largely in the picture, an issue to which we will return later in this chapter.

Gender is clearly also an important dimension when we consider how day-care services such as we have discussed impact upon people's entry into the labour market, and thereby, of course, impact upon the poverty of families and their children. As we have said, when we discuss the interaction of day-care service provision with economic activity, in the vast majority of cases we are talking about the activity of women. The poor level of day-care services therefore has important implications for women's employment. To some extent, it explains why the relatively high female economic activity rates in the United Kingdom include a very considerable portion of part-time working (Hantrais and Letablier 1996: 94). It also partly explains why the United Kingdom is one of the Union states in which the employment of women is most concentrated in clerical jobs and public sector employment, 'where working conditions are more flexible and "women friendly", but where pay is lower than in the private sector' (Hantrais and Letablier 1996: 97). All these features, of course, have direct implications for women's, and thereby families', incomes. Not surprisingly, all these issues become particularly pointed in the case of lone parents, 90 per cent of whom are women.

In 1986, about 40 per cent of the income of lone parents came from state benefits (Williams 1993: 93), and Millar (1994) concluded that lack of childcare was the largest single barrier to the employment of lone mothers. Another part of the vicious circle in which many British lone parents find themselves can be seen in the massive impact of pre-school day-care costs (Ruxton 1996: 113). The proportion of these costs as a percentage of gross half average earnings for a lone parent with one child is

56 per cent, easily the highest in the Union. If alternative childcare is vital for the employment of lone mothers and many cannot possibly afford the costs of that alternative, partly owing to female unemployment and low wages plus the interaction of those wages with the benefits system, then their plight is plain. And the plight of their children is plain too.

For the overall impact on families and children of the benefits system, the labour market and day-care services, the most eloquent evidence is provided by data on poverty in Britain. In terms of general poverty rates, 1994 Eurostat data from the European Commission's POVERTY 3 programme (Ramprakash 1994: 124) are revealing. On the basis of a poverty line drawn at 50 per cent of average equivalent incomes, the United Kingdom had a poverty rate of 22.4 per cent, the worst of any of the countries measured. Using the British government's own data published in 1994, Ruxton (1996: 179) demonstrates that the percentage of two-parent families with children who had below half the average income in the United Kingdom tripled from 8 to 24 per cent between 1979 and 1991/2. The comparable figure for lone parents was an increase from 19 to 59 per cent. He goes on:

> Extrapolations from the same data suggest that child poverty increased between 1979 and 1990/91 from 10% to 31%, with another 10% living on the margins of poverty. Another study ... showed that up to the mid-1970s inequality was decreasing, but that since then it has grown sharply, with a shift in the composition of the poorer groups away from older people and more towards families with children.
>
> (Ruxton 1996: 179)

These statistics really do speak for themselves. So too does the fact that in Britain a baby from a household headed by an unskilled father is twice as likely to die in its first year as a baby from a household where the head is a professional (Ruxton 1996: 188). Moreover, while infant mortality has decreased by about two-thirds between 1970 and 1994, so that it now stands at about the average for the European Union, the decrease has been far less marked in socially deprived urban areas than in affluent ones (Ruxton 1996: 230–1). Similar connections have been posited between poverty, class and children's educational achievement. For instance, Ruxton (1996: 187) draws on data illustrating that in the United Kingdom over the past thirty years, 'the educational gap between the children of professional parents and those of unskilled manual workers has not narrowed significantly.' It is clear from what has already been said that for the structural reasons outlined above the families of lone mothers will be disproportionately represented in those sectors of society characterized by poverty, greater child health risks and limited educational achievement.

Racism and childcare provision

However, it is not only the intersections of class and gender which should concern us when we consider the combined impact on children of discriminations arising from labour market, benefits and day-care systems. As we have already noted in passing, 'race' and racism are also powerful sources of discrimination in Britain, and they too intersect with class and gender.

Cochrane (1993a: 208–10) well summarizes many of the main features drawn from research. He notes that both African Caribbean and Asian men tend to earn substantially less than white counterparts, and both women and men are more vulnerable to unemployment, especially younger adults. There is also some tendency for an overconcentration in semi-skilled or unskilled manual jobs, just those types of occupations most affected by recession. Moreover, it is often black women who occupy the most peripheral, low-paid and insecure jobs. Further intersections are obvious, as Cochrane points out that African Caribbean families are more likely than white families to be headed by a lone parent and that black families are overrepresented in precisely those inner-city areas associated with poverty, poor infant health and limited educational achievement. For instance, there is recent evidence from the Department for Education and Employment that black African and Caribbean pupils are six times more likely than other pupils to be excluded, suggesting they may often be stereotyped as troublesome (Ruxton 1996: 220). In addition, benefits are increasingly restricted to those with 'right' immigration status (Cochrane 1993a: 209), and recent moves by the government against the welfare rights of asylum seekers underline this process.

Clearly all these factors interact with the generally negative situation which I have described relating to day-care in Britain. Writing in the light of repeated attacks by right-wing politicians and academics on lone parent families for allegedly undermining the fabric of British society (Pringle 1995: 55–8), Cannan puts the situation in what, for me, is its true perspective:

> part time, temporary work and homeworking characterize women's employment, in a labour market which is becoming increasingly segregated, diverse and flexible as regards organization of production and labour conditions. It is ethnic minority and lone parents who are especially vulnerable to these insecurities of the labour market, and who have the most difficulty in gaining access to formal and informal sources of good daycare for children . . . Given the lack of childcare facilities and an increasingly unregulated labour market in the UK, it seems to me more reasonable to talk of a crisis *for* families, and especially for lone mothers, rather than a crisis

in the family. It is not changing family structures which cause social problems but the relationship between the family and the state, and policies and practices which the state implements to support or disadvantage certain family forms.

(Cannan 1992: 122–3)

On the other hand, in terms of 'race' and racism there are complexities within this picture when seen from a comparative European perspective. One example of this complexity relates to policies regarding black children in public day-care settings. There is evidence (Children in Scotland 1994; Vedder *et al.* 1996) that public day-care settings in Britain do tend to acknowledge positively and promote the cultural identity of black children to a greater extent than in many other European countries. Vedder *et al.* (1996: 65) reviewed practice in eight European countries and noted that in only two they found explicit use of anti-racist policies: Scotland and England.

There is certainly no cause for complacency in Britain given the levels of racism which permeate society there. Nevertheless, I feel that this relatively positive outcome is of importance because it may well be symptomatic of some much wider European issues regarding racism, which we explore further in later chapters. It has been pointed out that the United Kingdom has some of the most advanced anti-'race' discrimination legislation in the European Union, though its implementation leaves a lot to be desired (Mitchell and Russell 1994: 140).

Mitchell and Russell emphasize several major negative policies regarding issues of 'race' in the United Kingdom: British progress in this field has been achieved due to the commitment of certain local authorities rather than central government, and both those authorities and their anti-racist policies are constantly under threat (Mitchell and Russell 1994: 150); the position of black migrant workers and asylum seekers is similar to the parlous situation of their counterparts in the rest of the Union (p. 143); and 'the government has paid little more than lip service to the notion of a multi-cultural and multi-racial society in its recent health and welfare reforms' (p. 151).

Even so, it is possible to argue that in policy terms, and to some extent in practice, the United Kingdom is more advanced than many of its neighbours in Europe. That view is also echoed in Rex's (1992) comparative anaysis, where he seems to regard Britain's multicultural/anti-racist perspectives as preferable to both the assimilationist tendencies of French policy and the exclusionary tendencies in German policy (see also Chapter 3).

An alternative approach is suggested by Cooper (1994b) and Cooper *et al.* (1995: 130–43). Comparing French and British perspectives on 'race' and racism, they suggest that the French approach offers a more

sophisticated and perhaps positive way forward, along the lines advocated by Gilroy (1993): via the concept of multiple cultural identity.
These are complex debates and I offer a detailed critique of Cooper *et
al.*'s (1995) position in Chapter 3, which surveys the French situation.
At this point, I merely note that it is clear, on a number of grounds, that
racism is just as prevalent in France as it is in Britain.

Returning to the situation in Britain, we can summarize our analysis
as follows. Even if in some respects this country may be more progressive about issues of 'race' than others in Europe, nevertheless the pattern
of welfare provision for children is still deeply affected by oppressive
power relations associated with racism in terms of benefits, the labour
market and day-care provision. Those oppressive relations also intersect
with other dimensions of power, two of which are gender and class.

LEAVE ARRANGEMENTS FOR PARENTS

Gendered power relations seem to be most important when we try to
understand the pattern of leave arrangements in Britain. That pattern is
in many ways as distinctive and as unhelpful to the welfare of children
as is the system of day-care provision.

Let us consider in turn maternity leave, paternity leave, parental leave
and leave for family reasons. At first sight, British arrangements for
maternity leave seem generous: forty weeks in total, of which twenty-
nine are available post-natally. However, as Ruxton (1996: 140–3) points
out, the payment conditions are less generous from a comparative point
of view: 90 per cent of earnings for six weeks and a flat-rate payment for
a further twelve weeks, the remainder being unpaid. It is conditional on
two years' full-time or five years' part-time employment with the same
employer. Ruxton goes on to say that since new legislation in 1994 all
pregnant employees are entitled to fourteen weeks of leave and (with
some exceptions) a flat-rate payment.

This raises an important issue. The new legislation in Britain was only
the result of the European Union Directive on the protection of pregnant
women which the EU adopted in 1992. The British Conservative government fought that directive and produced a legislative response almost
under duress. Moreover, by 1992 the United Kingdom had been the only
(then) member state of the Union without a universal right to maternity
leave for women in paid employment (Hantrais and Letablier 1996: 132).

A similar pattern, but more extreme, emerges when we consider the
other leave categories. Unlike Belgium, Denmark, Finland, France, Spain
and Sweden, the United Kingdom offers no statutory entitlement to
paternity leave (Ruxton 1996: 143–4). Within the Union, only Ireland,

Luxembourg and the United Kingdom offer no statutory right to parental leave (Ruxton 1996: 144–8). Similarly, only Ireland, Luxembourg, the Netherlands and the United Kingdom have no statutory provision for leave on the grounds of sickness of children or other family reasons. Since the Union adopted a Directive in June 1996 requiring member states to provide laws on provision of parental leave and leave for child sickness, those other countries of the Union are now altering, where appropriate, their legislation. The Directive is discussed in detail in Chapter 7. However, we may note here that the United Kingdom was not bound by the Directive since it refused to sign the 1991 Agreement on Social Policy arising from the Treaty of European Union (Hantrais and Letablier 1996: 132).

The Labour administration in Britain, elected in 1997, has made a commitment to endorse the Agreement on Social Policy which clearly may have implications for the adoption of the Directive by the United Kingdom. However, regardless of what will happen, it is interesting that in fact many large companies in Britain have already granted their employees other considerable rights under the agreement. This is because those companies are based in Britain but have large offshoots in the rest of the Union, or because they are themselves based elsewhere in the Union and have offshoots in the United Kingdom (see Barrie Clement in *The Independent*, 7 November 1995; and Chapter 7).

Returning to the overall position of Britain in relation to the labour market and family issues, we may note that Hantrais and Letablier (1996: 124–34) seek to categorize the members of the European Union in terms of their national policies for reconciling employment and family life. They identify three primary categories (all have sub-categories as well): those which juxtapose family and employment with state support (Denmark, Finland, Sweden, France, Belgium); those which aim for sequential ordering of family and employment with state support (Austria, Germany, Italy, Luxembourg, the Netherlands); and non-interventionist states (United Kingdom, Ireland, Portugal, Greece and Spain). With regard to this latter category, the final three countries are identified as engaging in non-intervention largely because of economic restraints: on the whole, their policies are actually supportive of positive intervention. By contrast, it is only the United Kingdom and Ireland which have taken a state non-interventionist stance on largely ideological grounds.

The emphasis on the privacy of the family is a theme which recurs repeatedly in virtually all aspects of British social policy towards families – and it is a particularly idiosyncratic feature of the United Kingdom in the context of comparative European social policy. For instance, Hantrais and Letablier (1996: 143) reviewed the comparative history of member states in terms of the extent to which they assigned a recognized role for the state in family affairs. Ireland, Italy, Spain and the United Kingdom have been the strongest advocates of the family as a private domain. In the case of Spain (and perhaps Italy) one might regard this partly as a reaction to a previous history where fascist governments adopted the family as a social tool of the state. Or it may be linked to a strong Catholic tradition placing the family on a pedestal and at the centre of a patriarchal social existence – a factor which might well also apply to Ireland (see Chapter 4). It is far harder to speculate about the roots of the British non-interventionist philosophy. This theme of 'an Englishman's home is his castle' (with, of course, the emphasis on *man*) is addressed again later in this chapter, since it is central to many aspects of British child welfare policies.

Before we turn away from child social welfare provisions related to family benefits, the labour market, day-care and supportive parental leave arrangements, let us briefly summarize what we have reviewed so far. In many ways these policies are characterized by some of the features which Esping-Andersen identified as neo-liberal in his survey of much narrower data: a residual role for state intervention; a faith in the operation of market forces; and a wide reliance on private or privatized forms of provision. However, this analysis also confirms the degree to which Esping-Andersen's approach failed to address the way other dimensions of discrimination and oppression are generated by these systems of welfare, thereby interacting in complex ways with class differentials. We have particularly identified those dimensions of oppressive power related to racism and sexism. Moreover, we have seen the way in which these forms of discrimination bear down with force on the lives of children in terms of poverty, health, education and other life chances. Consequently, in this analysis it is important that we take into account those forms of oppression associated with the age and dependancy of children (Qvortrup *et al.* 1994). It is my contention that many of these themes, not least the oppression of children by virtue of their age, will be equally present in our analysis of social care services in Britain. It is to this analysis that I now turn.

SOCIAL CARE

At many points the legal framework for Scotland is at variance with that for England and Wales: for instance, in terms of child protection (Lister 1995) and criminal justice (Ruxton 1996: 305). In order to avoid confusion and also because of space limitations, I have therefore decided to focus in this chapter on social care for children in England and Wales. Moreover, I have provided in-depth critical analyses relating to various aspects of this subject elsewhere (Pringle 1995, 1996a, 1997a, b, c); in the limited space available here I will seek to summarize some of these critical issues.

Childcare or child protection

A major and highly idiosyncratic issue is the fact that for some commentators (including myself) it seems that social care services for children in England and Wales are targeted on the abuse of children, to the virtual exclusion of other forms of provision (Parton 1991). The process by which this has occurred is a complex issue (Parton 1991; Pringle 1997a) and we can only pick out a few key reasons for its development. One reason was undoubtedly the background issue of expanding demands on welfare and, from the mid-1970s onwards, a shrinking taxable resource base along with a crumbling of social insurance provision (Clarke and Langan 1993; Chapter 1, this volume). Part of this process inevitably entailed pressure on children's services (Parton 1991: 204–5).

Another factor was the public, political and professional concern about child abuse which burgeoned throughout the 1980s, prompted by a series of 'scandals' relating in particular to the alleged failure of social services to save a series of children from death at the hands of parental figures (Cochrane 1993b; Reder *et al.* 1993). In an era of shrinking, or at least relatively static, resources compared with the past, it was hardly surprising that such a climate of concern and fear would focus services on the area of physical abuse.

It is interesting that this massive concern about physical abuse in England and Wales occured in a country which, unlike its Nordic neighbours, has no legal ban on corporal punishment; and a country where research indicates that serious physical chastisement is a way of life for a very significant minority of children, most of whom never enter the child protection system (Hallett 1995: 39). It is also a country which, despite its bureacratic concern about abuse, has not allowed the introduction of statutory reporting laws relating to abuse, unlike Scandinavian countries and Austria.

A third factor shaping the idiosyncratic form of English social care services for children was the growth in the 1980s of a professional and public awareness about the occurrence of child sexual abuse. Several commentators have noted that, within the European context, this marked focus on sexual abuse seems to be a particular hallmark of British childcare practice (Armstrong and Hollows 1991; Pringle 1996b, 1997a). Once again, the reasons for this state of affairs are complex, and they will be addressed in more depth by Chapter 8. At this point, I will only mention that the explanation offered there involves the presence of an active and radical women's movement in Britain during the 1970s and 1980s. More broadly, I discuss in Chapter 8 whether there are structural reasons why awareness of child sexual abuse should be so heightened in England compared to the remainder of Europe. As we shall see in Chapter 8, I regard sexual abuse of children as a massive social problem and I have major doubts about the way it is being addressed by professional services, not only in England but also in continental Europe.

However, as far as England is concerned, the inadequacy of professional services there is largely the result of the procedural frameworks within which welfare professionals have to operate (see below). Some of those welfare professionals have by now absorbed at least a portion of the insights into the dynamics of sexual abuse offered by survivors and feminist commentators who first put the issue on the social agenda (Pringle 1995). These insights have entered into the mainstream of English welfare practice more than elsewhere in Europe, although the pressure for radical analysis to be dismissed continues to operate (Pringle 1996b, 1997a).

A final important reason for the shape of social care services for children developed in the 1980s relates to the election of Margaret Thatcher as Prime Minister in 1979 (Cannan 1992; Cochrane 1993b; Pringle 1997a). She openly proclaimed herself hostile to what she called the 'nanny state', in the process attacking the Swedish welfare system as the epitome of that alleged dependency culture (Gould 1988). Her stated aim was to roll back the frontiers of the state, including intervention in families. She and her ministers also made it clear that part of this process would involve the substitution of private welfare service provision for public provision.

As I have noted elsewhere (Pringle 1997a), one characteristic of Thatcherism across a range of diverse political issues was to identify supposedly 'dangerous' minorities who were alleged to be undermining the social fabric: so-called 'enemies within'. Such a strategy was useful in diverting attention away from far more concrete problems of a structural nature which the Conservative government was unwilling to acknowledge. That strategy also enabled Thatcherism to reassure the nation that the vast majority of citizens were good, law-abiding people and that the country would flourish if only this or that minority could be dealt with.

Such a skewed philosophy, when applied to childcare as it was developing in the early 1980s, had clear implications. The vast majority of families were assumed to contain good citizens who should be allowed to look after themselves without state interference. However, there was also the expectation that there would be a small minority of 'feckless', dangerous individuals who could not cope financially and/or harmed their children. This scenario, apart from being very reassuring to the majority of the population, also had the potential for being economically advantageous to the government. Once again, in this context, it is not hard to see why the resources of the personal social services for childcare should be concentrated on the issue of child abuse. Those services were to identify that (allegedly) small minority of (allegedly) dangerous individuals and families while leaving the rest of the public to enjoy their 'freedom' untramelled.

Thatcherism and the destruction of the British welfare state

If we recognize that Thatcherism was, and under her successors continued to be, critical in the shaping of British welfare services for children, then we need to ask ourselves why her policies had such a major impact. Although debates continue as to precisely how far Thatcherism destroyed the 'welfare state' of the post-war years (Clarke and Langan 1993: 53–6), many commentators (including myself) do believe that a massive change, qualitative rather than simply quantitative, has occurred between the mid-1970s and the late 1990s (Esping-Andersen 1996b: 10). How did Thatcherism manage to achieve this?

Other European countries have also been under immense economic pressure and have had established right-wing governments during the same period without quite the same result. Why? I suggest one reason may be that the principles of Thatcherism were particularly well suited to underlying and long-standing characteristics of Britain's social institutions – characteristics which are rather alien to much of continental Europe. Some welfare commentators (Cooper *et al.* 1995; Hetherington *et al.* 1997) have suggested that culturally and historically the institutions of English society are traditionally committed to values which favour individualism and privacy rather than principles of social solidarity and social consensus – those latter principles in fact being more characteristic of many continental societies. In the context of this perspective, the post-war solidaristic welfare settlement starts to appear as something of a 'blip' in the English welfare tradition. At the same time, we can see that the tenets of Thatcherism match well an English societal commitment to individualism which in the period 1979–97 was able to reassert itself. In all the chapters which follow, I revisit this concept of a differential commitment to principles of social solidarity across Europe. I believe it helps us to understand why various underlying forms of social oppression facing children and their carers in Europe have gone largely unchallenged by a range of welfare systems (see Chapters 8 and 9).

However, returning to our present focus, we have identified some of the reasons why childcare in English personal social services became dominated by child abuse issues throughout the 1980s. One of those reasons related to the influence of Thatcherite principles which, as we have already noted, constitute a political approach that can be legitimately described as neo-liberal.

Those same reasons also go a long way towards explaining the equally idiosyncratic manner by which the social care services in England and Wales have come to deal with child abuse. And, once again, the approach in England and Wales contrasts markedly with approaches in many countries of continental Europe (Pringle 1996b; Chapter 8, this volume). Consequently, in the next section of the chapter we survey the way services for the protection of children against abuse have operated in England.

The idiosyncracies of the English child protection model

The system for dealing with child abuse in England and Wales which developed throughout the 1980s and 1990s is often referred to as child protection. Its main themes can be summarized as follows (Pringle 1997a): a desire to reduce social work intervention to a minimum; a shift from treatment and preventative services to bureaucratic identification of dangerousness (i.e. investigation) and punishment; ghettoizing dangerousness in a small delinquent minority of the population confined to the lower orders of society. What has come to dominate personal social services' response to child abuse (and therefore childcare generally) in England and Wales is investigation of alleged cases, with very few resources remaining available for prevention or therapeutic help to those who have been abused (Saraga 1993; Pringle 1995; Gray *et al.* 1996, 1997).

As we shall see in the following chapters, this contrasts starkly with the kinds of approach developed in countries such as France (Cooper *et al.* 1995), Belgium (Marneffe *et al.* 1990), Germany (Hutz 1990), the Netherlands (de Ruyter 1990) and Austria (Pronay *et al.* 1995). The lack of attention paid to preventative and support services in England is enhanced by a structural characteristic of social work there which has quite a long tradition. Unlike their counterparts in many other European states, social workers in England do not have a primary responsibility for the allocation of financial benefits: social security and personal social services are administered quite separately (Madge and Attridge 1996).

What is also striking about the emphasis on investigation, or 'enquiry' as it is now known, is the degree to which it has become proceduralized and developed into a virtual welfare technology. The process of child protection in England and Wales is characterized by a mass of written procedures and 'guidance' produced by central and local government, to a far greater extent than anywhere elsewhere in Europe (Harder and Pringle 1997). This reflects a number of factors. First, 'proceduralization' is a means of protection for the personal social services agencies themselves, which, as we noted above, are working in an atmosphere of extreme fear about risk-taking as a result of public 'scandals' relating to child abuse (Parton 1996b, 1997; Parton *et al.* 1997).

Second, the emphasis on procedures is connected to the fact that child protection has increasingly been driven by an agenda set by the judicial system rather than by the welfare professions (Hallett 1995). Indeed, when one considers some of the most important government guidance on the conduct of child abuse enquires, such as the so-called 'Memorandum of Good Practice' (Home Office 1992), it almost seems that social workers have become judicial assistants to the central figures in the process, who are, apparently, the police.

Third, proceduralization may also say something quite important about the balance of power in England and Wales between central and local government. As we shall see, many European countries possess a history of federalism and of an importance attached to local government. Moreover, in recent years for various reasons devolvement of responsibilities to the locality has occurred in many states. By contrast, for largely historical reasons England and Wales has one of the most centralized government machines in Europe. This tendency has been increased by the attacks of successive Conservative administrations on the powers of local government. In the context of English child protection, the system is administered and coordinated locally but the mass of guidance (as well as the bulk of funding) comes from the centre and largely prescribes local practice. One illustration of this centralized approach is provided by the issue of national registers. As Madge and Attridge (1996: 141) point out, England and Wales has had a central register of children who have been abused since the 1970s. The only other member of the Union with a closely comparable system is Ireland.

Let us summarize at this point. Childcare in England and Wales, in terms of the personal social services, is largely focused on child abuse, certainly far more than anywhere else in Europe. Within the English child protection model there is an emphasis on enquiries, with few resources available for preventative or therapeutic work. This is also characteristic of England and Wales within a comparative perspective. The enquiry process is heavily proceduralized, again far more than anywhere else in Europe, and that process is dominated by judicial considerations and by the prescripions of central government, even though it is nominally coordinated locally by public social work agencies.

Many of these features, including the emphasis on justice considerations rather than welfare ones and the requirement to target 'dangerous' persons, are paralleled in other branches of English social care services for children and young people. We have already noted the move towards surveillance and the identification of dangerousness in public day-care services (Cannan 1992). The field of youth work betrays the same signs: targeting of services and an emphasis on justice displacing issues of welfare more rapidly in the United Kingdom than elsewhere in Europe (Ely and Stanley 1990; Junger-Tas 1992; Downes 1994; Pitts 1994; Ruxton 1996: 304–5).

Before ending this analysis of the principles underpinning the child protection approach, we should note that there were clear signs from 1995 onwards that the Conservative administration was seeking to shift the emphasis of practice away from child protection and closer to a 'family support' model. The principles underpinning that model appear similar to perspectives dominant in many continental countries (Department of Health 1995; Parton 1996c; Pringle 1996b). The reasons for this apparent policy shift are complex, and its success in practice seems doubtful for a variety of reasons (Parton 1996c; Parton *et al.* 1997; Pringle 1996b). Whether the advent of a Labour administration in Britain will affect this change of direction seems unlikely. I will discuss the child protection and family support models at more length in Chapter 8, where I compare welfare approaches towards child sexual abuse across Europe.

Preventative and therapeutic services

It would be wrong to suggest that no preventative or therapeutic services for children exist within the area of social care in England and Wales. In terms of preventative work, as Madge and Attridge (1996: 139) note, the breadth of the British health visitor service is wider than its counterpart, the *puericultrices* of France. On the other hand, Madge and Attridge also point out that for health visitors, unlike the *puericultrices*, one of their main roles is detection of child abuse. Referring to health visitors, they add that 'their decline – real in recent years and apparent in the future – is currently causing considerable alarm within their professional organisation' (Madge and Attridge 1996: 139–40). The reason for this decline, of course, is economic.

Considerable educational work around general issues of parenting also occurs in English family centres and nurseries. However, once again, the shadow of child protection is not far away – in an earlier section of this chapter we have noted that such public services are often targeted on families with children deemed to be at risk.

In the area of child protection itself, some therapeutic work is of course undertaken, but it increasingly tends to be set within a particular context. Since a reform of the law in 1990, social care provision for adults has become organized around a split between, on the one hand, those agencies which assess need and then purchase the requisite services, and, on the other hand, those agencies which provide such services. Moreover, the Conservative government gave massive encouragement for the service providers to be as far as possible private rather than public.

Increasingly this pattern is becoming established in childcare too, although it is not quite as advanced. So far, not-for-profit charities have come to play a larger role rather than private profit-making concerns. Thus recent research in one region, the North East of England, concerning services for people who have been sexually abused revealed that remarkably little therapeutic or preventative work was carried out by the public social services, while people turned to small self-help oriented charities for quality therapeutic assistance (Gray *et al.* 1996, 1997). Such charities rarely gain major funding from either local or central government, largely depend upon the massive personal commitment of their members and rarely charge for their services. Earlier research in the same region around provision for children who have been sexually abused also highlighted the major role played by some large childcare charities in providing therapeutic help, although usually this depends upon funding from local authorities – which is of course increasingly scarce (Davis *et al.* 1987; Pringle 1990; Helm *et al.* 1993).

Some of the provision reviewed in that research was foster care. This reminds us that in England and Wales, within the field of social care, there are considerable family placement services and smaller but still significant residential services for children (Bullock 1993: 212–31). Such provision may be available for many possible purposes, sometimes on a specialist basis: for instance, assessment, to maintain children on remand from courts, or short-term placements to cover a temporary family crisis. However, on the whole both residential and family placement services are, at least in theory, aimed primarily at providing positive therapeutic assistance to children placed there, often on a medium-term or long-term basis. Although children enter what is known as the 'care system' for a variety of reasons, there is no doubt that many are now there as a result of child abuse or have suffered such abuse at some points in their lives even when that has not been the primary reason for their admission to care (Pringle 1995: Chapter 3). Out-of-home placements (family placement and residential) clearly constitute a major segment of social care services for children in England, and we discuss these in the next section.

Children in out-of-home placements

English trends in these forms of provision are similar to those throughout much of Western Europe. For instance, Ruxton (1996: 329) notes that across the Union there has been a switch from residential to foster care, partly due to research findings on the potentially detrimental aspects of the former. Certainly such a switch is very clear in England and Wales: indeed, no other member state of the Union has carried this transfer of provision quite as far as England (Ruxton 1996: 330). What is rarely commented upon but surely significant in this transfer process is the fact that foster care tends to cost less than residential care.

On the other hand, in England and Wales there is increasing use of better-paid 'professional' family placements: foster carers are given reasonably large fees in addition to boarding-out allowances. Usually these carers are expected to accept children and young people who previously would have been restricted to residential care, such as those in their teens, children deemed to have serious 'problem behaviours' and disabled children (Pringle 1990; Bullock 1993). This is a trend seen in other European countries, such as Sweden, Denmark and Germany (Ruxton 1996: 335; Harder 1997), but England was one of the pioneers in the early 1970s (Bullock 1993: 219). Increasingly, family placement and residential care are being provided by not-for-profit charities, having in the past largely been the preserve of the public sector.

Other European trends are also common to England and Wales: for instance, the use of smaller units in residential care and the greater use of voluntary rather than compulsory parental arrangements when children are placed away from home (Madge and Attridge 1996; Ruxton 1996). At the same time we are seeing some local authorities in England and Wales divert considerable resources away from both fostering and residential care to fund community-based provision aimed at preventing children entering care settings (Bullock 1993: 213). However, it is probably fair to say that such initiatives have been developed far more intensively in other Union states, particularly the Netherlands, Denmark, Belgium and Germany (Madge and Attridge 1996; Ruxton 1996). This is surely not surprising given our discussion above about the idiosyncratic balance of services in England and Wales.

It is clear from research that the following factors are associated with entry of children into the care system and thereby into out-of-home placements: lone parenthood; being of multiple heritage; being in receipt of income support (Berridge 1994: 134). Of course, many of these factors connect with issues identified earlier relating to the differential experience of poverty in British society. No doubt there is a connection in some cases between social stress and the entry of children into the care system – and it is that connection which Berridge himself emphasizes. However, I have suggested elsewhere (Pringle 1995: 44–5) that there is ample evidence to indicate that these characteristics of children in care can often be explained by biases within the way assessments and community-based services are carried out. Sexism, racism, classism and other forms of oppression also operate widely in the very structures of the English welfare system which have (allegedly) been designed to counter oppression. This is a point that cannot be stressed too strongly.

For instance, there has been considerable research and critical analysis revealing the sexism and racism which operates in the way young women find their way into the care and court systems (Frost and Stein 1989; Pitts 1990) or the way young black men are treated by the courts (Walker 1988), and the intersections between 'race', gender and class discriminations which may occur in these processes (Carlen and Wardhaugh 1991). Moreover, there is one particularly heinous form of oppression bearing down on some children within the English care system which we have not yet mentioned: abuse of children in out-of-home placements.

Abuse of children in out-of-home placements

There is an important trend in England and Wales which on the whole is not common to most West European countries. That trend is the high degree of suspicion which now attaches to the quality of residential care and, increasingly, to foster care as well. Many of these doubts relate to a wide range of issues. However, the most high profile and serious doubts relate to the physical and sexual abuse to which some children are subjected by welfare workers in these welfare settings and other locations such as nursery care (Pringle 1992, 1993, 1995, 1997a, b, c). The central points to note about this issue are: first, professional and public awareness of the problem seems far more extensive in Britain than almost anywhere else in Europe, either West or East; second, the issue of gender has become prominent in British debates about maltreatment of children in welfare settings, particularly in relation to sexual abuse.

This latter feature reflects the partial recognition in England that issues relating to masculinity are a highly significant factor in the generation of sexual violence as a whole with regard to children abused either inside or outside home settings and also in relation to adults who are sexually abused (Pringle 1995). Although such a focus on masculinity is still open to controversy in Britain, there is undoubtedly a much greater professional welfare and public acceptance there than elsewhere in Europe that gender is an important dynamic. The reasons for this greater professional and public awareness compared to continental Europe concerning both the extent of sexual abuse and the importance of gender as a causative factor will be further analysed in Chapter 8. We may just mention here that once again the women's movement in Britain has played an important part in raising awareness about those issues. As we saw above, there is reason to believe that some elements of feminist discourse around the dynamics of sexual abuse have entered into the

practice of a significant number of welfare professionals – and the same
to a limited extent might be said about public attitudes.

We should also note that there is increasing evidence from the United
Kingdom and the United States concerning the links between sexual
violence and other oppressive power relations, such as those associated
with issues of disability, age, 'race', sexuality and class (Pringle 1995: 172).
Those complexities are often ignored in the literature. Such an observation illustrates why in this volume we must address the full range of
forms of social oppression as they interconnect with one another.

Let us summarize what we have seen so far about the nature of preventative and therapeutic services regarding the social care of children
in England and Wales. Therapeutic services are slightly more in evidence than preventative ones. However, what exists of either of them
is often associated with issues of child protection directly or indirectly.
Therapeutic provision is offered to children increasingly by not-for-profit
charities, whether the children are living at home, in residential care or
in foster placements. For-profit agencies are not so far a significant feature in childcare provision, unlike adult care: however, their importance
is likely to grow. There are high profile doubts about the quality of care
settings, with a particular focus on the occurrence of sexual abuse there
and the relevance of gender as a factor in that abuse.

This concern reflects a wider professional and public acknowledgement
in Britain of gender as an important variable in understanding the problem
of sexual abuse throughout society as a whole. That focus on gender
in debates about sexual violence also marks out Britain from most of its
European neighbours. We noted that in understanding and challenging
sexual abuse we needed to address the same range of interconnected social oppressions which, as we have seen, structure other forms of social
disadvantage to which children and their carers are subjected: racism,
heterosexism, disablism, sexism, ageism and classism. These oppressive
power relations also appear to structure welfare services themselves,
with the result that, as we saw, they tend to compound the disadvantages suffered by children and their carers rather than alleviating them.

Neo-liberalism and social care

In the first part of this chapter, we discussed how far the pattern of child
welfare services in the United Kingdom centred on issues such as benefits, day-care and parental leave conformed to the kind of characteristics
located in a neo-liberal stereotype. We saw that in many respects there
was a fair degree of conformity. However, we also found that the neo-
liberal paradigm failed to account for the profound way in which those

welfare structures shaped, and were themselves shaped by, a complex of oppressive power relations.

In the second part of this chapter we surveyed child welfare services in the form of social care provision in England and Wales, primarily the personal social services. Once again, the pattern of services demonstrates some neo-liberal features: the identification of a residual population to whom stigmatizing services, of frequently questionable quality, are directed with a largely punitive rather than therapeutic intent. Moreover, there is clearly a shift away from public service provision, largely (so far) to not-for-profit charities.

On the other hand, once again we find that Esping-Andersen's neo-liberal paradigm fails to pick up some very significant trends without which it is impossible to understand the British situation. In view of what we have already said about the gaps in Esping-Andersen's analysis, these trends predictably relate to a whole range of oppressive social dynamics, including those associated not only with class but also with gender, 'race', disability, sexuality and age. We have seen that these forms of oppression manifest themselves in many different ways throughout children's care services.

We have given particular attention to one especially serious manifestation of oppression: child sexual abuse, both inside and outside the care services. As I shall demonstrate in Chapter 8, there is no better comparative example than child sexual abuse for demonstrating how different approaches to child and family welfare problems are structured by those interconnected forms of social oppression.

Moreover, in Chapter 8 I will use the topic of child sexual abuse to explore important respects in which Britain's response to welfare issues seems in advance of its continental neighbours despite the undoubtedly negative social policy context which existed in the United Kingdom between 1979 and 1997. As we have seen in this chapter, these progressive British features include a greater level of professional and public awareness about major social problems such as sexual violence and racism and the (albeit tenuous) development of radical welfare challenges to them. Those progressive elements in the British picture are also at odds with what one would expect in terms of Esping-Andersen's neo-liberal paradigm.

First, however, in the chapters which follow we will survey in detail the patterns of childcare provision across Europe to which I have briefly alluded in the previous chapter. We will start with those allegedly conservative corporatist countries, France and Germany.

3

CHILDREN, SOCIAL WELFARE AND CONSERVATIVE CORPORATISM

INTRODUCTION

We noted in Chapter 1 that some commentators who adopt a feminist perspective have suggested that Esping-Andersen's conservative corporatist model splinters quite markedly when confronted with issues of gender. In Chapter 2 we found that the characterization of a neo-liberal model failed to encompass significant dimensions of oppression in addition to gender. To assess whether this is also true of the conservative corporatist model, I will review the evidence for two European states, both defined by Esping-Andersen (1990) as approximating to that welfare model: France and Germany.

Readers will also recall from Chapter 1 that some of the central features of this model were: insurance-based social protection systems which maintain power differentials in society; strong principles of subsidiarity which place a clear home-making, domestic role on women, with men as family earners; a strong commitment to principles of solidarity; a welfare consensus largely determined by constructive cooperation between employers, trade unions and governments. How far do France and Germany conform to this stereotype when we consider a wide range of welfare services devoted to children and their carers? Once again, we will review in turn benefits and other financial supports, day-care provision and parental leave arrangements; followed by a separate analysis of social care provision.

FINANCIAL SUPPORT

As regards the relationship of the state to the family, a marked contrast exists between these countries and Britain. In the United Kingdom the family was, and is, generally regarded as a private sphere open to legitimate public intervention only in the most dire emergencies. As Hantrais and Letablier (1996: 26–7) make clear, both France and Germany in their constitutions recognize the family as a social institution and undertake to give it protection. However, even those constitutional commitments betray major differences between France and Germany in the way they interpret the idea of protection. For instance, France's 1946 Constitution justifies state intervention in support of the family unit and recognizes it as an important social institution (Hantrais and Letablier 1996: 27). By contrast with this broad and enabling formulation, Germany's constitution acts as 'a source of rigidity, focusing attention on the legitimate family as sanctioned by marriage' (Hantrais and Letablier 1996: 26).

In terms of central government structures, both states have demonstrated a long-term commitment to the family: for instance, by regularly appointing government ministers with the family as a remit. Moreover, in France since 1984 there has been the influential advisory body entitled, rather significantly, the 'l'Haut Conseil de la Population et de la Famille', and presided over by the President of the Republic no less. As we will see, few countries in Europe have been as explicit as France in pursuing pro-natalist policies (Hantrais and Letablier 1996).

One manifestation of this pro-natalism in France is a strong commitment to horizontal redistribution of resources towards families with children by, in particular, use of relatively generous family allowances and tax concessions (Hantrais and Letablier 1996: 161–2; Ruxton 1996: 118). This horizontal redistribution tends to favour larger families and more highly earning ones. By contrast, family allowances in Germany are comparatively low and are means-tested after the first child. It is clear that the overall impact of these benefits is vertical rather than horizontal redistribution, which at least provides more help to lower earning families. However, since they are also taken as income (like Britain) for calculation of other benefits (Schweie 1994: 218), that positive effect is partially offset. The tax policy towards families in Germany enhances the redistibutive effect and also reinforces the impression of strongly gendered and traditional assumptions about families (Schweie 1994: 218).

Both Schweie (1994) and Hantrais and Letablier (1996) describe the way the policy of *Ehegattensplitting* (splitting of marital incomes for tax purposes) disadvantages both cohabitation (which is not eligible for this process) and women's participation in the labour market: a double blow for traditionalism. Hantrais and Letablier (1996: 56) note that French co-habitees actually possess a tax advantage over married couples in cases where they have one or two children and unequal incomes. These different attitudes in France and Germany to cohabitation run more or less consistently right across the benefits systems in the two countries.

Even at this stage in our analysis, I believe a certain pattern is discernible as regards public and family policies in France and Germany: unlike Britain, both countries are quite at ease with the idea of overtly using public policies to shape family issues; but in France, these policies are directed towards promoting family well-being and pro-natalism, with, comparatively speaking, few gendered assumptions; in Germany, public policies are explicitly directed at promoting traditional family norms, norms which implicitly contain highly gendered and sexist assumptions. As we shall see, these themes are echoed in other policies and practices.

However, we should note that in the first four years of Jacques Chirac's presidency, means-testing and welfare cuts in France have to some extent eroded the supportive benefits structure. One central impetus for this policy has been the approach of European Monetary Union (EMU). Of course, France has not been alone in this: a similar path has also been followed in Germany (Ruxton 1996: 118). As far as France is concerned, the election of a left-wing government in June 1997, working in 'cohabitation' with a centre-right President, does not seem to have markedly slowed down the process of benefits erosion and targeting (Masters 1997).

Means-testing already has some established place in the French system in the form of *complement familial, allocation de parent isolé* and, perhaps most significantly, *revenu d'minimum d'insertion* (RMI) for the long-term unemployed (Hantrais and Letablier 1996: 166; Cannan 1996: 2). Hantrais and Letablier point out that the latter two benefits are administered by the Caisse Nationale des Allocations (CNAF), a specialized non-governmental administrative agency, and both benefits are based on ideas of national solidarity. This seems an appropriate moment at which to comment on the issue of solidarity as regards the French approach to social welfare.

Social inclusion, social welfare and poverty

In Chapter 2, focusing on the United Kingdom, I suggested that welfare policies in the period 1979–97 were characterized by a perspective which was actively hostile to any notion of social solidarity – and that to a large extent the predominance of this perspective in Britain may be due to its congruence with historic values permeating British society on a broad basis.

In delineations of the conservative corporatist welfare model (Wilson 1993), historic notions of social solidarity are often instanced as one characteristic of that model. In this respect, France certainly conforms to the stereotype and apparently presents a strong contrast with Britain. For instance, Cannan (1996: 1–4) has recently described how, in order to gain RMI, recipients make contracts about what training, community service or work placements they will undertake. Thereby, recipients may be 'inserted' into society, countering social exclusion. Moreover, the scheme fits into a wide range of French anti-exclusion policies (Cannan 1996: 2). I want now to consider in more detail the specific issue of RMI and solidarity.

Social workers have a central role in the financial administration of RMI. This is only one example of how some social workers in France are intimately involved in social security matters, unlike their peers in Britain but in line with social workers in many other European countries (see Chapter 2). Spicker (1995: 10) has suggested that in fact RMI has further increased the social workers' role as bureaucratic *fonctionnaires*. Spicker (1995: 13) is also perhaps more sceptical of RMI as a solidaristic welfare tool than Cannan (1996). He points out that such policies as RMI often fail to achieve insertion of unemployed people and are more successful in deterring welfare claimants by stigmatizing the latter as deviants. He believes the take-up is poor and that instead of helping families with children, RMI seems to have been used more by single men.

His comments raise the important point that the concept of solidarity may be a double-edged phenomenon. On the one hand, viewed from a British perspective it may well seem to some commentators on the left that a policy of social inclusion would make a welcome change from the welfare policy trajectory of the United Kingdom from 1979 to 1997. Certainly the concept of social inclusion has made its way into the lexicon of the new Labour administration in Britain. On the other hand, we begin to see in RMI that the concept of social inclusion may often be social control in another guise – and therefore not as distant from Mrs Thatcher's Britain as we might think. We shall observe a similar blurring of purposes later in the chapter, when we consider the role of French assimilationist policies towards migrants and black people in France.

However, returning to our concern here with poverty in France, we can say that it remains a very significant problem in terms of child welfare (Ruxton 1996: 176). Ramprakash's (1994) Eurostat data suggest that 16 per cent of young people below fourteen years in France are living in poverty (where the poverty level is defined as 50 per cent of average equivalent expenditures) and 19.4 per cent of those aged fourteen to sixteen. With regard to lone parents, it seems that the French benefits/tax system is more helpful to those with higher earnings (Ruxton 1996: 109), illustrating the degree to which that system has been characterized by horizontal redistribution – even though, as we have seen, vertical redistribution is increasing.

Poverty and social assistance in Germany

When we turn to social assistance strategies in Germany, we see a certain consistency with other benefit patterns there in the heavy emphasis on targeting and means testing. Owing to economic recession and the social pressures bearing down on most West European states, outlined in Chapter 1, the demand for social assistance in Germany has increased rapidly. This is a major source of welfare system strain where provision has traditionally been dependent on social insurance schemes.

Based on recent German data, Ruxton (1996: 176–7) reports that between 1984 and 1993 the proportion of German nationals with incomes below 50 per cent of the national mean doubled from 10 to 20 per cent. Perhaps significantly, the figure for non-nationals was nearer 25 per cent. Ruxton goes on to note that the households most affected by poverty are lone parents (33 per cent), households with five or more persons (23 per cent) and households with older children (19 per cent).

Lone parents, as we have seen, represent a major element of the population in poverty and, of course, in receipt of social assistance. Based on recent data from the European Observatory on National Family Policies, Ruxton (1996: 109) estimates that in comparative European terms, lone parents with relatively low incomes are treated quite generously in Germany due to targeting measures, while those on relatively high incomes also benefit considerably. Certainly lone parents in both Germany and France seem to have, as a whole, an advantage over their British counterparts, largely because of the cost differentials in relation to childcare (Ruxton 1997).

One particular feature of German social assistance worthy of note is that because of the differentiated mode of payment, children in a family aged fifteen years or over can themselves be in receipt of income support, though their entitlement is offset against child support payments and publicly advanced maintenance payments (Schweie 1994: 219).

As we shall see throughout this chapter, principles associated with the concept of subsidiarity thread their way through the whole of child welfare provision in Germany. The social security system is no exception. For instance, Germany's policy regarding dependent relatives is striking:

individuals with the means to do so are legally obliged to assume responsibility not only for their parents but also for unemployed, unmarried children under 25 and for their offspring's lone parent families.

(Hantrais and Letablier 1996: 59)

German reunification and financial supports

One important variable in the case of Germany I have not yet mentioned: the impact of reunification. This is important in many aspects of child social welfare. Although I shall review the situation of the former German Democratic Republic (GDR) as part of Eastern Europe in Chapter 7, I will note in this chapter some specific issues related to reunited Germany.

Prior to reunification families with children were relatively better off when compared to other households in East Germany than in West Germany, particularly families with smaller numbers of children (Hauser *et al*. 1994: 283). Similarly, lone parent families benefited more in the East than in the West, especially if they had one or two children. Setting the poverty level at 50 per cent of the national average, poverty among children also seems to have been avoided more successfully in the East than the West, though it is not clear how far this resulted from the number of women working there and how much from a greater equalization of family incomes (Hauser *et al*. 1994: 283). If, as seems very possible, the former factor was important, then we need to consider the burdens carried by working mothers in the East (Einhorn 1993; Makkai 1994).

Following reunification, it seems that overall income inequality has increased slightly in Eastern Germany over the first three years without reaching Western levels (Hauser *et al*. 1994: 286). More specifically, while smaller families have maintained their position, larger families and one-parent families with two or more children fell behind in average terms (Hauser *et al*. 1994: 291). Significantly, in view of what we have just said about the role of working mothers in the GDR, Hauser *et al*. (1994: 288) attribute this loss of position to the fact that 'in most of these cases there is only one person working, thus increasing the risk of income losses in case of unemployment.' As we shall see later, this situation is also influenced by trends relating to other forms of provision, in particular day-care services.

Financial support: a summary

In summarizing the overall position in France and Germany regarding financial support systems to families, we can make the following points.

First, in some important respects they both manifest characteristics which one might expect from states which have been labelled as possessing conservative corporatist welfare systems. In both cases, social insurance remains a central component of the benefits systems, though social assistance has come to play a far more important role in France and Germany under the impact of unemployment and demographic pressures.

Moreover, we can say that the principles of subsidiarity and social solidarity are embodied within both welfare systems, albeit sometimes manifested in rather different ways. As regards subsidiarity, for instance, this concept is reflected in the French system by the important administrative role played by the CNAF and its local Caisses d'Allocations Familiales (CAF), and the general decentralization of welfare responsibilities which has occurred since the early 1980s (Grevot 1996b: 5). In Germany, the application of subsidiarity principles is widely apparent in the highly overt importance placed on the family as the primary source of welfare for children, and within the family the traditional role of women as exclusive carers and home-makers, which contrasts to some extent with the position in France.

In terms of solidarity, I have already commented on the centrality of this principle in the French context. As regards Germany, although there are other less positive ways of viewing the emphasis on targeted social provision there, one perspective is that it demonstrates a certain social commitment to some sections of the population who are increasingly unprotected by traditional social insurance networks – whether this commitment is equally extended to non-citizens is, however, more open to doubt.

As we have seen, there are other respects in which welfare approaches in the two countries differ quite extensively. This is particularly obvious, as we have noted, in relation to the role of women and the family, where many of the German financial supports, linked to the nature of the labour market, encourage women to take on predominantly 'home-maker' roles (Lewis 1993; Wilson 1993). By contrast, French policy, with its emphasis on family well-being and building (Hantrais and Letablier 1996), is less concerned with strengthening traditional family roles *per se*. This contrast between France and Germany has been noted by many recent commentators seeking to classify European welfare systems, particularly those influenced by feminist perspectives (Duncan 1995). Similarly, Hantrais and Letablier (1996: 124–34) characterize France as a state which aims at a juxtaposition of family and employment with state support, while Germany is included in those countries which strive for sequential ordering of family and employment with state support.

In addition, solidarity may be interpreted rather differently in the two countries when it is applied to issues of citizenship. This difference is even more apparent in other policy areas. As we shall see later, in some respects France and Germany are diametrically opposed as far as this subject is concerned, particularly in relation to people who are migrants or whose antecedents were migrants.

Let us end this section on financial supports by concluding that while the label of conservative corporatist welfare regime does have some validity in relation to France and Germany, it also ignores major differences between the two systems, particularly in relation to issues of gender and 'race'. Some of these features are equally apparent when we turn to parental leave arrangements and day-care.

PARENTAL LEAVE ARRANGEMENTS

In terms of leave arrangements, there is considerable similarity between the two countries, although there are some significant differences. For instance, there is no statutory paternity leave entitlement in Germany: a fact which may be unsurprising in view of what we have said in the sections above about the buttressing of traditional gender roles there. France offers three unpaid days (European Commission 1996a: 144; Ruxton 1996: 143), which is an advance on Germany and, of course, on the United Kingdom. On the other hand, this paternal leave is quite limited compared to provision in Sweden (see Chapter 5).

Maternity leave in France for single births extends from sixteen to twenty-six weeks, depending upon whether the baby is the third-born or beyond, and is paid at 84 per cent of earnings. In Germany, for single births, maternity leave is normally fourteen weeks paid at 100 per cent of earnings (Ruxton 1996: 142). The difference regarding the increased entitlements for additional babies in France may well be a reflection of those pro-natalist policies upon which we have already commented.

Arrangements for parental leave are similar, in that it is available until the child reaches 36 months. However, there are differences in some details. For instance, in France the replacement benefit (APE: see above) is only paid for the second and additional children (previously it was only for the third child or above). Once again, there are overtones of pro-natalism here (Hantrais and Letablier 1996: 129). It may also be significant that the flexibility for combining part-time work with taking parental leave is considerably greater in France than in Germany, returning us to the theme of different approaches to family/employment relations (Ruxton 1996: 147). On the other hand, Germany is more generous in relation to leave for other reasons (for instance, child sickness), providing at full earnings ten days per parent (twenty-five days if there are two children or more) compared with France's three unpaid days (increasing to five if the parent has a child under three years or three or more children) (European Commission 1996a: 145).

DAY-CARE PROVISION

The divergences between France and Germany become far clearer when we consider their respective policies towards day-care provision. In essence, such provision in France is far more extensive than in the former West Germany. Coverage in France extends to 23 per cent of children under three and 99 per cent for three to six year olds (1993 figures). This compares with 2 and 78 per cent respectively for the former West Germany (1990 figures). Significantly, the respective 1990 figures for the former East Germany are 50 and 100 per cent (European Commission 1996a: 148).

Day-care provision in Germany

In the GDR much day-care provision had been based at the workplace. In fact, even by the standards of the Eastern bloc the GDR had very extensive day-care provision (Makkai 1994: 193), though as we noted earlier such provision was nevertheless geared to a very marked dual role for women. We should also point out that the currently increasing and marked unemployment among women in the former GDR is partly a function of the vertical and horizontal job segregation which characterized women's situation in the labour market there before reunification (Makkai 1994: 196; Einhorn 1994: Chapter 4). In the former West Germany that emphasis in family policy on bolstering traditional family roles, which we have observed previously, clearly impacted on the historically poor day-care provision there.

Reunification thus brought together two wholly different approaches to day-care. This bifurcation has had some influence on present German policy. As the Childcare Network notes, a new law in force will by 1999 give every pre-school child of three years or more the right to a kindergarten place. However, this has imposed tremendous pressure on local government in Western Germany, with consequent variations, lowering of standards or cuts in other service areas (European Commission 1996a: 41). Provision in the former West Germany was already, and still is, marked by considerable local variation. Delivery is via a mixture of service providers, including public authorities, not-for-profit charities and trade union organizations (European Commission 1996a: 42). That pattern of service provision is typical of the social care system, as we shall see later, and (like the emphasis on the primacy of family care) conforms strongly with the principle of subsidiarity – which one would expect in a conservative corporatist welfare system.

Reunification has also resulted in different, less authoritarian and more child-centred approaches to childcare from Western Germany being adopted by day-care services in the former GDR (Ruxton 1996: 151). However, the latter has also been forced to adapt to other, perhaps less benign, policy characteristics brought over from the West: for instance, those relating to abortion. Since reunification this has been one of the most controversial issues in Germany, with a chequered legal history over the past few years (Makkai 1994: 197; Einhorn 1994: Chapter 3; Hantrais and Letablier 1996: 34). The controversy arises from the fact that abortion was widely available in the East, while the Basic Law in the West allowed abortion only where the mother's life was in danger or there was other serious risk to health (Wilson 1993: 142). As the law now stands, throughout Germany termination of pregnancy remains illegal, though not punishable provided certain conditions are met for abortions carried out in the first three months of pregnancy (Hantrais and Letablier 1996: 34). Such a policy clearly conforms to the patriarchal theme of traditional family roles associated with the concept of subsidiarity in terms of both its principle (regarding women's lack of power over their own bodies) and its practical implications (regarding employment) (Makkai 1994: 197).

Further restrictions on women's ability to participate in the labour market in Germany relate to provision focused on schooling. As the Childcare Network (European Commission 1996a: 42–3) point outs, the German school system operates only on a half-day basis. Although there is some provision to cover out-of-school hours, in Western Germany this is rather limited, with the result that many women with school-age children only work part-time. In East Germany the situation differs because of higher levels of provision there.

Day-care provision in France

As implied earlier, when we turn to childcare provision in France we find a rather different overall situation. We have already noted the much higher levels of provision there for both the under-3 and 3–6 age groups than in either the western part of Germany or the United Kingdom. As the Childcare Network report (European Commission 1996a: 59) points out, there is a wide variety of forms of day-care provision in France, some welfare-oriented, others education-centred. In terms of spread of provision, especially for the under-3 age group, there is considerable variability in the extent of publically financed day-care on a geographical basis, with a tendency to higher levels in the metropolitan centres (Windebank 1996: 153).

The programme of *contrat enfance* (introduced in 1988) has been partly responsible for considerable expansion of provision in recent years for pre-school children, and this appears to be ongoing (European Commission 1996a: 61–2). On the other hand, it is important to remember that the majority of children under 3 in France are not looked after in nursery schools, crèches or child-minding centres. Windebank (1996: 154) reports that 54 per cent are looked after by their mothers at home. Of the remaining 46 per cent, about a quarter are cared for by other family members (most often grandmothers), the rest being largely accounted for by out-of-home and out-of-family provision. Significantly, class mediates gender in this respect, with greater use of informal and familial care by those lower down the social scale. As we shall see in Chapter 5, this profile of under-three care is considerably different from that which pertains in Sweden, another country which is often identified in positive terms for its childcare provision.

While Sweden makes greater use of publicly funded out-of-home facilities for this age group, French provision relies more heavily on various forms of financial subsidy to parents to assist employment of carers both outside and inside the home: for instance, *Aide à la famille pour l'emploi d'une assistante maternelle agrée* (AFEAMA) and *Allocation de garde d'enfant à domicile* (AGED) (European Commission 1996a: 64). Moreover, we have already seen the way in which fiscal and benefit arrangements are designed to achieve considerable horizontal and, to some extent, vertical redistribution of resources towards families. Once again, though, readers need to bear in mind the impact on family benefits of the policy of welfare cost-cutting in France, initiated in the first four years following the presidential election of Jacques Chirac, mentioned earlier (Smart 1996; Ruxton 1996: 118). These changes, particularly in terms of the desire to cut unemployment levels, also had implications for mothers owing to the then government's increased eagerness to promote their care of children at the expense of women's presence in the labour market (European Commission 1996a: 61).

The present reality is that France, like the Nordic states, still retains relatively high female and maternal labour participation rates (Hantrais and Letablier 1996: 93–6; Windebank 1996: 153). What distinguishes France from, say, Sweden is that a far greater proportion of this labour participation is full-time rather than part-time. Women's labour participation also tends to differ in that respect from the profile of female working patterns in Britain. The French profile is partly the outcome of those childcare packages noted above plus the greater non-availablity of 'woman-friendly' part-time working hours compared to the situation in Sweden or Britain. Clearly, though, both Sweden and France provide far more extensive childcare packages, in terms of day-care and/or benefits, than is the case in Britain (Windebank 1996).

Another difference between women's employment patterns in France on the one hand and those in both Sweden and Britain is that French mothers' labour participation rates tend to fall away significantly not with the birth of the first or the second child but only with the third one (Windebank 1996: 153), a feature clearly linked in part to the nature of the French pro-natalist child-rearing allowance (Ruxton 1996: 118).

Summary

Partly for the reasons given above, Hantrais and Letablier (1996: 126–35) define France as a country (along with Belgium) which aims at a juxtaposition of family and employment with state support. By contrast, they class Sweden (along with Denmark and Finland) as a state which provides a similar juxtaposition, but one which aims at equality rather than family support *per se* (see Chapter 5 for a detailed consideration of that characterization). We noted in Chapter 2 that Britain is classified as an ideologically based non-interventionist state by Hantrais and Letablier (1996: 132–3).

It is clearly significant that in reviewing family policies Hantrais and Letablier (1996) place Germany, particularly Western Germany, in a very different category from France. They characterize Germany as a country which belongs to a cluster where family policies aim at sequential ordering of family and employment with state support. Our analysis here fully bears out that categorization given the way German childcare policies place such emphasis on family care of children – and of course family care in most cases equates with care by mothers.

It is important not to overstate the difference between Germany and France on these issues. For instance, we know that conditions in Eastern Germany regarding day-care, despite their erosion, are in some respects closer to the French situation. At the same time we also know that changes in French welfare policy in the first four years after Jacques Chirac's presidential victory presaged some degree of convergence between French and German family policies, and that lower income French families do already rely to a considerable extent on family-based care. Similarly, Windebank (1996) correctly notes that French childcare policies, like those in both Sweden and the United Kingdom despite their great variations, ultimately rely in one way or another on the caring role of women, whether in day-care centres, as childminders or as alternative family carers. Therefore, in a way France, no more than Germany, truly escapes this particular gender trap.

Nevertheless, the overall direction of our analysis clearly underlines significant divergences in child welfare policies between Germany and France regarding tax, benefits, parental leave and day-care provision. It is hardly surprising to find that other analysts have also divined such differences and therefore expressed major reservations about the value of Esping-Andersen's classification of France and Germany as being both 'conservative corporatist' systems, particularly in relation to gender issues (Lewis 1993; Duncan 1995). Moreover, we also need to bear in mind once again Duncan's point that regional variations in welfare policy and provision can often belie broad national categorizations.

We have now surveyed French and German childcare policy and seen the severe limitations of the concept of 'conservative corporatism' in relation to issues such as parental leave, tax and social security, day-care provision and family policies. Those limitations related partly to the divergences between the two countries in terms of policy and practice. However, they also reflected the fact that Esping-Andersen's formulation fails to embrace many dynamics of disadvantage which operate against children and their carers. In the remainder of this chapter we need to examine how far our analysis can be extended to the social care services of the two countries.

SOCIAL CARE PROVISION

Although there continue to be considerable disjunctures between French and German approaches in relation to social care, nevertheless there also seem to be more points of convergence than were observable in the preceeding parts of this chapter. Certainly there are more commonalities between these two countries than exist between either of them and England in this context. We can illustrate that judgement by focusing on the degree to which the principles of subsidiarity and solidarity, associated with 'conservative corporatism', permeate social care services in France and Germany.

Principles of solidarity and subsidiarity

Subsidiarity in France
Subsidiarity is a central feature of social care provision in both France and Germany. As far as France is concerned, decentralization of children's social care services really dates from 1983 (Grevot 1996b), with the focus of control henceforth largely located within the *departements* (Cooper *et al.* 1995; Munday 1996b). Moreover, such services tend to

have a strongly multidisciplinary element which is largely, though not wholly, absent from the English situation.

While the framework of children's social care services is clearly centred within local government, it is important to realize that the not-for-profit 'voluntary' sector plays a highly crucial part, far more high profile than has hitherto been the case in Britain. For instance, Cooper *et al.* (1995: 30) point out that rather 'than providing supplementary services to the statutory sector, French voluntary agencies carry formal responsibility for key aspects of child protection', funded by contracts from local government. Grevot (1996b: 5) notes that these voluntary agencies, *associations*, constitute 'a large component of the French social welfare system and this is reflected in the major role they play in the life of the community as a whole.' He goes on to estimate that within the field of social welfare generally, there are hundreds of thousands of *associations* throughout France.

Another reflection of the subsidiarity principle within French practice is the heavy emphasis on the birth family as the most desirable location for children:

> Enormous emphasis is placed on the need to keep children in their families or, if they are removed, to return them. The family has a reality in France that is much stronger than in England; the child is part of the family, and there is nothing that one can do to change that fact. So, one has to try to change the family. The French legal system reflects that reality.
>
> (Hetherington 1996: 104)

As Cooper *et al.* (1995) make clear throughout their volume on French and English child protection practice, the English cultural emphasis on the privacy of the family, its disconnectedness with wider society, may restrict the ease of professional intervention within the family compared to the situation in France. However, they also note that this same disconnectedness accounts for the relatively more serious legal consequences of such intervention when it does occur in England. Moreover, this contrast in approaches to the birth family is at its starkest in relation to adoption: in France it is virtually unheard of without the birth parents' permission (Hetherington 1996: 103).

In the light of this French perspective, it is therefore not surprising that children's social care services tend to be focused on ideas of prevention (Cooper *et al.* 1995: 29, 52–61) and therapeutic help (Hetherington 1996: 100), concepts both of which have become almost redundant in the bureaucratized English system dominated by child protection enquiries and assessments (Saraga 1993; Cooper *et al.* 1995; Pringle 1997a; Chapter 8, this volume).

Subsidiarity in Germany

As far as subsidiarity in German services is concerned, the situation is rather similar to France in a number of respects, at least as far as the former FRG is concerned. Once again we find a mix of state and voluntary provision (Colla-Muller 1993; Madge and Attridge 1996; Munday 1996b), the state being represented by the local tiers of government rather than those of the centre. However, the 'voluntary' not-for-profit sector plays an even more extensive role than is the case in France, ranging, as Munday (1996b: 43) notes, from numerous grass-roots organizations, often with radical political underpinnings, through to the six massive central 'voluntary' associations that so dominate welfare provision in Germany and tend to be centred on religious or labour affiliations. Once again, funding for 'voluntary' provision is largely state-based.

If anything, the principle of subsidiarity is more clearly evident in German social care services than in French ones. For instance, there is no home visiting service in Germany, with mothers being expected to consult family or child doctors themselves (Madge and Attridge 1996: 140). As we shall see later, this contrasts with French practice – and even more with the surveillance role performed by health visitors in Britain.

The picture in the former GDR is considerably different (Colla-Muller 1993; Von Strandmann 1994; Munday 1996b). In the old GDR relatively few resources were devoted to child welfare services for children presenting problematic behaviour, largely because such problems were not supposed to exist to any great extent: social work and social care were reminders that the system did not function perfectly and so had little official approval. Welfare was very much on a community basis, using volunteers to befriend families with difficulties such as physical and emotional neglect, alcoholism and minor delinquency. Sexual and physical abuse did not 'exist' in the GDR: in other words, they were not looked for or recognized. Employed social carers supervised volunteers. In some respects this approach seemed to work well: for instance, in networking local resources. However, apart from non-recognition of some major problems, it also had other important disadvantages. One of them was the serious overlap of social control and surveillance with social care.

Residential care was highly underdeveloped and even more so foster care. Such residential units as existed were very large and often staffed by untrained workers. In fact, social work training in general in the GDR was considerably less developed than in the FRG.

Now Eastern Germany is having to adapt to the methods of the former FRG: pluralistic, rather than highly coordinated and centralized, services; contracting out to voluntary/private organizations; more emphasis on family care; an influx of Western trained social work staff; new approaches to residential and foster care. Social work training centres in the west are paired with training centres in the east to improve and adapt social work training methods. There is some suggestion that although these developments may well improve welfare services in the east, some assets may be lost: for instance, the community networks and coverage that the older system developed, and more emphasis on women having less choice about their domestic roles; which echoes our findings in the earlier parts of this chapter on issues such as childcare provision and abortion rights.

Solidarity in France

When we turn to the principle of solidarity, which is said to be influential in conservative corporatist welfare systems, we once again find some similarities in the France–Germany comparison – as well as considerable complexities. On the face of it, child and family social care services in France have a highly solidaristic component. After all, we have already noted several commentators who emphasize that a strong two-way responsibility between family and society, rather alien to English eyes, pervades French service provision. Moreover, many British commentators (Cannan 1992, 1996; Cannan *et al.* 1992; Cooper 1994a, b; Cooper *et al.* 1995; Hetherington 1996) set great store by the emphasis placed on the concept of social inclusion within French social care practice.

For instance, in contrast to the highly targeted and stigmatizing focus of English childcare practice on child protection (see Chapter 2) and the place of family centres within that system, Cannan (1992) considers the role of *centres sociaux* and other French services in providing a relatively universal resource which families most at risk can then be encouraged to use. Similarly, Madge and Attridge (1996: 139) note that the work of British health visitors is far more intensive, intrusive and child abuse focused than the remit of their equivalent in France, the *puericultrices*. In terms of juvenile justice policies as well, Downes (1994: 8) notes that the French system stresses familial and societal integration far more than the more individualistic English system.

Although I acknowledge the validity of those specific judgements, I nevertheless want to critique some of the general premises about social solidarity and social inclusion which lie behind them. In the context of social care I would like to suggest again that sometimes the line between 'social inclusion' and social control is a thin and uncertain one. In terms of social care this is particularly pertinent given the fact that one of the central tasks of some local government social workers in France has been the distribution of family benefits (Madge and Attridge 1996: 135). As we have already noted, such a financial role for social workers is not unusual in Europe: Britain is an exception. In Germany, a similar financial role is fulfilled by one branch of social work there (Munday 1996b). In both Germany and France we might ask ourselves how far regulation of service users' resources impacts upon that delicate balance between care and control which seems to characterize social care provision in all countries. As we saw above, this balance has been further imperilled in France by the fact that some public social care staff are centrally involved in the operation of RMI – and I have already outlined serious concerns about the role of RMI as an instrument of social control.

This issue refers us to other possible fissures in the discourse of solidarity, centred on inclusion and the degree of inclusion available to various sections of the population. Discussion in Cooper (1994b) and Cooper *et al.* (1995) about the French ideology of citizenship, integration and social solidarity offers clues about the problems with that ideology. Cooper *et al.* (1995: 143) regard these principles as being on the whole positive:

> in France there is a prevailing attitude that given time, good professional help, the presence of a benign authority, and a determination to interfere only where absolutely necessary, people may be able to handle matters for themselves. If the apparent cohesion of French society in terms of shared norms and values, or at least shared debates about these, has its claustrophobic side, equally it has its liberating aspect too.

They note that these principles are also central to French practices in the protection of children. They represent those practices as a 'cycle of trust and optimism in social work–family relationships' which 'operate in a positively reinforcing manner'. This French family support model is contrasted with the English child protection system, where a cycle of mistrust and pessimsm operates. In Chapter 8 I will critique Cooper *et al.*'s (1995) interpretation by suggesting that while the English child protection model is indeed wholly inadequate, the French family support model is also often dangerous to children. What is missing from Cooper *et al.*'s analysis of child protection (1995) is a sufficient attention to the reality of oppression and power imbalance within families where child abuse occurs. As we shall see in Chapter 8, one can argue that the much-vaunted social inclusion promoted by French protective services to families may in reality advantage abusing parents rather than their vulnerable children. The general point I am making here is that social inclusion may be mediated by a whole series of power differentials. In the specific case of child abuse one of the most important differentials relates to age and ageism: the relative lack of power held by children.

The same failure to recognize the pervasive nature of structural oppression also marks Cooper *et al.*'s (1995: Chapter 10) over-optimistic analysis of 'race' and racism in France. Although there is an ambiguity about this analysis, there seems to be a clear implication that they approve of the French approach to 'race', racism and cultural diversity more than the British approach, which seeks to challenge structural oppression and focuses on anti-racist strategies. The allegedly more sophisticated French approach fosters multiple, unfinished cultural identities and Cooper *et al.* (1995: 138–9) draw parallels between this approach and Gilroy's (1993) critique of anti-racism.

Unfortunately, the analysis offered by Cooper *et al.* (1995) centrally ignores two issues of power. The first is the lived and multiple oppression of many black people in France regardless of whether they possess French citizenship or not. This is reflected in urban civil unrest and the popularity of the National Front. After all, in the first round of the 1997 French parliamentary elections the National Front gained over 15 per cent of the national vote. Second, there is the privileging of one identity (French citizenship) over others in France, so that, for instance, there is virtually no provision made for Muslim practices within the education system (Rex 1992). Once again, social inclusion is mediated by relations of power, this time centred on the phenomena of 'race' and culture.

We can extend this critique to issues of gender and other dimensions of oppression. In Chapter 8 I will demonstrate that the awareness of child sexual abuse in France (and many other continental countries) is much more limited than in England: and this includes awareness of abuse perpetrated by welfare professionals (Pringle 1996b). At the same time, I will suggest that the family support approach to dealing with child sexual abuse which is predominant in France (and, once again, many other continental countries) is dangerous because it fails to address the fundamental power dynamics which generate that social problem. In Chapter 8 I will relate both the French lack of awareness and their inadequate welfare response to the fact that forms of oppression central to the genesis of child sexual abuse are ignored there. These forms of oppression relate not only to gender but also to sexuality, age and disability. This fits with the pattern we have already seen in French power-blind approaches to other social problems. It is as if the passion for social cohesion and solidarity in France creates a resistance within the French welfare context to acknowledging and challenging fundamental social fissures.

Solidarity in Germany

Social care practice in Germany also demonstrates certain solidaristic elements, particularly when these are contrasted with the marked lack of solidaristic principles characterizing social care for children in England.

Despite some cuts in provision owing to economic recession and the
EMU criteria, German social care services tend to be more inclusive
than those in England. For instance, let us take the example of juvenile
justice. In comparing diversion from custody policies on the continent
and in England, John Pitts (1994: 34) comments:

> it is clear that in France, Germany and Holland social and economic pol-
> icies are developed with an eye to their impact upon the quality of social
> relations and community life.

Lorenz (1995: 6), discussing the disadvantages of youth work in England,
notes that in France, Germany and the Netherlands the 'concept of
"pedagogy" gives youth workers a clearer mandate to explore, to experi-
ment, to be creative.' While recognizing that there is still a long way to
go, Speiss (1994: 38) can nevertheless summarize German diversionary
policies as follows:

> The expansion of diversion as well as of probation in Germany demon-
> strates that practicable alternatives to formal sentencing and to imprison-
> ment do exist and that it is promising and justifiable to go further on this
> path.

This contrasts sharply with punitive British policies, which have, since
1992, sent the latter country 'into reverse' compared to its continental
neighbours (Pitts 1994: 33). We should note in passing, however, that
Speiss also emphasizes the massive variations in diversionary policies
not only between the German *Länder* but also within individual ones:
demonstrating how principles of subsidiarity and solidarity can interact
in a complex and potentially contradictory manner (1994: 34–5).

If we now turn to the example of child abuse and child protection
practices in Germany, we again find that solidaristic principles are prominent compared to England – but that the picture is not straightforward.
Whereas in England we have reached a point where social work in
the field of childcare has become almost wholly confined to the issue
of child abuse (see Chapter 2), in Germany public childcare services,
combined with youth services, tend to be more broadly based and less
exclusively focused on child abuse (Munday 1996b). Of course, as I shall
discuss more fully in Chapter 8, one needs to be cautious in the way one
interprets such a broader approach. While it may well have advantages,
it may also indicate a less developed awareness of the extent of child
abuse than is the case in England. Certainly, there are fewer statistical
data available in Germany on child abuse (Wustendorfer 1995), and that
includes abuse which is perpetrated by welfare professionals (Pringle
1993, 1996b). This is highly reminiscent of the criticism we made earlier about low levels of child abuse awareness in France: the same criticism can be aimed at the situation in Germany.

The German Children and Young Person's Act places stress on issues of prevention and therapeutic assistance, though, like the Children's Act in England, it depends upon adequate resourcing to fulfil its potential (Wustendorfer 1995). As far as Germany is concerned, this point returns us to the issue of local variations in terms of both different local authorities and the former FRG/GDR divide. In the former FRG territory there is more awareness than in the former GDR about child abuse, and protection infrastructures are less developed in the latter than in the former (Armstrong and Hollows 1991: 153–4).

In the western part of Germany, 'voluntary' and charitable organizations play a major role in providing therapeutic assistance, as one might expect. In terms of child abuse, one of the most important of these since the mid-1970s has been the child protection centres which have grown up in major cities (Wustendorfer 1995). In Chapter 8 I will discuss their approach to child abuse, and specifically child sexual abuse, in detail.

At this point, we need only note that although the German child protective structures are different from those in France, nevertheless the basic principles used by the centres in Germany are very similar to those solidaristic ones which underpin protective services in France: a heavy emphasis on family support and the social integrity of the family as the fundamental unit of society. Consequently, the strictures which I outlined above regarding the French system apply equally to the solidaristic practice of the German child protection centres. That practice may deny fundamental power imbalances within the family and might therefore tend to leave children insufficiently protected. The power imbalances involved in the genesis of child abuse which the centres do not seem to address sufficiently relate, again, to issues of age, gender, sexuality and disability.

All these issues are explored much more deeply in Chapter 8. We now see that the central point I make in that chapter is directly relevant to Germany as well as to France: a strong commitment in a welfare system to principles of social cohesion and solidarity may lead to the denial of fundamental social oppressions and a reluctance to challenge them in welfare practice.

Let us now summarize this section. Compared to social care practice in England, German practice may well be broader, less targeted and not so focused on concerns about child abuse. In these respects we may justifiably see it as being more socially inclusive. On the other hand, the relative lack of awareness about child abuse and the greater dominance of family support approaches to this issue in Germany indicate that those inclusive solidaristic elements may be adversely mediated by oppressive power relations associated with, for instance, ageism, sexism, heterosexism and disability.

CONCLUSIONS

In the first part of this chapter, we concluded that the model of a 'conservative corporatist' welfare system was seriously fractured when French and German child welfare policies were compared in relation to topics such as financial support and day-care. This fracturing partly arose from their different responses to issues of oppression along dimensions of gender, 'race' and age. We might note that such divisions within the conservative corporatist model around child and family issues are not confined to Germany and France. For instance, had we chosen to study the situation in Belgium (another allegedly 'conservative corporatist' system), we would again have found large divergences in provision of day-care and benefits between that country and Germany (Schweie 1994), as well as a few much smaller differences between Belgium and France (Hantrais and Letablier 1996: 129).

In this chapter we also observed that the concept of 'conservative corporatism' is fractured by the extent of regional and local variations in the level and form of service provision within individual countries (Duncan 1995). Regionalism is probably especially relevant to those states, such as France and Germany, where the principle of subsidiarity has particular salience. Moreover, the issue of regional variation exhibited an additional dimension when we surveyed the differences in childcare policy and practice between the eastern and western parts of reunified Germany.

Our analysis of French and German social care practices in the second half of the chapter has not revealed such a marked contrast between the two countries. Both of them seem to share more commonalities here than either of them do with England. On the other hand, some differences of emphasis between French and German approaches were carried over from the first to the second half of the chapter. This was most apparent in the even greater stress placed in Germany on subsidiarity. Indeed, this was sometimes at the expense of solidarity in terms, for instance, of family responsibilities, the role of charities and local variations in service provision. However, in both countries social care was heavily influenced by the dual principles of subsidiarity and solidarity, with a range of relatively supportive welfare measures being provided in France and Germany compared to Britain. A question mark still exists about how far these supportive measures can remain a realistic policy objective for either French or German governments in the light of the drive towards EMU (Begg and Nectoux 1995; Grevot 1996a). The election of the left-wing government in June 1997 suggests that at least in France considerable public resistance remains towards austerity policies when they reach a certain point. It will be interesting to watch future developments: particularly since the left-wing victory in France resulted to some extent from the strength of the ultra-right vote in the parliamentary elections. So far, as we noted earlier, initial evidence suggests that the new administration will continue some degree of cutting and targeting (Masters 1997).

In this chapter another major issue central to the theme of the book emerged strongly, which places existing French and German welfare approaches in a less favourable light. We demonstrated how a strong welfare commitment to principles of social solidarity in both countries seemed to create a denial of fundamental social oppressions and the welfare problems generated by them. Consequently, there also appeared to be a lack of welfare responses which might effectively challenge those forms of oppression. On the contrary, in the case of child abuse it seemed that welfare responses might sometimes compound the oppression of children by failing to offer sufficient protection to them. As we noted in Chapter 2, welfare systems themselves may be structured by those same forms of oppression which permeate the society of which they are a part: hence their frequent tendency to collude with oppression rather than challenge it. To some extent, this point seems relevant to the situation in France and Germany. In Chapters 8 and 9 I shall argue that it is in fact even more relevant to continental countries such as France and Germany than it is to Britain, where at least some coherent, albeit tenuous, concept of anti-oppressive welfare practice has emerged.

4

CHILDREN, SOCIAL WELFARE AND 'RUDIMENTARY' WELFARE SYSTEMS

INTRODUCTION

As we noted in Chapter 1, it was partly as a reaction to a perceived gap in Esping-Andersen's (1990) welfare typology that a fourth welfare model was defined (Leibfried 1993) encompassing those countries of Western Europe with less extensive formal welfare systems. We also noted in Chapter 1 that the labels appended to this model tended to be pejorative to a greater or lesser extent: for instance, the Latin rim, thereby implying a certain marginality; and the term 'rudimentary welfare model' itself has a patronizing quality.

It is probably fair to say that there is more dispute about the conceptual validity of this model than any other. A reflection of that is the lack of clarity over the countries which belong to it. Sometimes, under the rubric of Catholic corporatism, Ireland is included on the grounds that it displays the typical features of 'subsidiarity, family solidarity and social consensus' (McLaughlin 1993: 206). Other commentators, such as Katrougalos (1996: 57), concede that Ireland shares in common with the countries of the Mediterranean a relatively low level of social expenditure, the insurance principle and sexist attitudes to women's family role. However, Katrougalos goes on to suggest that the largely tax-financed basis of Ireland's social protection and the latter's semi-universalistic profile justify categorizing it as a 'laggardly' partner to Britain, combining neo-liberalism with a 'Bevridgean' [sic] influence.

Similarly, Italy also holds an ambiguous position, having originally been included by Esping-Andersen (1990) within the domain of 'conservative corporatism'. Much of the confusion over the position of Italy within welfare typologies surely derives from the massive divergence between the social profiles of the north and south of the country (Ferrara 1996: 21–2; Spano 1996).

At a more general level, one recent commentator has critiqued the alleged 'rudimentary' quality of this typology in the light of the generous pensions programmes offered by many Mediterranean states. He has also questioned the alleged centrality of Catholicism in the development of their welfare systems (Ferrara 1996: 18). However, Ferrara retains the concept of a South European model (Greece, Italy, Portugal, Spain) on the grounds that it displays four idiosyncratic features: a highly polarized 'corporatist' income maintenance system, with a massive divergence between extreme generosity and lack of social protection for differing sectors of society; national health services of various extents; a 'highly collusive mix' between public and non-public providers of welfare; and the existence of highly developed clientalist networks (Ferrara 1996: 17).

By contrast, Katrougalas (1996) rejects the notion of a discrete South European model, seeing it as a sub-set of conservative corporatism. Although he acknowledges that a limited breadth and depth of social protection is common to the countries of that region, their welfare lag 'simply reflects the delay in the construction of the welfare state, and more generally, the relative economic underdevelopment of the Mediterranean South' (Katrougalas 1996: 43). He concludes that these countries are now catching up with the conservative corporatist ones (pp. 43–4). In making this judgement Katrougalos seems in harmony with the approach of Esping-Andersen (1996b: 66–87) in his later writing, where there is only reference to an all-embracing continental European welfare model. On the other hand, most of the countries of South Europe are in fact accorded only minimal attention by Esping-Andersen (1996a): Greece and Portugal do not even merit a mention in the index of that work, and neither does Ireland.

In this chapter we shall bear in mind these ongoing debates as we consider the resources and services available for the welfare of children and their carers in those countries which may, or variously may not, constitute a distinct welfare typology: Greece, Ireland, Italy, Portugal and Spain. How far does such a typology help us to understand child welfare in those states? We will survey welfare provision for children and their carers under four headings: financial support; parental leave arrangements; day-care services; and social care.

FINANCIAL SUPPORT

Socio-economic similarities

As we have seen, in their recent survey of family policies in Europe, Hantrais and Letablier (1996) eschew any simplistic global taxonomy of European welfare systems, preferring instead to make empirical, often overlapping, classifications based on particular themes of social policy. In their analysis, the countries of the Mediterranean and Ireland do cluster together in important ways. For instance, drawing on a British research study, Hantrais and Letablier (1996: 162) note that the least generous European Union member states in terms of child benefit packages (including housing costs) are Portugal, Italy, Ireland, Spain and Greece. Excluding housing costs does not alter the cluster, only the ordering of countries within it, largely because of the particularly high housing costs in Spain and Greece (Ruxton 1996: 116). When they consider how far the family is constitutionally designated as an object for promotion and protection, a similar clustering occurs (Hantrais and Letablier 1996: 45–6, 183), although the precise form of constitutional support varies between the relative interventionism of the state in Portugal and the more 'hands-off' stance of Italy, Spain and Ireland (Hantrais and Letablier 1996: 143).

Moreover, if we consider health provision it is striking that all these countries (including Ireland) have been developing public national health services (Ruxton 1996: 257), albeit with varying degrees of success (Saraceno and Negri 1994; Ferrara 1996: 22–5). This contrasts rather markedly with the six allegedly conservative corporatist states of the Union which are, in this respect at least, commonly characterized by more pluralist health systems. This is a fact which casts some doubt on Katragoulas's (1996: 42–3) argument that the Mediterranean countries are simply developmentally 'laggard' members of the conservative corporatist model.

In this book one particular focus within our survey of child welfare is the gendered operation of welfare systems, a consideration virtually absent in Esping-Andersen's initial analysis (1990) and still given a low profile in his more recent work (1996b). In terms of the way social protection systems are gendered, the cluster of Mediterranean countries and Ireland once again seems to offer a useful, though not all-encompassing, point of reference. As regards a wide range of relevant issues, such as encouragement of women's labour market participation, vertical and horizontal labour segregation, differential levels of social protection, provision for lone-parent families and divorce rates, these countries generally present a relatively patriarchal profile compared to the rest of Western Europe. This is widely reflected in a series of comparative studies focusing on issues of gender, social protection and family policy (for instance, Lewis 1993; Siaroff 1994; Duncan 1995).

This clustering also occurs in relation to other statistical evidence crucial to the welfare of children: for instance, comparisons of national poverty rates. Of course, measures of poverty are notoriously problematic (Ramprakash 1994; Nolan and Whelan 1996). However, it is surely significant that European Union data analysed under the POVERTY 3 programme placed the same five countries among the six poorest in the Union using either expenditure or income as a measure (Ramprakash 1994: 124). This state of affairs has a direct impact on the social welfare of children. One statistical survey suggests that in all the Mediterranean countries, plus Ireland, at least 15 per cent of children below the age of fourteen years were living in poverty towards the end of the 1980s: the figure for Ireland was actually 21 per cent; and this was surpassed by Portugal with 22 per cent (Ruxton 1996: 175).

Socio-economic dissimilarities

On the other hand, we should not be deluded into thinking that this clustering means we can always simply talk about these countries in one breath. For instance, even in terms of the patriarchal features of their welfare systems, which we discussed earlier, complexity exists. This is demonstrated by a consideration of female labour market participation, where Portugal, in particular, presents a rather different profile from other members within the cluster owing to the relatively high, and full-time, female employment rates pertaining in that country. Moreover, Hantrais and Letablier (1996: 98) point out a whole series of smaller complexities around female employment in this cluster that further underline the dangers of oversimplification.

The issue of poverty provides an even broader example of the limits of generalization. Here the complexities within the overall picture are, at the very least, twofold. On the one hand, the sections of the population most affected by poverty differ from country to country in the cluster (Ruxton 1996: 176–7). In Greece older persons are particularly vulnerable, while in Ireland families with children loom large in the poverty statistics. Poverty rates in Portugal are very high, but it is single people and older people there who seem more vulnerable than families. A similar situation seems to occur in Spain, though lone mothers are highly at risk there and structural discrimination against women is especially marked (Cousins 1995). By contrast, Greece and, to a lesser extent, Italy provide some financial protection for lone parents (Ferrara 1996: 22). In Italy itself families with three or more children seem in most danger (Ruxton 1996: 177).

The situation in Italy alerts us to the second example of complexity within the statistics on poverty: the importance of local variations (Ferrara 1996: 21–2; Ruxton 1996: 176–7). In previous chapters we have sought to emphasize the importance of regionalism in understanding the operation of welfare systems 'on the ground', as recently pointed out by Duncan (1995). Nowhere in Europe is this more apposite than in the countries of the Mediterranean: perhaps slightly less so in relation to Ireland. The importance of regionalism partly relates, of course, to actual differentials in levels of poverty. So, in centre–north Italy the average poverty rate is 9 per cent, while in the South it reaches 26.4 per cent (Ferrara 1996: 22). Similarly, in Spain regions such as Catalonia and the Canaries (and to a lesser extent Madrid, Navarra and La Rioja) exhibit much higher disposable income measures than, say, Extremadura or Andalucia (Ayala 1994: 161–2). In some countries (for instance, Spain and Italy) social assistance and minimum income schemes will themselves depend upon local variation in practice (Ruxton 1996: 116). We may also note in passing that neither Greece nor Portugal has any general assistance scheme at all (Hantrais and Letablier 1996: 148).

Regionalism also influences the precise forms of poverty as well as the sheer amount. A particularly clear example of this is provided by Italy (Ruxton 1996: 177). As Spano (1996: 19) notes, in the north 'poverty is concentrated in one or two person households . . . the majority of the poor population . . . is elderly . . . there is a remarkable level of "feminisation" of poverty.' She contrast this with the structure of poverty in the south, where 'almost half of poor people live in large families: . . . the main age group living in poverty is the youngest (under 30 years old) . . . poverty affects the people with children and the young.' Moreover, Spano (1996: 22) argues that strategies for dealing with poverty must also be differentiated between north and south. In the north, she believes, material social services are the priority. While she acknowledges that these services are required for the south too, Spano (1996: 22) emphasizes that:

> since here, most poverty is caused by, or at least connected with, unemployment, and as most of the poor are children and the young, policies against poverty appear much more relevant. And policies against poverty in the South necessarily mean economic and, in particular, employment policies rather than social policies.

Defining characteristics of a Mediterranean cluster?

To a greater or lesser extent a similar differential analysis could be applied to all the Mediterranean states. Indeed, despite the fact that regionalism complicates any oversimple social policy analysis, we could, paradoxically, argue that 'hyper-regionalism' itself can be seen as a defining characteristic of the Mediterranean cluster, partly as a result of geography and partly due to history (Ferrara 1996).

This reference to history and geography reminds us of reasons for the limited social welfare developments in the Mediterranean zone, some of which also apply to Ireland, and some of which do not. On the one hand, all these countries (including Ireland) have historically, and more recently, relied on agricultural economies to a greater extent than the rest of the Union (Ferrara 1996). Katragoulas (1996: 43) himself emphasizes this point, which seems to be at odds with his assertion that the social protection lag in the Mediterranean has no institutional basis (p. 42).

While household size in the Mediterranean countries, as well as Ireland (Hantrais and Letablier 1996: 21–2), has decreased, it is still the highest in Europe (Katragoulas 1996: 43). A similar pattern exists with regard to the number of one-person households (Hantrais and Letablier 1996: 20).

As we saw above, a marked tendency towards clientalism has also been identified as a defining feature of this welfare model, although it is considerably less relevant to Ireland. Such clientalism and patronage within the welfare systems distorts delivery of support and services across the board, including provision for child welfare. This clientalism is itself partly a function of yet another alleged defining characteristic of the Mediterranean countries, a historical one again not shared with Ireland: the legacy of totalitarian government in the relatively recent past (Ayala 1994; Cousins 1995; Ferrara 1996; Katragoulas 1996). This legacy has contributed to the idiosyncratic timing of welfare developments in the Mediterranean countries. That timing varies between countries but clearly differs from the social welfare chronology of other Union member states.

Likewise, fascist history was partly responsible for the dualism in social protection common to Mediterranean states which we mentioned earlier. On the one hand, there is the *iper-garantismo* selectively granted to the labour market core (Ferrara 1996: 21), heavily weighted in favour of men (Cousins 1995). On the other hand, we also find varying degrees of lesser protection available to different sectors of society, with an absence, or limited availability, of general assistance schemes (Ruxton 1996: 116). Ferrara (1996: 21) notes that this latter phenomenon results in a structure of social protection which is in fact far more complex than simply dualism.

The financial well-being of families has tended in the past to depend upon at least one family member falling into the category of *iper-garantismo*. The increasing failure of this to happen is one reason why the incidence of poor households is now so high in Portugal, Spain, Greece and South Italy (Ferrara 1996: 21–2; Katragoulas 1996: 56), with

clear implications for the welfare of the children within those households (Ruxton 1996: 175), as we noted earlier. The levels of unemployment, centrally linked to much of the poverty in the Mediterranean and
Ireland, are relatively high from a European Union perspective, ranging
from 7.2 per cent of the workforce in Portugal and 8.5 in Greece to 11.7
in Italy, 12.3 in Ireland and 13.8 in Spain (*The European* 7–13 November
1996: 20).

This incidence of poverty and low employment may well be linked to
the postponement of marriages and deferment of first births which has
resulted in a marked decrease in fertility rates across all these countries
between 1980 and the nineties (Cousins 1995: 185; Ruxton 1996: 80–1).
Indeed, particularly low rates are characteristic of the South European
countries relative to other Union members. However, once again we
need to limit our generalizations: Portugal has a medium-level fertility
rate compared to Germany, which actually has the third lowest (Ruxton
1996: 81). As for Ireland, it still has the second highest fertility rate in
the Union, even if it has almost halved since 1970 (Ruxton 1996: 81).
This is yet another important example of Ireland's divergence from the
Mediterranean cluster.

The economic pressures on the systems of social protection in South
Europe are likely to increase further given the drive in those states towards EMU and the massive problems which all of them face in achieving the requisite financial criteria (Begg and Nectoux 1995: 293; Ferrara
1996: 31–2), not least the large size of their national debts as a ratio of
GDP (Naudin and Clarke 1996: 19). In fact, all the Mediterranean states
are doubtful as far as the first round of EMU is concerned. By contrast,
again, Ireland is one of the few member states which may well be eligible,
partly because it has a dispensation regarding the size of its national debt.

To summarize: we may conclude from the discussion so far that in
terms of financial support measures and the cultural/social/historical/
economic factors associated with them, some form of a case can be made
out for a limited clustering of the welfare systems in Greece, Ireland,
Italy, Portugal and Spain. However, we have also noted variability between these countries around issues such as benefit coverage, female
labour market participation, regionalism, birth rates and socio-cultural-
historical backgrounds. This is particularly true of Italy and Ireland,
though for different reasons. Perhaps of all these countries, Ireland seems
most out of step with the others, and one questions the utility of associ-
ating it with them in this way.

That state of affairs is reflected in the relatively sophisticated categorizations offered by Hantrais and Letablier (1996) regarding various
aspects of family policy and practice. Thus when they attempt to categorize the countries of the Union in terms of national policies towards

reconciliation of women's family and employment roles, Portugal, Spain and Greece are clustered together as representing 'financially constrained state intervention' (pp. 133–4). Ireland is placed in the same category as the United Kingdom as a state which has rejected the principle of state interference in family life and 'has concentrated on the problems of poor families and equal rights between spouses, rather than the family–employment relationship' (p. 133). Finally, Italy is grouped along with those countries (Austria, Germany, Luxembourg and the Netherlands) which have adopted a supportive approach regarding 'the family–employment relationship in terms of organising paid work and family life sequentially by redistributing economic resources from productive (paid) workers to reproductive (unpaid parents at home)' (p. 130).

They then define three clusters, one of which encompasses the member states of South Europe, including Italy, but which also overlaps with other clusters. I will quote their useful summary regarding this cluster, which skilfully balances the value of generalization against a recognition of true complexity:

> Divorce rates are low in Greece, Italy and Spain. Divorce, remarriage and cohabitation are viewed less negatively in Spain than in the three other countries. Fertility rates are among the lowest in the Union, particularly in northern Italy and Spain . . . Extramarital births are particularly low in Greece, Italy and Spain but higher in Portugal than in some of the central EU member states. Lone parenthood is less widespread than elsewhere in the Union and is viewed negatively, especially in Greece. Female economic activity rates in Greece, Italy and Spain are consistently below the levels reached in other member states, whereas Portugal registers some of the highest initial rates and maintains them for women with young children.
>
> (Hantrais and Letablier 1996: 180)

Significantly, Hantrais and Letablier (1996: 180–1) cannot fit Ireland into any particular cluster.

On the whole, my review of the financial context for child and family welfare systems within these countries supports the judgement of Hantrais and Letablier (1996): the Mediterranean states can be clustered usefully together for analytic purposes, but with clear and extensive limitations in mind. Moreover, including Ireland in this cluster seems even more problematic.

This is far less definite than the kind of welfare model proposed by Leibfried (1993) and others in the spirit of Esping-Andersen. Once again, we conclude that such a framework fails to grasp the complexities of welfare provision and ignores many of the diverse forms of oppression which bear down on children and their carers.

In the next section of this chapter I consider whether these judgements about clustering extend to welfare provision in the form of parental leave.

PARENTAL LEAVE ARRANGEMENTS

Greece, Ireland, Italy, Portugal and Spain all grant maternity leaves of varying lengths and with different levels of financial support. With regard to the latter, full earnings are provided in Greece, Portugal and Spain; payments in Ireland are at 70 per cent of earnings apart from the last four optional weeks, which are unpaid; Italy's payments are at 80 per cent of earnings (European Commission 1996a: 144–6; Ruxton 1996: 140–3).

Statutory paternity leave exists solely in Spain (two days) (European Commission 1996a: 145). The only country in this cluster not previously to grant any statutory parental leave has been Ireland (Ruxton 1996: 144). However, the recent European Union Directive on parental leave now applies to Ireland: at least three months in case of birth or adoption to be taken up until the child becomes eight years old (Pochet *et al.* 1996a: 68). But the issue of payment has not been dealt with, so that the worker taking parental leave must rely on her or his own social security benefits (Pochet *et al.* 1996b: 166). All the South European states already had at least this level of provision prior to the Directive. Some had considerably more provision. For instance, the entitlement in Portugal was between six and twenty-four months per family, although this was unpaid. In fact, in all the countries of South Europe parental leave is unpaid, except in Italy, where parental leave of six months (strictly speaking mother's entitlement, which can be transferred to the father) is paid at 30 per cent of earnings (European Commission 1996a: 145; Ruxton 1996: 147). With regard to leave for pressing family reasons (such as the child's health), this is also covered by the new Directive (Pochet *et al.* 1996a: 68). In reality, all the countries in the cluster, apart from Ireland, already had some form of provision in this respect, paid in Spain and unpaid elsewhere (European Commission 1996a: 144–6).

Although it is difficult to balance out how these provisions compare with those available in other member states because of the number of variables pertaining, we can say that the South European states tend to be considerably more generous than the United Kingdom (see Chapter Two), with Ireland closer to the latter than the former until the Directive came into force. Provision by the South European states is also considerably less generous than that offered by the Nordic states in terms of monetary compensation for parental leave and, particularly in the case of Sweden, regarding the amount of parental leave available (see Chapter 5). As we have seen, the allegedly conservative corporatist category of member states is more variable in terms of these provisions and so harder to compare with the cluster focused on in this chapter (see Chapter 3). For instance, the Netherlands provides for six months of parental leave without any financial compensation, while both France and Germany allow for thirty-six months with mainly flat-rate compensation (European Commission 1996a: 145). Generally speaking, though, provision in conservative corporatist countries is more generous than that offered by those of South Europe (including Italy), while being rather less generous than Sweden and, to some extent, Finland.

Once again, we see that a clustering of South European countries offers some degree of conceptual value in terms of analysing patterns of child welfare provision. On the other hand, in terms of leave availability Ireland was clearly closer to the model associated with the United Kingdom than to South Europe. To some extent that is still the case, though implementation of the Directive on parental leave now brings Ireland nearer to the South European cluster.

This clustering does seem to bear some correspondence to the concept of a rudimentary welfare model. However, once again there are a mass of complexities to which such a taxonomy does not do justice. In part the inadequacy derives from the fact that this model, like those of Esping-Andersen (1990, 1996b), fails adequately to address the multilayered and multiconnected range of social oppressions which bear down on children and their carers: a point which has been, and will be, repeated throughout this study.

DAY-CARE PROVISION

In these countries the level of publicly funded day-care for under-fours is generally rather low, ranging from about 2 per cent in Ireland and Spain, through a level of 6 per cent in Italy, to 12 per cent in Portugal. This is comparable with, or higher than, the United Kingdom/Western German rates of 2 per cent and of Austria's 3 per cent, but also much lower than the level in all the Nordic European Union member states, the Eastern parts of Germany and pro-natalist countries such as France and Belgium (European Commission 1996a: 148).

In relation to provision for 3–6-year-olds, the lowest rate in the cluster is achieved by Portugal (48 per cent coverage) and the highest by Italy (91 per cent), Spain (84 per cent) and Greece (an estimated 70 per cent). These latter levels are comparable with those achieved by the Nordic states and are surpassed only by the huge rates of provision in France, Belgium and Eastern Germany (European Commission 1996a: 148).

Several other features of day-care provision are worthy of particular note in this survey. First, distinctions also need to be drawn between the majority of countries in the cluster, which do not provide any financial subsidy for childcare costs, and those such as Greece where parental contributions are low and/or major subsidies are available (European

Commission 1996a: 52; Ruxton 1996: 112). Such distinctions may well be linked to degrees of awareness regarding the pro-natalist potential of day-care provision. For instance, the Childcare Network notes that a 1994 Greek parliamentary committee report on demographic problems concluded that:

> the issue of inadequate services for the children of working parents is a major factor in the decline in the birth rate . . . The Committee recommended legislation that would require the Ministry of Social Welfare to establish services for children below compulsory school age within 2 years and following an assessment of need.
>
> (European Commission 1996a: 49)

However, in some countries the desire to expand day-care provision is frustrated by economic pressures, including the drive towards EMU, as we discussed earlier. Greece is yet again a case in point (European Commission 1996a: 49–50), as are Italy (European Commission 1996a: 75) and Spain (European Commission 1996a: 55). The European Union Structural Funds, including the Social Fund and New Opportunities for Women (NOW) projects, have played some role in helping to develop day-care provision, particularly regarding their quality, in the Mediterranean countries as well as in Ireland (European Commission 1996a: 49, 68). However, in both national and Union terms the size of the Structural Funds are so small (Wise and Gibb 1993: Chapter 5) that it is impossible for Union social spending to have a major impact in this or any other welfare field (Begg and Nectoux 1995: 286; Chapter 7, this volume).

The extent and role of private agencies in day-care provision vary across this cluster of states. For instance, in Portugal private organizations play an increasing part in managing publicly funded services (European Commission 1996a: 98). In Ireland private non-subsidized services seem to perform a more substantial, and indeed increasing, function than in the South European countries, since much public welfare provision in the former is narrowly targeted on 'at-risk' children. Thus there occurs a sharp bifurcation in Irish day-care availability similar to that which exists in Britain (European Commission 1996a: 68). This once again underlines the relatively anomolous position of Ireland in terms of the cluster of countries we are surveying in this chapter. On the other hand, the low levels of labour market participation by Irish women with children are far more reminiscent of Greece and Spain than of the United Kingdom (Hantrais and Letablier 1996: 95).

These findings serve to remind us that no simple link can be made between the extent of day-care provision and women's labour market participation when they have children. While generous day-care services may well assist the high participation rates achieved by France, Belgium,

Denmark and Sweden, they do not explain the high activity rates for women with children under seven in Portugal, or the moderate levels achieved by British women with children under two years who lack generous day-care (Hantrais and Letablier 1996: 95).

Nor is there any simple or comprehensive linkage between women's labour market participation and fertility rates across Europe. Relatively low levels of female economic activity in countries such as Greece, Italy and Spain can coexist with low fertility rates. Similarly, relatively high female labour market participation coexists with relatively high fertility rates in Sweden (Hantrais and Letablier 1996: 89–97; Ruxton 1996: 81). As Hantrais and Letablier (1996: 186) note, the evidence for a link between greater family size and increased level of benefits is even more inconclusive, which throws into some doubt pro-natalist family policies focused on financial provision, such as exist in France (see Chapter 3, this volume). Instead they endorse a 1993 Eurobarometer report suggesting that the most important factors in influencing couples' decisions about the number of children they want are:

> housing, the economic situation and unemployment, the cost of bringing up children, worktime flexibility, the availability of good quality childcare and parental leave, in that order . . . Neither family benefits nor tax relief had much importance, suggesting that it may not be the direct and visible family-labelled policies which are most effective in persuading couples to have children, but rather the wider social and economic environment.
>
> (Hantrais and Letablier 1996: 186)

Returning to the specific issue of day-care provision, another important feature in many of the Mediterranean states, though of less note in Ireland, is the marked local and regional variation which occurs within them. This is particularly striking in Italy where the gulf between the North and South which we noted earlier in relation to poverty and unemployment also applies to service provision:

> in the North, there are areas where asili nido [centres for children aged 3–36 months] serve about 30% of children and staff have received continuous training for years; while in other areas of the country, in particular the South, these services do not even exist.
>
> (European Commission 1996a: 74)

These local variations are exacerbated by a serious lack of coordination between service organizers and service providers (European Comission 1996a: 74–5). As we shall see in the next section of this chapter, these characteristics extend to the form and degree of social care provision in Italy – and in the other member countries of the South European cluster.

Before ending our brief analysis of day-care services in the countries of this cluster, we should note one specific area of European development where some of these countries, most especially Italy, have played a lead-ing role – and in some ways a role which may be a little surprising. As we shall explore more fully in Chapter 7, the Childcare Network has for a number of years been actively developing several initiatives which have had considerable impact across the European Union: for instance, its long-term work contributed significantly to the Directive on Parental Leave which we discussed earlier. Here I want to draw readers' attention to one facet of the programme: the need to promote a fuller role for men in childcare, both as parents (European Commission 1993) and as workers in childcare services (European Commission 1996b). That specific issue is also discussed more fully in Chapter 7. What we need to note here is that some of the most vital contributions to this aspect of the Network's activity have come from agencies and individuals located in Italy.

For instance, a ground-breaking seminar on 'men as carers', held in 1993, took place in Ravenna, was jointly organized by the Childcare Network and the regional government of Emilia-Romagna and drew almost half its delegates from Italy (European Commission 1993). Like-wise, the (undated) Childcare Network report on 'fathers, nurseries and childcare' is an account of the close cooperation between two pioneering agencies in this field, a nursery in the United Kingdom and another in Emilia-Romagna.

Given our comments earlier in this chapter about the marked patri-archal relations which structure welfare provision (and indeed society as a whole) in the countries of the Mediterranean, this may seem to be a surprising phenomenon. In response I will make three comments at this stage. First, it may be significant that such a development is being spear-headed in a prosperous area of north Italy rather than in the south, given what we have already said about the differential spread of provision. Second, we should not perhaps be so surprised that anti-sexist initiatives can sometimes occur in social contexts which may be hostile to them: indeed, such hostile contexts may occasionally accompany the develop-ment of relatively progressive initiatives. This is a theme I develop far more broadly in Chapters 8 and 9. Third, I suggest that the policies and practices advocated by the Childcare Network around the greater in-volvement of men in welfare work are only anti-sexist up to a certain point, as viewed from some radical feminist and pro-feminist perspect-ives (Pringle 1997a, b). This is also an argument I develop further in Chapter 7.

Let us now summarize the general picture for day-care in our cluster of countries. In many ways it seems similar to the pictures drawn earlier relating to financial support and leave arrangements. There is a degree of commonality for the Mediterranean states, less so in relation to Ireland. That commonality does bear a resemblance to some features of the rudimentary welfare model but there are numerous levels of complexity which the model does not embrace. This partly reflects the model's relative insensitivity to issues of oppression such as gender and age.

SOCIAL CARE

Some of the features which we have noted in earlier sections of this chapter also pertain to the issue of social care:

1 Some structural similarities between patterns of provision in the countries of the Mediterranean and Ireland combined with significant variations both between them and, at local levels, within them.
2 The particularly ambiguous position of Ireland as regards this cluster of countries.

In the survey which follows, I will focus particularly upon the Republic of Ireland and Italy partly because more data are available in relation to them. However, I will also refer to the position in the other states where appropriate.

Child abuse

The topic of child abuse and child protection usefully highlights some of the idiosyncracies of this group of countries in relation to child welfare. In all the countries of South Europe, awareness of child abuse is considerably less than in most other European states to the north (Sale and Davies 1990; Armstrong and Hollows 1991), and this is particularly so in relation to child sexual abuse (Armstrong and Hollows 1991; Bini and Toselli 1997). Reasons for this relative lack of recognition are various. For instance, as regards Greece, Armstrong and Hollows (1991: 154) note that in cultural terms 'physical punishment of children is not stigmatised and only the most serious cases receive an official response.' Certainly none of these countries operates bans on physical chastisement such as exist in the Nordic states and Austria (Madge and Attridge 1996).

Bini and Toselli (1997), referring to Italy, emphasize familistic ideology as presenting a major obstacle to the recognition and discovery of child abuse. Armstrong and Hollows (1991: 156–9) also identify this 'traditional' family approach as a factor in their explanation of differential attitudes to child abuse across the states of the European Union. Their explanatory model for this differential spread consists of three elements which they apply to the various countries: extent of denial; societal attitudes to child, family and/or state; and definitions of abuse. Significantly, Armstrong and Hollows include the degree to which gender roles and the liberation of women are prominent on the social agendas of each country within the second of those elements. I believe this issue is even more crucial than Armstrong and Hollows allow, and I will seek to develop the importance of that theme in Chapter 8.

Even though it may be at a relatively low level, there is probably more awareness of child abuse and of child sexual abuse in Italy than in the remainder of South Europe. This is particularly true of north Italy (Bini and Toselli 1997). However, the greater level of awareness in the north only represents a variation in quantity, not quality: awareness even there is far more variable and tenuous than in many other parts of Western Europe.

By contrast, the current heightened level of awareness in Ireland does seem to represent a difference in quality. It is clear that there is still considerable resistance to recognizing these issues in Ireland, largely owing to the same traditional familistic and patriarchal values which operate so powerfully in South Europe (Armstrong and Hollows 1991). Nevertheless, it is also clear that the Irish situation, unlike the Mediterranean one, has been influenced by recent events in Britain and the United States (Otithearnaith 1990), particularly the periodic 'scandals' which have occurred in Ireland around the topic of violence to children. Moreover, organizations such as the Irish Society for the Prevention of Cruelty to Children (ISPCC), whose origins stretch back to the late nineteenth century, have also played an important long-term role in highlighting the issue (Buckley 1997). No real parallel exists in the countries of the Mediterranean. The history and impact of these various influences has recently been well articulated by several Irish commentators (Ferguson 1996; Buckley 1996a, b, 1997).

Buckley (1996a, b, 1997) documents the way official Irish responses mirror some of those in England, such as the narrowing focus of childcare on child protection, the primacy of 'investigation' within child protection practice and the conflict between the rights of children and of their parents (Pringle 1997a; Chapter 2, this volume). On the other hand, she also points out the major differences with England, not least the fact that, so far anyway, Ireland has avoided the plethora of bureacratic regulation which dominates the English system of child protection.

The future trajectory of services for the protection of children in Ireland remains uncertain and will be interesting in view of the diverse influences bearing down upon it. As we noted earlier, the danger is that such services will come to dominate Irish childcare provision in the same way as they have done in England. By contrast, when we look at provision in the countries of South Europe the relative lack of awareness about child abuse in both public and professional circles is reflected in a relative absence of specifically child protective services (Sale and Davies

1990). One result of this is that such provision for abused children as does exist tends to be part of general childcare services.

This is still particularly true in Greece (Armstrong and Hollows 1991: 154). Acosta (1990) suggests that a similar situation exists in Spain, even though awareness does appear to have begun developing from a low base (Casas 1993). In Portugal both awareness and provision seem to have moved further ahead, but the concept of specific services is still at a relatively early stage (Clemente 1990). To some extent Italy presents a picture akin to that of Greece, given that in many regions there are few social workers assigned specifically to child physical or sexual abuse and more are available to deal with other childhood issues relating to, for instance, mental health or social marginalization (Bini and Toselli 1997). As one might expect from previous discussion, local variations in relation to child protective services in Italy are massive, and this situation derives from a number of factors.

Above all, national laws relating to the issue of child maltreatment are purely framework in nature, relying on regional implementation and municipal resourcing for service provision. Added to this is the fact that collaboration between judicial and welfare systems is highly variable at the local level (Bini and Toselli 1997). As one might expect, the most focused provision tends to be in northern conurbations, particularly Milan (Vassalli 1990). However, such provision still tends to take the form of pilot programmes. Most of the specific services that do exist in Milan, which are public–private in funding, are family therapy centred (Bini and Toselli 1997), which is unsurprising given our earlier comments about the strong familistic theme in Italian social life.

Yet there are other important and contrasting initiatives in Italy which, like the project on men's participation in childcare described earlier, are at first sight more surprising. For instance, there is the work of the *case delle donne* (protective 'women's houses'), which are especially prevalent in the cities of northern and central Italy. One such *casa* is Artemesia: Centro donne contro la violenza Catia Franci in Florence. As its name suggests, this *casa* began as a resource focusing on violence to women, but for several years now the logic of its work has carried over into the subject of violence to children, especially sexual violence. The centre provides written information and guidance. Apart from raising awareness about the issue, Artemesia also provides counselling services where possible, depending upon funding. Much of this funding has to be negotiated with the various local, municipal and regional authorities.

Unlike the family therapy oriented service we noted above in Milan, many *case delle donne* seem to use a range of feminist perspectives on sexual abuse. It would be a mistake to portray the *case delle donne* as mainstream resources. Unfortunately they tend to have a somewhat marginalized position, and their financial existence often seems precarious. However, their presence is important to this study for several reasons. First, the work they struggle to provide in their localities often represents examples of good practice. Second, their continued existence, and hoped for expansion, in what might be regarded as an inhospitable ideological environment, reminds us about the dangers of overgeneralizing. It also reminds us never to underestimate the creative potential of survivor-led and/or survivor-focused community services. That potential is a topic to which we shall return in Chapter 8.

Another important feature of protective services in Italy which raises wider issues is the situation of ethnic minority groups. Bini and Toselli (1997) emphasize that insofar as some services do exist to protect children in Italy, they are often not geared to the needs of minority groups like Romany people or Albanian refugee children. Such difficulties can be extended to the whole area of social care and minority groups. This is particularly the case because the welfare of children in Italy, as in much of the Mediterranean, still often relies on extensive social networks which, perforce, are closed to those regarded as 'outsiders' by the dominant culture (Bini and Toselli 1997).

Similar considerations apply to Ireland in relation to 'travellers' (O'Higgins 1993; Buckley 1997), though Gilligan (1993: 127) notes that some specialist provision has recently been developed within the care system for their children. It would be a mistake to think that such difficulties around service provision for minority groups are confined to the countries which are the subject of this chapter. After all, in Chapter 3 we highlighted the contrasting but equally worrying plight of minority groups in France and Germany, while the inadequacies of Britain's child welfare system for that country's black population are becoming increasingly well documented (Barn 1993, Pringle 1995; Jackson 1996; Chapter 2, this volume).

We should address one final issue in relation to child abuse. Several commentators mention that the problem of extra-familial child abuse has come to the fore in several Mediterranean countries, particularly Italy (Madge and Attridge 1996; Ruxton 1996) and Greece (Madge and Attridge 1996). Given the highly familistic ideology of these countries, it may be easier for abuse outside families to be acknowledged than abuse inside them. However, once again we should be wary of generalizing too extensively: after all, it appears that extra-familial abuse has not been so clearly recognized in, for instance, Spain (Madge and Attridge 1996). As for Ireland, what is striking is the way that in recent years a public realization has developed concerning extra-familial sexual abuse within the Catholic Church itself, that bastion of traditional Irish society (Buckley 1997).

In concluding this discussion about child abuse, it is perhaps appropriate to emphasize again the ambiguous position of Ireland among our cluster of countries. While it shares some important cultural features with the countries of the Mediterranean, it is also influenced as a result of its history, language and geographical location by the United States and the United Kingdom. In this account we have noted several outcomes of the latter connection. However, unlike the United Kingdom, Ireland does not so far possess a centralized child abuse registration system. In this it shares common ground with Greece, Italy and Spain (Madge and Attridge 1996).

Out-of-home placements

Child abuse is not the only barometer of social care we should consult to assess provision in the Mediterranean states and Ireland. After all, child abuse tends not to be a high priority on the child welfare agendas of the South European countries. Consequently, in some ways we may gain a more extensive appreciation of child welfare interventions by looking at other issues: for instance, the profile of out-of-home placements. On the whole a far greater proportion of children are cared for in institutions across the Mediterranean states than in other West European countries, though Germany and Belgium come close to Mediterranean levels (Colton and Hellinckx 1993; Madge 1994; Ruxton 1996: Chapter 12).

However, we should recognize that in recent years the numbers of children residentially placed have fallen around the Mediterranean, with some concomitant increase in the use of family placement, reflecting general West European trends (Colton and Hellinckx 1993). However, these shifts are considerably less marked than in many other West European states (Ruxton 1996: Chapter 12). There are several reasons for this pattern, which no doubt vary from country to country. For instance, in Greece the slow move to foster care may partly result from professional resistance (Colton and Hellinckx 1993). In Spain, one problem seems to be the relative novelty of foster care and the lack of experience in recruiting appropriate carers (Ruxton 1996: Chapter 12). Reductions in residential care are to some extent a reflection of more preventative services and not simply a transfer from residential to foster care, as can be seen from the statistics in many countries. However, behind both these trends there remains the crucial issue of cost and the relative expense of residential care.

Ireland certainly differs from the Mediterranean states in terms of the residential care–foster care ratio, being far closer to the European Union 'pioneers' in fostering such as Sweden and the United Kingdom (Gilligan 1993; Ruxton 1996: 330). Moreover, the range of family placements available in Ireland is considerably wider than in virtually all the South European countries (Colton and Hellinckx 1993), with perhaps the exception of services available in some northern and central Italian areas (Vecchiato 1993). This reminds us that once again it is important to make allowance for local variations. That applies not only to Italy. In Spain too the central role of the autonomous regions ensures that variability is a factor, though in general Spanish fostering provision tends to be less developed than in Italy (Casas 1993; Vecchiato 1993).

Ireland has also been notable in recent years for moving in the reverse direction to much of the rest of the European Union in terms of its greater use of compulsory legislation for admissions into care (Ruxton 1996). Gilligan (1993: 124) provides various explanations for this trend, one of the most important being the more pressing nature of social problems such as unemployment, drug misuse, AIDS and, last but not least, the growing number of child abuse referrals.

Juvenile justice

Turning to the different ways in which countries deal with crime committed by young people, it is particularly difficult to find meaningful methods of directly comparing practice due to variations in the forms of provision available in these countries (Ruxton 1996: Chapter 11). However, it is relatively clear that the incarceration of young people is considerably higher in Ireland than in the Mediterranean countries (Ruxton 1996: 314). Indeed, this is yet another occasion where practice in Ireland seems closer to the idiosyncratically punitive British response from the early 1990s onwards (see Chapter 2).

It would be wrong to suggest that diversion from custody strategies are widespread and uniform in South Europe. As usual there is a wide range of responses with much local variation, as evidenced by Spain (Ruxton 1996: 310). Perhaps not unexpectedly, the most advanced diversionary practice seems to be developed in the more wealthy and cosmopolitan regions, such as Catalonia (Barberan 1996). However, the overall impression is of a more welfare-oriented response in South Europe than may currently be found in the United Kingdom or Ireland.

CONCLUSIONS

Our review of certain aspects of social care provision for children in those countries often allocated to the Catholic corporatist/rudimentary welfare category provides similar conclusions to our earlier survey of benefit, leave and day-care services. First, it is clear that this rigid form of categorization tends to mask wide variations between all its members. In other words, heterogeneity has to be recognized as a considerable factor in the picture. On the other hand, it would perhaps be even more misleading to suggest that the states encapsulated by this alleged welfare model are simply 'delayed' versions of conservative corporatism as Katragoulas (1996) suggests. Even allowing for the fact that Chapter 3 heavily critiqued the very concept of a conservative corporatist model itself, Katragoulas's argument seems unconvincing when applied to the field of social care.

There are significant parallels between the Mediterranean countries: the structure of their health provision (Ferrara 1996); their relatively low levels of awareness about child abuse and their limited services dedicated to that problem; patterns and levels of residential and foster care; approaches to juvenile crime.

The ambiguous position of Ireland in this categorization has been apparent in relation to many of the issues just mentioned. For historical and cultural reasons, Irish practice has clearly been influenced by idiosyncratic approaches found in England and Wales. Nevertheless, our discussion of child abuse in particular suggested that it would be wholly wrong to align Ireland with England: policy and practice in the former are not the same as in the latter even if there are some commonalities. Irish culture is a complex fusion of many different influences, not least its own Celtic history: its culture and its welfare responses are unique.

Taking this chapter as a whole, there appears to be some analytic value in recognizing a certain clustering of the Mediterranean states as regards welfare policies and practices directed towards children and their carers. However, given the degree of variation and complexity we have found in our survey, actually positing a rudimentary-type welfare model does not seem helpful. As for Irish child welfare policies and practices, on balance it seems doubtful whether it is useful to cluster that country with the Mediterranean states, even though there is a limited degree of commonality between them. This overall conclusion echoes our thoughts expressed in earlier chapters that overarching welfare taxonomies seem to have little analytical value when one is trying to understand the complex play of social disadvantages and oppressions relating to the welfare of children and their carers; or in understanding the range of welfare responses to those disadvantages and oppressions.

5

CHILDREN, SOCIAL WELFARE AND NORDIC WELFARE SYSTEMS: TROUBLE IN PARADISE?

INTRODUCTION

For what was designated by Esping-Andersen (1990, 1996b) as the 'social democratic' or 'Scandinavian' welfare model, I prefer the term 'Nordic' for purposes of geographical clarity, due to uncertainties about the definition of 'Scandinavia'. In using the concept of Nordic welfare systems, however, I will restrict my focus to those in Sweden, Norway, Finland and Denmark.

As we saw in Chapter 1, the welfare parameters of this model have been relatively clearly drawn by Esping-Andersen and those building on his analysis. One of the latter has provided a neat summary of the model's characteristics:

> broad, usually universal, coverage, high income replacement rates, the scope of citizenship rights, and service intensity are four of the basic institutional parameters of the Scandinavian welfare states.
>
> (Stephens 1996: 36)

That definition alerts us again to one of the main limitations of Esping-Andersen's analysis: its primary and rather narrow focus on highly quantifiable elements of welfare support. Once more, this chapter like its predecessors will survey welfare provision for children and their carers more widely, in both cash and kind, to see if that largely positive characterization of these welfare systems holds true.

In Chapter 1 we noted some feminist critiques of this model (Langan and Ostner 1991; Lewis 1993; Gustafsson 1994; Daly 1994; Sainsbury 1994). However, all these critiques to varying extents acknowledge that the welfare systems in the Nordic countries are more broadly generous *and* generally less oppressive to women than others in Western Europe. This chapter, like its predecessors, will re-evaluate Esping-Andersen's typologies, with specific reference to children and their carers, along a range of dimensions of power.

WELFARE TRENDS IN THE NORDIC STATES

Before we focus on services to children and their carers, let us approach this issue first of all from the point of view of general welfare trends. Several recent commentators have sought to qualify Esping-Andersen's analysis on the grounds that it represents only a 'snapshot' in history, whereas welfare systems are in reality dynamic and constantly reforming over time. Perhaps the most influential critique from this point of view has been offered by Kangas (1994). His critique, written very much from a Nordic perspective, sought to compare over time the progress of the welfare systems in Sweden, Finland, Germany and the United Kingdom. Among Kangas's conclusions were two observations especially pertinent to our analysis. First, he pointed out that in some respects by the beginning of the 1990s Finland's welfare system was even more typically 'Scandinavian' than Sweden's. Of course, Kangas also noted that this situation was subject to further dynamic change given the dramatically worsening economic climate in Finland.

Second, he discerned some distinct trends towards welfare system convergence, particularly between Sweden and Finland on the one hand and Germany on the other. These convergences partly related to changes in Germany. However, to a large extent they reflected adaptions to welfare support systems in the Nordic countries under the force of adverse economic pressures. As regards these adaptions, Kangas made specific reference to factors such as the shrinkage of welfare coverage and the increase in social transfers apparent in Sweden and Finland, as well as greater reliance on employee contributions to social insurance in Finland (Kangas 1994: 91–2).

Arthur Gould has made similar points, but with specific reference to Sweden:

> Sadly, the Swedish experiment would seem to have reached the limits of reformism. Decommodification could only go so far. The use of unemployment as a policy device, the privatisation of public services and reductions in welfare benefits, which elsewhere have re-established the primacy of

market discipline and social control, are painfully and slowly dismantling 'the People's Home'.

(Gould 1993: 233)

From these perspectives one could easily draw the conclusion that the characteristic Nordic model of welfare outlined by Esping-Andersen, and partly acknowledged even by his feminist critics, is well nigh dead and buried. Moreover, no doubt there is considerable truth in the analyses of Kangas and Gould. The economic crises recently endured by Sweden and Finland, as well as the more long-term financial pressure suffered by Denmark (Stephens 1996), have taken their toll and we will see this reflected in the welfare supports for children and their carers which we survey below.

However, there is reason to believe that the announcement of the demise of the 'Scandinavian' or Nordic model has been somewhat premature. We need to bear in mind that both Kangas and Gould were writing at the beginning of the 1990s when the economic crisis, at least in Sweden, was at its worst and when the forces of social democracy seemed to be politically in flight. Writing only a few years later, Gould's analysis, though similar, seems to have a rather different tone:

> It needs to be said . . . that despite the recent cuts in welfare, Sweden still possesses one of the most comprehensive and generous systems of welfare provision in Europe and the world . . . the very scale and institutional significance of the Swedish model means that it will be some time before the Swedes descend to the levels of deprivation and inequality seen elsewhere in Europe.
>
> (Gould 1996: 91)

By then a social democratic political influence had been restored in many of the Nordic states, including Sweden. Such a restoration did not mean that negative welfare trends were going into total reverse. After all, in Sweden the Social Democratic Party had previously been involved in welfare retrenchment itself both as the government at the very end of the 1980s and as a relatively cooperative opposition during the 'bourgeois' administration of 1991–4 (Gould 1996). However, as Gould himself acknowledges, the re-election of the Social Democrats in September 1994 demonstrated in part 'a reluctance on the part of Swedes to further dismantle their welfare state' (Gould 1996: 89).

This change in the emphasis of Gould's analysis reminds us how difficult it is to make social policy judgements in the present volatile economic and political climate of Western Europe. As we shall see in Chapter 6, what is difficult as far as Western Europe is concerned becomes almost impossible when it is the social policy trends in Eastern Europe which are being assessed.

Returning to the Nordic states, perhaps the most judicious assessments of the present welfare situation there, in terms of Esping-Andersen's criteria, have been offered by Esping-Andersen (1996b) himself and by Stephens (1996). Both acknowledge the major challenges presented to these welfare systems but neither regards the wholesale dismantling of the 'Scandinavian' welfare state as by any means inevitable. Stephens (1996) makes another important point about the Nordic states which has central relevance to our analysis here. He stresses the need to dis-aggregate the experience of these countries to an extent. It may be that there is more overlap between the welfare systems of the Nordic states than there is with any other of Esping-Andersen's typologies. However, this very commonality means that we have to be particularly alert to those situations where divergences between the Nordic welfare systems may be hidden by the 'social democratic' or 'Scandinavian' labels.

That is why, at a general level, Stephens's analysis is so useful. He points out that the recent macroeconomic conditions in the Nordic states demonstrate divergences as well as convergences. The economic and industrial profile of each country has specific features which have impacted on the precise form of the financial pressures bearing down on their welfare support systems: for instance, Sweden's greater emphasis on an internationalized, large-scale corporate structure focused on the export of capital and finished goods; the disastrous impact of Soviet economic collapse on Finland; the reliance of Norway on oil revenues; Denmark's longer-term economic difficulties and its greater economic reliance on agrarian industry (Stephens 1996: 38–43). We need to bear these wider contexts in mind as we now turn to the more specific focus of our attention: children and their carers.

CHILDREN AND THEIR CARERS: GENERAL TRENDS

The issue of commonalities and divergences immediately arises once we look at these trends. Without doubt, many of the common family features for which the Nordic states have become well known are based on fact, as the collation of data offered by Ruxton (1996) demonstrates. Relatively speaking, the legal frameworks for divorce are more relaxed (Ruxton 1996: 125–8) in the Nordic region: in 1993 Sweden, Denmark and Finland had the highest divorce rates of all the current European Union members apart from the United Kingdom (p. 88). Within the Union, Sweden and Denmark do have the lowest rates for couples with children and the highest rates for couples without children (p. 76) as well as for one-person households (p. 72). It is also true that in 1993 Sweden and Denmark had by far the highest rates in the Union for extra-marital births (p. 82). Finally, in contrast to much of Western Europe, the fertility rates in the Nordic countries are relatively buoyant: Sweden's is the highest in the Union, Finland's is the third highest and Denmark's equal fourth. Moreover, the rates in Denmark and Finland have actually risen very considerably since 1980 (p. 81).

However, one cannot help feeling that sometimes commentators overstate the Nordic picture. Take, for instance, this recent evaluation by Vic George:

> The traditional long-lasting monogamous, male-dominated, two-parent family is everywhere in retreat in Europe, though the pace and the timing of the retreat varies from one part of Europe to another. The move away from this type of family began in the Scandinavian countries, spread to north European countries and more recently to the Mediterranean countries.
>
> (V. George 1996: 187)

Although there are some valid points encompassed by this summary, there are several general criticisms we could level at his diffusion thesis, including the fact that the family is a dynamic organism and changes within it may signify different processes in different contexts (Hantrais and Letablier 1996: 177). In terms of our particular concern with the Nordic states, George also seems to overgeneralize. After all, Finland does not follow the same trends as Denmark or Sweden in relation to couples with children or without them (Ruxton 1996: 76). Moreover, the three Nordic members of the European Union have the lowest rates for lone-parent families expressed as a proportion of households (Ruxton 1996: 72), Greece being the next lowest. Finally, the rates of extramarital births in the Nordic states primarily represent the growth of cohabitation rather than the decline of the two-parent family *per se* (Ruxton 1996: 87). As Ruxton notes, cohabitation is virtually a norm there and may sometimes act as a prelude to marriage after the birth of one or two children. Even the idea of a decline in marriage across the whole Nordic region has to be treated with caution. Hantrais and Letablier (1996: 16) note that in the European Union marriage rates have been maintained at relatively high levels in Denmark and Portugal. In fact, marriage rates actually rose in Denmark between 1980 and 1993 (Ruxton 1996: 85).

All this bears out our earlier call for a considerable degree of disaggregation when one is surveying social welfare typologies, including the Nordic one. On the other hand, we have also seen that there are some common features characterizing the contexts in which children live across the Nordic states. We will bear these in mind in our survey of welfare support mechanisms for children and their carers. Given the particular degree of coordination between benefits, parental leave arrangements and daycare provision in the Nordic states, in the next section we will address all of them together. Later in the chapter, as in previous chapters, we will separately review several crucial aspects of social care services for children in these countries.

FINANCIAL SUPPORTS, PARENTAL LEAVE PATTERNS AND DAY-CARE PROVISION

In these three associated fields, the Nordic states are generally portrayed as being among the most generous in Western Europe. Let us take, for example, the categorizations suggested by Hantrais and Letablier (1996) in their study of family policies. They characterize Nordic policies as promoting state supports aimed at a juxtaposition of family and employment, with gender equality as the objective:

> In Denmark, Finland and Sweden, where women display high levels of continuous economic activity, albeit often part-time and interrupted by periods of parental leave, governments have intervened actively to help parents combine paid work outside the home with childraising in accordance with egalitarian principles ... emphasis has been on provisions that apply to men and women in an attempt to encourage a more equal sharing of paid and domestic work.
>
> (Hantrais and Letablier 1996: 126)

Later, they add that:

> The Nordic states have pursued social policies ensuring a high level of support for all families with the objective of encouraging the sharing of childcare and household tasks in a context where individual rights, including those of children, have been actively promoted.
>
> (Hantrais and Letablier 1996: 170–1)

The question then is: how far do the facts support these judgements?

Our initial point has to be an open acknowledgement that all the countries in the Nordic region do make some of the most universal and generous provisions in Europe regarding financial support for families, parental leave arrangements and day-care provision (Ginsburg 1992, 1993; Gould 1988, 1993, 1996; European Commission 1996a; Hantrais and Letablier 1996; Ruxton 1996). In this context, it may be useful to explore the distinctions between the Nordic states and France, another leader (along with Belgium) in the field of European childcare provision (see Chapter 3).

As Hantrais and Letablier (1996: 129) note, there is some difference of emphasis, in that France places more stress than the Nordic states on the health and well-being of mothers as workers and the expectation that they will continue in full-time paid employment even when the children are very young. Moreover, and perhaps significantly in view of our later discussion, French arrangements for parental and maternal leave are less generous than those in the Nordic states, and less effective in giving women choice about the labour market in the child's early life.

Instead of now simply detailing provisions for children and their carers in the Nordic states, I want to spend the remainder of this section noting the variations in provision which exist and highlighting some of the complexities in the pattern of these services which are not always sufficiently prominent in surveys of them.

Limitations on provision in Nordic states owing to economic factors

First, we will review how far these provisions have been affected by the welfare cuts made in all the Nordic states owing to economic pressures. While still retaining the most generous overall provision, Sweden has certainly not escaped such cuts. For instance, ten months of the earnings-related coverage of parental leave was reduced to 80 per cent (Gould 1996: 83–4), one waiting day was introduced for parents claiming benefit for child sick leave and child allowances for large families were reduced (Gould 1996: 90).

At the same time, there have been pressures placed on Sweden's day-care provision. The most recent review by the European Commission Network on Childcare notes a series of concerns: potential variations in service between local authorities due to funding changes; some reductions in staffing levels and group sizes in day centres as well as some local variation in length of opening; increased parental fees, and local variations in level of fees, both factors hitting low-income families most seriously. Moreover, the Swedish system is geared to the needs of employed and student parents rather than the unemployed, who now make up a larger proportion of the population than hitherto. An increase (currently about 10 per cent of provision) has also taken place in private but publicly funded services. Finally, there is an ongoing shortage of provision.

On the other hand, we should add some positive developments which have recently taken place, especially as regards day-care in Sweden: from 1995 a right in law for employed/studying parents to local provision for children aged from one to twelve years, with a considerable increase in services; a significant level of bilingual provision for children from different ethnic minorities; integration of children with disabilities in recent years (European Commission 1996a: 109–16).

As for Norway, we noted earlier that economic pressures have so far been cushioned by oil revenues. Consequently, Norway has avoided many of the cutbacks which can be noted in other Nordic countries, such as increases in waiting days or reductions in coverage rates for various benefits (Stephens 1996: 52–3). While there has been some overall tightening of criteria for benefits, in fact the provision for maternal leave has recently been upgraded, making it second only to Sweden in generosity (Stephens 1996: 52).

By contrast, over recent years provision for children and their carers in Finland has been adversely affected, along with other welfare supports. For instance, replacement rates for parental benefits have been cut and the benefit period has been similarly reduced, though only marginally (Stephens 1996: 53). Nor has day-care been unaffected:

> The rapid growth of unemployment . . . and cuts in public expenditure in the early 1990s led to rapid changes in quality and quantity in services. Between 1992 and 1994, the need for services decreased by 16%, while the number of places decreased 15%. As a result of increased unemployment, there is no longer a shortage of places.
>
> (European Commission 1996a: 105)

On the other hand, once again we should note elements of progress: a more flexible combination of parental benefits ('home care allowance') and day-care provision for under-4-year-olds; the right to a publicly funded place for all children under school age, created on the whole by more flexibility in provision rather than by an absolute increase; successful efforts to integrate children with disabilities into mainstream day-care and education (European Commission 1996a: 105).

Finally, we turn to Denmark, where financial pressure on provision is more long-standing and where a gamut of general welfare restrictions has been imposed over time, including selectivity, means testing, use of waiting days, tighter qualifying criteria and alterations to indexation (Stephens 1996: 54). On the other hand, maternity leave has been improved (Stephens 1996: 54) and a more extensive scheme of parental leave was introduced in 1994 (European Commission 1996a: 32). Interestingly, this system resulted in more parents staying at home and in some reduction in demand for scarce under-3-year-old day-care provision (European Commission 1996a: 32). This may indicate that less urgency is now being attached to the need for a return of parents to employment. In 1991 Vedel-Petersen was noting the demand in Denmark for arrangements to allow parents more choice in deciding the balance between public care and parental care, and these changes seem, in part at least, to be a response to this need. However, another impetus may well be the shortage of day-care places which, though reduced, still remains a problem largely because of the rising birth rate. In some local authorities, the shortage has meant that unemployed parents are given a lower priority for places and/or cannot obtain them. At the same time, concerns are expressed in some areas (as they are in Sweden) about staffing levels and larger children's groups in day-care (European Commission 1996a: 33–4). There is an informal central government commitment to provide public places for all children aged from 1 to 6 years, a commitment which many local authorities have attempted to meet, although considerable shortfalls remain, particularly in the Copenhagen area (European Commission 1996a: 32).

We might note in passing a significant feature of Danish provision which is paralleled in Finland and Sweden as well: the growing responsibility for service provision allocated by central government to local government at a time when pressure on resources makes such provision difficult to achieve. We have seen this phenomenon of welfare decentralization in virtually all the countries we have so far surveyed. Moreover, we will encounter it again later in this chapter when we consider Nordic social care services.

It is important to offset this negative picture of the Danish situation by noting some ongoing advances in provision there: the priority accorded to integration of children with disabilities (European Commission 1996a: 30); and the importance devoted to meeting the needs of children from ethnic minorities (Children in Scotland 1994).

Moreover, we need to set the discussion above regarding the Nordic states as a whole in context. Although restrictions on provision to greater or lesser extents have indeed occurred in each country, nevertheless levels of service remain high compared to those in most other welfare systems in Europe.

Feminist critiques of the 'Scandinavian' regime model in relation to family care

Of course, we still need to beware of overgeneralizing about the Nordic states. One caveat relates to the welfare situation in Norway, because in some respects Norway diverges from trends in the other countries. The clearest analysis of this phenomenon is provided by Leira (1994). She notes that historically the preference 'for the gender-differentiated nuclear family was more pronounced in Norway, where this family form has attracted stronger political and popular support than in the neighbouring countries' (p. 95). Partly as a result, in the 1970s and 1980s there was in Norway a characteristic lack of coordination between economic policies and social/family policies, with childcare not envisaged as being an element in 'women's policies':

> In Norwegian policies, the concept of the employed mother who is both earner and carer made only slight impact. Childcare policies were more

exclusively oriented towards the socialisation of the child . . . Danish and Swedish policies in this field appear as comparatively similar, while Norway's policies have a different 'profile'. Denmark and Sweden, the two countries in which reproduction policies were more closely co-ordinated with labour market policies, were more successful with regard to meeting the employed mothers' demand for childcare than was Norway, where childcare policies were introduced as in the 'best interests' of the child . . . The lack of attention paid to the problems of employed mothers made private and informal labour markets in childcare much more important in Norway than in Sweden and Denmark. Up to the late 1980s, informal child-minding in Norway provided more services for working mothers than did the state system.

(Leira 1994: 96–7)

At the same time the extent of support for working mothers in the other Nordic states, though genuinely impressive, has itself often been overstated. Leira points out that the day-care provision of the Nordic countries is not so massively different from that in some other welfare systems: a 'comparison of publicly funded childcare services across western Europe . . . modifies the image of the Scandinavian welfare states as particularly interventionist as regards early childhood education and care' (Leira 1994: 97).

Using more recent statistics than Leira possessed for the fifteen countries of the European Union (European Commission 1996a: 148; Ruxton 1996: 156), we can see that Denmark is far ahead of all other European Union members in terms of publicly funded services for children up to 3 years of age (48 per cent), apart from the former GDR. However, the second ranking country, Sweden with 33 per cent, is only slightly ahead of Belgium; while France outstrips Finland. The alleged predominance of the Nordic states seems even more precarious when services for 3–6-year-olds are considered: apart from the former GDR, all the Nordic states are outstripped by France, Belgium, Italy and Spain; Sweden is also overtaken by Western Germany, Austria, the Netherlands and Greece; and Finland's provision is only higher than Portugal's.

In this context we should also note a point made by Windebank (1996) in her comparative analysis of France, Britain and Sweden. She emphasizes (p. 152) that a significant proportion of pre-school children in Sweden (perhaps 40 per cent) are still cared for at home by a parent, usually the mother: and care at home is more likely in poorer families. The most recent statistics (European Commission 1996a: 116) suggest the figure is now around 37 per cent for Sweden. The same source reveals that in Finland 48 per cent of children under compulsory school age had a parent receiving benefit payment while taking leave, and another 15 per cent of children either went to private services or were cared for at home by a parent not on leave and receiving benefit payment (European Commission 1996a: 109).

Moreover, there are several other related issues that cause us to question the extent to which the welfare policies of the Nordic states are geared towards the objective of gender equality, as Hantrais and Letablier (1996) and many other commentators suggest. Let us return to the analysis offered by Windebank (1996). She notes that despite the much applauded levels of provision offered in Sweden, the vast bulk of childcare there is carried out by women in a variety of contexts: taking parental leave; working part-time and full-time; extended family members; service providers in the form of state-funded childminders or nursery workers.

Leira (1994) raises many of the same issues emphasized by Windebank. Leira also alludes to the massive extent of vertical and horizontal job segregation in favour of men, not only in Sweden but across the Nordic states. As regards the levels of men employed in day-care, we do need to acknowledge that in most of the Nordic states some meaningful attempt has been made to introduce more men as workers into professional day-care, although it is only in Norway that really significant change sponsored by central government seems likely in the relatively short term (Flissing 1997; Haughland 1997).

The overall picture offered by Windebank and Leira brings into focus a series of critical features worthy of further comment. One is the marked lack of involvement by men in taking parental leave across all the Nordic states despite a range of structures designed to promote that involvement. Ruxton (1996: 161–2) notes the problems in Denmark and Finland but is more positive about the situation in Sweden, pointing out that about half of fathers there take some parental leave, which seems to be a considerable improvement on the situation in the other two countries. However, his optimism about Sweden, though justified, may be too great. For what Ruxton fails to mention is the extent of parental leave taken by men. In 1994 the average number of days taken was forty-eight, i.e 11.9 per cent of all the used days in the paternal leave for that year. Admittedly this is an improvement on the position a decade before: in 1986 the corresponding figure was 6.2 per cent. However, in 1995 the figure actually fell to 10.3 per cent (Back-Wicklund 1996).

Various reasons have been adduced for this lack of take-up by men (Ruxton 1996; Back-Wicklund 1996): for instance, the relative financial penalties to many families of men taking leave as opposed to their female partners; the limited extent to which it is easy for men to obtain leave if they work outside the public sector. Certainly, recent comparative research has indicated that many men in both Sweden and Britain still express aspirations about fathering which outstrip their actions in practice (Mansson *et al.* 1996; Pringle 1996c).

The greater financial penalty attached to men's absence from the labour market reveals the significant gender segregation within that market, both vertical and horizontal. Recent comparative research on men's parenting has again highlighted this feature. Plantin and Mansson (1997: 3) note that in a qualitative research sample of twenty heterosexual couples:

> we see that the men and women have a relatively equal level of education; there is even a slight overweight of women in the sample who have a higher formal education than the men. On the other hand, the men still earn more than the women.

This segregation casts further doubt on the degree to which the welfare system in Sweden has achieved gender equality both inside or outside the home. As Windebank (1996: 152) comments:

> The majority of care needs for children outside compulsory schooling in Sweden are met by a combination of state regulated and sponsored care ... and the adaption of parents' (usually mothers') work arrangements, sanctioned by the state.

That comment can be applied across the Nordic states. Part of the maternal adaption mentioned by Windebank consists of taking parental leave, which, as we saw earlier, seems to be an increasing feature of Nordic welfare systems. The other main form of adaption is the dual earner–carer role of many women. In Sweden and Denmark, in particular, that configuration is clearly assisted by the very high rates of part-time working in the labour market undertaken by women. In Finland, full-time labour market activity is far more prominent than part-time in women's employment profile, although this does not seem to reduce their role as primary child carers (Hantrais and Letablier 1996: 94).

In summarizing these data, Leira draws some highly important conclusions. First, she casts doubt on day-care provision, at least in the Nordic context, as a gender equalizing strategy:

> While in the European Community the promotion of equal opportunities for women provides the basis for the Commission's proposals concerning childcare policy ... equal status legislation in Denmark, Norway, and Sweden has not treated day-care for pre-school children as a crucial issue.
>
> (Leira 1994: 91)

The European Commission's most recent documents in this area continue to pursue the approach noted by Leira (European Commission 1996b). She goes on to suggest that in practice neither Nordic day-care services nor leave provision have massively influenced gender equality in the home or in the workplace:

Considering the Scandinavian commitment to equal status between women and men, the continuity of sex/gender as an organising principle in society is quite striking, though it appears as less pronounced than in other forms of the welfare state. After almost 20 years of active welfare state intervention to promote gender equality, the division of labour between women and men remains a feature of the Scandinavian societies in the early 1990s. This is clearly evident when the distribution of paid and unpaid work is considered, or when the employment and family responsibilities of mothers and fathers are assessed together. As some of the work of social reproduction was collectivized, what was formerly unpaid work was transformed into paid employment. The sexual stereotyping of this kind of work proved resistant to change. Some of the 'old' equal status issues are still important in the 1990s, for example, questions concerning the division of time, money, power, and care that remain unresolved. Violence by men in the family directed towards women and children persists. If equal status policies neglect the private sphere, gender inequality will remain.

(Leira 1994: 100)

She emphasizes that in the Nordic states, traditionally and currently, paid employment is the most important basis of citizenship, so that:

Even advanced welfare states, such as the Scandinavian ones, have not granted women full citizen status ... Scandinavian citizenship was modelled on the worker. The more generous and more institutionalized benefits are reserved for the citizen as a wage worker while, in comparison, the citizen as carer is excluded from access to a series of welfare state benefits.

(Leira 1994: 101)

Leira concludes by placing this Nordic gendering of access to citizenship entitlements within a transnational context:

This situation is not unique to Scandinavia. Processes excluding women from some of the social rights of citizenship may well be more characteristic of 'liberal' and 'conservative' welfare states as opposed to the 'social democratic' welfare state.

(Leira 1994: 102)

The analysis offered in the previous chapters of this book bears out Leira's judgement. Women's exclusion from full citizenship is a common feature of social organization in all West European countries and is always intimately bound up with their role as primary childcarers. There seems little doubt that this feature is even more pervasive in many other West European countries (see Chapter 2). However, women's relative exclusion does still occur to a marked degree in the Nordic states.

Windebank (1996) comes to similar conclusions and correctly pinpoints the issue of men and childcare as a central one to be addressed. She asserts that if women are to be placed on an equal footing with men in the labour market:

then the only answer is for fathers to be more responsible for their children's well-being and to provide more of the flexibility necessary to reconcile childcare and parental employment. Social policies which do not address this issue will result in a 'zero sum game' for women.

(Windebank 1996: 160)

This suggests something of a 'Catch-22' situation, since we have seen that one reason for a lack of parental involvement by men in the Nordic countries appears to be the financial logic of the current labour market. Thus the evidence from these countries suggests that far more radical and all-embracing policies than those adopted will be required for any realistic hope of change. This of course also casts into considerable doubt the potential for change inherent in the equal opportunities policies advocated by the European Commission Network on Childcare and other measures to reconcile employment and family responsibilities, largely based as they are on Nordic models (European Commission 1990, 1996a, b; Chapters 2, 4 and 7, this volume). Meaningful change may well entail far broader and deeper gender equality approaches than have occurred in the Nordic states or have been fully considered by the European Union.

Commentators such as Ginsburg (1993), Leira (1994), Sainsbury (1994) and Hantrais and Letablier (1996) note that the historical reasons for extensive day-care and parental leave policies in the Nordic states were varied and included: concerns about the birth rate; the need to mobilize women further as workers for labour market purposes; the desire to promote children's well-being; and the objective of gender equalization. It may well be that the first three aims have been achieved to a considerable extent. By contrast, our foregoing discussion indicates that the last objective has only been addressed to a very limited degree.

Nordic commitments to child welfare and the principle of social solidarity

Partly to balance what has gone before, I want now to end this section by asking a rather different question: insofar as the Nordic states have instituted, and are still implementing, welfare policies for children and their carers which are relatively generous compared to much of Western Europe, why is this happening – especially in times of such economic distress for them? After all, we have already seen evidence of their apparent determination to resist a dismantling of their welfare systems even if they do accept a need to modify them.

To explore this issue, it may well be useful to compare the situation in the Nordic states with that in Britain. Such a comparison is particularly pertinent because in some respects the United Kingdom possessed a welfare system not dissimilar to the Nordic ones less than twenty years ago. We have seen (Chapter 2) how over the intervening period much of that British welfare system was dismantled. Despite being under similar economic pressures (albeit with different timescales) the present welfare trajectories of the Nordic states now look very different from the United Kingdom's. Why?

A clue to the answer may perhaps be found in some of the discussions in previous chapters regarding Britain's almost unique welfare trajectory in Western Europe. In Chapter 3 we considered the differences between British and French approaches to child welfare. One of our major conclusions centred on the different responses to the principles of solidarity in the two countries. Post-1979 Britain evidenced welfare policies which were more individualistic rather than solidaristic in orientation. How far does that comparison extend to the Nordic states?

Discussions of the welfare systems in those states frequently make reference to the importance of solidarity and to a concept of 'society' in their development (Ginsburg 1993). Let us turn once again to Leira:

> the public–private split is essential to the liberal conceptualization of the state. In the social democratic welfate state, the public–private distinction does not hold the same importance. In fact, Scandinavian vernacular does not always make a clear distinction between the terms 'state' and 'society'. Scandinavians often refer to the welfare state as 'folkhem', literally 'the people's home'. The metaphor identifies – perhaps naively – the welfare state as 'people-friendly', made by the people for the people.
>
> (Leira 1994: 95)

Such a conceptualization, very similar to that which inspired the British Labour government in 1945, would be almost unthinkable in post-Thatcher Britain. Nor should we forget that, in Margaret Thatcher's rhetoric against what she considered the pernicious 'nanny state', she attacked Sweden directly and explicity (Gould 1988). Moreover, the comparison between the eighteen years of continuous Conservative government in the United Kingdom (1979–97) on the one hand and, on the other, the swift rejection of a far more consensus-oriented centre-right Swedish government in 1994 is surely revealing. In order to understand the welfare trajectory of the Nordic states it seems we need to take account of the immense cultural importance attached there to the principles of social solidarity. In the next section, which addresses social care services, we shall see the importance of that principle manifested again – in ways that may be construed as both positive and negative.

SOCIAL CARE

When we survey social care services for children in the Nordic states we find a pattern similar to that outlined in the section above. These services are, as often portrayed, relatively universal, adopting reformist principles designed to promote the positive well-being of all children. Some significant variations in service provision exist between the different countries. Finally, certain welfare features of these services betray important and often disregarded fissures in the fabric of the apparently cohesive Nordic societies. Let us now consider these matters in more detail.

Public social services

One critical difference between these services in most Nordic countries and those in the United Kingdom is that social workers in the former often carry a central responsibility for assessing and 'gate-keeping' the financial needs of service users (Gould 1988; Melhbye 1993; Madge and Attridge 1996; Harder 1997). Some commentators (Gould 1988) have suggested that the financial aspect of the social worker task in the Nordic countries may increase the degree of social control exercised over service users there. This is similar to the point explored in Chapter 3 relating to RMI in France. These concerns have particularly been expressed about Sweden, where social workers have had relatively coercive powers (either explicitly or implicitly) in certain situations, such as in relation to parents who indulge in alcohol or drug abuse (Gould 1988).

The underlying social control element in Swedish social work practice (Gould 1988) may connect with our discussion above about the importance of solidaristic principles in Nordic social welfare provision. In Chapter 3 we similarly explored the ambiguous relationship of RMI with the concepts of both social inclusion and social control: at what point does the former become the latter? We might ask more or less the same question regarding the strongly solidaristic characteristics of some Swedish social welfare approaches: when does social protection become social control?

What is certainly clear about the financial control aspect of social work practice in Sweden and Denmark is that it increasingly absorbs social work time as the economic crisis continues and unemployment remains at relatively high levels. This then has implications for the extent of therapeutic provision available to service users.

Preventative social care

Despite what has been said about elements of social control in some Nordic social services systems, we should note that they are also generally characterized by a massive commitment to preventative work. This contrasts particularly with the situation in the United Kingdom, where prevention in social work has been attenuated (Pringle 1997a; Chapter 2, this volume). For instance, since 1988 the Danish government has invested relatively huge resources for the local development of preventative and innovative welfare projects with children and families (Vedel-Petersen 1991; Melhbye 1993; Madge and Attridge 1996; Harder 1997). Similarly, a survey of child welfare services in Finland has identified continuing scope for preventative work with children and their carers (Tuomisto and Vuori-Karvia 1997). The same survey indicated that active therapeutic work with service users was also carried out by fieldwork services, a finding echoed in a parallel Danish study (Harder 1997).

Social care and marginalized social groups

What is not very clear from the data is how marginalized groups fare as regards social care provision. We know, for instance, that in Sweden young people, single mothers and immigrants/refugees seem to have been especially damaged by the recent welfare cuts which have taken place across the board (Gould 1996: 88). Gould also points out that racial attacks and harassment are increasing in Sweden, often carried out by dispossessed young people who have joined fascist organizations around some of the major cities (Gould 1996: 79). This process seems paralleled by an apparently more ambivalent attitude expressed in government procedures and practices towards migrants and refugees (Alund and Schierup 1993).

Out-of-home placements

There is evidence in many Nordic states of a clear preponderance of children from financially poor families being removed from home (Melhbye 1993; Harder 1997; Tuomisto and Vuori-Karvia 1997), which has led some commentators (Melhbye 1993) to suggest that a considerable number of these removals might be preventable. On the whole, there is a great reluctance in the Nordic states to remove children (Kemppainen 1994; Madge and Attridge 1996; Pringle and Harder 1997). Where removal does occur the trend is very much towards voluntary rather than compulsory placement in most Nordic states. For instance, since the legal reforms of 1982 in Sweden this trend has been clear, and the voluntary path has also become much more common in Denmark (Ruxton 1996: 333–4). However, Kemppainen (1994: 42–3) reports that while the total number of admissions to care in Finland has not increased, the number of compulsory removals has risen, accounting for about 20 per cent of new admissions. To some extent this is attributed to public criticism of social workers in recent years, which may have then encouraged them to act more forcefully and rapidly than they would hitherto have done.

Interesting variations exist in the Nordic states around the mechanisms for compulsory removal. In Denmark cases are decided by a social committee in each local municipality, consisting of three municipal politicians, one judge and one psychologist. In other words, the body which sanctions removal belongs to the administrative unit (the municipality) that is seeking removal (Melhbye 1993; Harder 1997). Although the other Nordic states use mechanisms which also have strong democratic elements, they avoid this direct overlap of functions. Of course, the Danish system contrasts even more strongly with procedures in many West European countries outside the Nordic zone. For instance, since 1989 the routes by which young people may enter care on a compulsory basis in England and Wales are all channelled through the courts (Allen 1992).

In most Nordic countries there has been a significant reduction in the number of children being removed from home over the past few decades, particularly in Denmark (Colton and Hellinckx 1993; Ruxton 1996). No doubt this is partly owing to more preventative efforts. However, financial considerations and the costs to the state of out-of-home placements are no doubt also relevant factors (Vedel-Petersen 1991; Melhbye 1993).

Of those children who are removed, a greater proportion are now also being placed in foster homes, although the pattern varies across specific countries. For instance, Sweden is one of the European leaders in the use of foster care and has a relatively long experience of it (Ruxton 1996). Denmark has more balance between residential and foster provision than Sweden (Ruxton 1996), but this balance still represents a considerable shift away from residential care (Melhbye 1993). Once again, cost may be an issue in this change (Merrick 1990). Finland is also shifting towards more fostering, but still makes very considerable use of residential provision (Ruxton 1996; Tuomisto and Vuori-Karvia 1997). However, Kemppainen (1994) indicates that the traditional boundaries between residential and foster care are anyway breaking down in Finland with the creation of intermediate forms of provision such as family homes. In addition, Kemppainen (1994) emphasizes the increasing development of open care measures. Both these points have wider applicability to other Nordic states (Ruxton 1996: 337).

Another relatively common feature across these countries is the considerable resources they devote to the after-care of young people who have been in care, though local variation in provision manifests itself in this sphere as well (Ruxton 1996: 341–2).

Child abuse

Child abuse is another important issue which reveals similarities and divergences between the Nordic states. For instance, a recent transnational comparative survey (Harder and Pringle 1997) highlights more awareness about child abuse, particularly sexual abuse, in Denmark than in Finland, with a consequently higher priority attached to it in the former country (Pringle and Harder 1997). Reasons for this difference appear to be several. One may be the fact that in Denmark organizational structures dedicated to child abuse have existed since the late nineteenth and early twentieth centuries, very much along the same lines as in the United Kingdom, the United States and Ireland. For largely historical reasons (for instance, political subjection to Sweden, then Russia, then civil war), an early institutional framework was not similarly established in Finland (Pringle and Harder 1997).

As regards child sexual abuse, there seems evidence that awareness about it has also increased in Sweden to some extent over the past few years, partly owing to feminist groups pushing the issue on to the public and professional agenda. It also appears that social services are improving their procedures and their training to deal with this problem (Eklund 1993). Awareness of sexual abuse in Norway also appears to have grown to an extent. Certainly more research seems to have been carried out into its prevalence there than in most Nordic countries (Heap 1990).

Moreover, there are other differences of emphasis between Nordic states in relation to child abuse. For instance, Tuomisto and Vuori-Karvia (1997) note that about 60 per cent of child protective measures in Finland occur because of alcohol or drug abuse by mothers. This reflects the point discussed in Chapter 1 about the different social constructions made in different countries regarding the nature of social problems. No doubt alcohol and drug abuse also pose problems in Denmark, but the intense emphasis on these issues does not seem in evidence there as it does in Sweden and Finland (Pringle and Harder 1997). Certainly, our survey in previous chapters does not suggest that this extremely close association between alcohol, drugs and child abuse is shared by many other West European countries to the same extent.

It is important to register an important fact about child maltreatment which does separate the Nordic countries in a positive way from other West European states, excepting Austria. They have all made corporal punishment of children illegal (Sale and Davies 1990; Ruxton 1996: 418). This of course contrasts markedly not only with some Mediterranean countries such as Spain, but also with Britain (Ruxton 1996: 418–9).

As we have noted, awareness of child abuse has been generally developing across the Nordic states over the past few years. However, it is clear from comparative studies (Sale and Davies 1990; Harder and Pringle 1997) that the public and professional awareness of child abuse in all the Nordic states is still considerably less than in the United Kingdom – and this is especially true in relation to child sexual abuse. For instance, the debate about the role of men in professional childcare arising from concerns about sexual abuse has only been initiated recently in Sweden (Back-Wicklund 1997), whereas in the United Kingdom that debate is now very well established (Pringle 1997d; Chapters 2 and 8, this volume).

Reasons for this difference are open to debate. One hypothesis recently put forward by the author (Pringle and Harder 1997) is that the relative lack of a commitment to solidaristic principles in the British welfare context (see Chapter 2) may paradoxically permit a greater recognition of oppressive power relations in that country and the social problems to which they give rise. As we have noted in previous chapters, child sexual abuse is a particularly clear example of such a social problem, since it is associated with a complex range of oppresssive power dynamics centring on such issues as gender, sexuality, age and disability (Pringle 1995; Chapter 8, this volume). Thus it is probably no accident that awareness about, and challenge to, child sexual abuse has developed so much more in the British context. Conversely, in societies such as the Nordic states which place a high premium on social cohesion and consensus, cultural resistance may be greater against recognition of social problems which reveal the fabric of those societies to be less cohesive than they would like to believe. This point is similar to one made in Chapter 3 regarding French and German responses to child sexual abuse. The issue of sexual abuse seems to possess the capacity to highlight with particular force some major lines of structural inequality in societies. So once again it may be no accident that welfare contexts heavily committed to solidaristic principles, such as France, Germany and the Nordic states, have not addressed child sexual abuse very closely. In Chapter 8 I explore this topic more deeply and extend my analysis to social welfare issues more broadly.

Childhood disability

In the field of childhood disability, an issue which is conspicuous by its absence in surveys of social welfare in many other countries, the Nordic states do demonstrate a uniformly liberal and progressive approach. In Denmark, Finland and Sweden policy, and often legislation, provides for relatively extensive service provision within the community wherever possible, or in specialist settings where it is not (Ruxton 1996: 382–3).

Juvenile justice

When we turn to the field of juvenile justice (as it is significantly called in Britain), we find a relatively consistent pattern across the Nordic states and one which makes the term juvenile justice relatively inappropriate for those countries. In contrast to the punitive British trend throughout much of the 1990s (see Chapter 2), the predominant approach in the Nordic states is very much a welfare one, with a major emphasis on diversion from judicial proceedings (Ruxton 1996: 308–9). For instance, in Sweden the main responsibility for under 15-year-olds and crime lies with the social authorities and not the courts at all. As for over 14-year-old juveniles, only 15 per cent are prosecuted and the vast majority who are found guilty avoid custody (Sarnecki 1989; Ruxton 1996).

Interestingly, in Sweden there has also been a marked decline in recorded juvenile crime committed by white boys since the late 1970s. However, records for girls and for young immigrant boys have increased (Sarnecki 1989: 8–9). We might note again that the authorities in Sweden do not seem to set a particularly good example in the way they deal with immigrant and refugee youth. For instance, Ruxton (1996: 453) points out that the penal authorities tend to take foreign children into custody under the Aliens Act, while Swedish children cannot generally be taken into custody until after the age of 18 years. This example of discrimination and others noted earlier (both official and unofficial) make one reconsider how far the concept of Swedish *Folkhem* extends to marginalized groups within Swedish society. More than once we have been forced to recognize that powerful cultural support for principles of social inclusion and cohesion may have some undesirable outcomes, the most obvious being potentially a strong element of social control. This may yet be a further example of the latter.

CONCLUSIONS

The picture of social welfare for children and their carers painted in this chapter is again a complex one. In many ways our survey has confirmed the familiar welfare image of the Nordic states: relatively generous and universal provision geared to the promotion of social equality and cohesion, with social protection for the more disadvantaged members of society. However, we have also highlighted the limitations of that image. These limitations have taken several forms: wide variations between practices in different countries on some issues; welfare retrenchment to a greater or lesser extent dictated by economic pressure and having a differential impact on various sections of society; perhaps most important of all, significant fault lines criss-crossing Nordic societies, created by oppressive power relations associated with gender, 'race', age and poverty. And all these features remain heavily disguised beneath that glowing image of Nordic social solidarity.

In Chapters 8 and 9, I will take forward elements of this analysis. In particular, I will develop the comments I have made in this and previous chapters about the need for an overtly radical anti-oppressive welfare practice in the countries of Europe if the many social disadvantages bearing down on children and their carers are to be effectively challenged. Central to that argument will be a discussion about the problems of developing such a practice within welfare contexts deeply committed to principles and images of social consensus and cohesion – such as the Nordic states.

6

CHILDREN IN A WELFARE CRISIS: EASTERN EUROPE

INTRODUCTION

As readers will recall from Chapter 1, Esping-Anderson's (1990) original formulation regarding regimes of welfare capitalism naturally enough did not embrace the communist states of Eastern Europe. However, at the end of the 1980s political, economic and social changes in that region presaged the end of Soviet-dominated communist regimes and massive shifts in the welfare contexts of the people who lived in those countries (Deacon 1992). Since then a variety of commentators have attempted to analyse the welfare transitions there to a greater or lesser extent in terms of Esping-Andersen's categorizations (for instance, Deacon 1993; Ferge 1993; Gotting 1994; Esping-Andersen 1996a; Standing 1996). Once again in this chapter I have two interlinked aims: first and foremost to analyse the situation of children and their carers in Eastern Europe; second, to see how useful those categorizations are in making our analysis.

Before starting that analysis, I want to mention three general points. First, although the speed of change at the current time in welfare systems is a problem for analysis right across Europe, nowhere is this more true than in the East. When discussing Eastern Europe, we need to recognize that most of the welfare systems there have been/are undergoing a social revolution. As a result, readers must regard the analysis which follows as particularly provisional.

Second, at the outset it is important to emphasize that the states of Eastern Europe are heterogeneous culturally, politically, socially and economically – and this is true of their past, of their present and, no doubt, of their future as well. This point has been made strongly on the general level by certain commentators (Kurczewski 1994; Standing 1996) and is apparent in some more specific studies: for instance, on the position of women (Bacon and Poll 1994; Leven 1994). Even so, in analyses of welfare systems across Europe, these countries are perhaps too often overclassified together. The survey which this book undertakes is also to some extent guilty of that overclassification; hence the fact that these countries are aggregated here. My decision to aggregate them is based on two interrelated factors. First, as I hope will become apparent as we proceed, there are some issues which cause these welfare systems to have more in common with each other than with any other country addressed in this book – despite their undoubted heterogeneity. Second, it has to be admitted that material on these countries is on the whole still rather limited and in that context it makes sense to bring them together for convenience – but in a way which, I hope, does not distort reality.

My third and final preliminary remark relates to the shape of this chapter. Because the situations we are surveying in Eastern Europe are in some ways markedly different from those surveyed in previous chapters, the format of this chapter is different from that of the others. After a review of trends before the fall of communism, I turn to an exploration of the current position. This exploration includes a survey of general social problems as they are differentially experienced across Eastern Europe and moves on to look at social disadvantages and social supports relating specifically to children and their carers. I then discuss the situation of social care services across the countries of Eastern Europe. I conclude by considering the validity of various categorizations of these welfare systems in the light of the data reviewed in the chapter.

Having made these three general points, I now want to focus in a more detailed fashion on the histories of these welfare systems in terms of their points of divergence and convergence, for it is clear that the past has played a significant role in shaping current trends (Sipos 1991).

PAST TRENDS

As regards the medium-term past, commentators such as Gotting (1994) and Standing (1996) make the important point that some countries of Eastern Europe, such as Hungary and the Czech Republic, have a close nineteenth- and early twentieth-century association with welfare traditions in Germany and Austria, unlike other states, such as Bulgaria and Romania. They suggest that this association may have some bearing on the relatively different welfare trajectories of these countries past and present.

Nearer to the present time, we may note other significant historical variables, of which I now mention two. First, there was more diversity between these countries in the post-war communist period than has often been acknowledged regarding gender-oriented policies. Einhorn (1994) underlines the degree to which apparently gender-oriented policies in many countries were really labour-market-oriented or population-oriented instead. Like Makkai (1994) in relation to nursery provision, Einhorn (1994) singles out the policies of the former German Democratic Republic from other communist states as at least approximating to a woman-friendly strategy in terms not only of day-care but also of reproduction. Once again, present welfare trajectories have to be considered in the light of this history (see Chapter 3 for some of the outcomes in the former GDR).

My second example of welfare diversity in pre-1989 Eastern Europe focuses on income differentials. Vecernik (1996) has noted that there were already important differences between many of these countries prior to 1989 regarding their levels of income inequality. As we shall see later in this chapter, events after 1989 tended to preserve those relative differences while massively increasing the levels of inequality in all these countries.

It is important to recognize that before 1989 the communist regimes to a considerable extent regarded social policy as essentially the servant of economic and industrial policy (Ferge 1991; Corrin 1992; Gotting 1994). The measures concerning day-care and reproduction noted above are a good example of this. Moreover, in allegedly perfect societies it was vital to ignore the existence of many social problems and to define them as the product of individual pathology (for instance, alcoholism) or the result of deviations from state-approved behaviour. The denial of child abuse in Poland is a highly relevant example of this phenomenon. Nor did such denial end in 1989: it lingers on now, as we discuss later in this chapter (Sobiech 1994).

Despite what I have said about the gross imperfections of social policy under communism, it may well be that a number of commentators (such as Deacon 1992) have perhaps underrated its achievements in some East European countries. For instance, there is no doubt that welfare supports for families with children in countries such as Hungary, the GDR, Czechoslovakia and Poland pre-1989 were, by many standards including some West European ones, quite impressive (Cornia 1991). As Cornia notes, such measures as universal family allowances, childcare grants, maternal allowances, provision in kindergartens and services in kind based at the workplace should not be dismissed. Similarly, Ferge (1991, 1993) notes that these supports had their roots in those longer-standing welfare traditions discussed above and were not purely the products of relatively short-term communist economic necessity.

Of course, even these relatively generous measures were by no means unproblematic. For instance, as we have implied, many supports were highly work-oriented and, indeed, workplace-centred (Cornia and Sipos 1991; Standing 1996). This was to present a major difficulty later when unemployment became a central issue. Even at that time, however, work-oriented welfare could be a potential problem, especially taken in conjunction with the gendered limitations of social policies. We have already noted that some allegedly woman-friendly policies in certain states should not necessarily be taken at face value (Einhorn 1994; Makkai 1994). However, feminist commentators such as Einhorn (1994) quite rightly go further and locate a major limitation of pre-1989 policies in the fact that they did not address the gendered advantages of men both inside and outside families.

It is interesting to speculate as to whether there are any parallels between this situation and that which we surveyed in the last chapter relating to the Nordic countries. The work-oriented nature of social provisions and the absence of policies directly addressing the situation of men are issues highly reminiscent of Leira's (1994) critique of the Nordic welfare systems. I am not, of course, pretending that countries such as Hungary, the GDR or Czechoslovakia pre-1989 are in any way directly comparable with the Nordic states. I am suggesting that when analysing the processes of change relating to children and their carers in some East European countries post-1989, we need to consider certain Nordic-type elements in their pre-1989 welfare configurations, particularly issues of public and private patriarchy (Einhorn 1994). Although the political, social and economic profile of the Nordic states bears no resemblance whatsoever to that of the pre-1989 communist countries, what they had in common was a high commitment to an ideal of social cohesion and solidarity. Such a commonality may account for certain similarities in some welfare features.

THE PRESENT

Overview

For the purposes of this study we do not need to enter into the complex debates about why certain economic, social and political changes occurred in the countries of Eastern Europe in the late 1980s and early 1990s; nor about the degree to which they were vital (Cornia 1991); nor about the relative pace of these changes (Gotting 1994). We can limit ourselves purely to noting the central elements of the economic changes instituted in different ways in all countries of East Europe. These elements are said to have included a macroeconomic stabilization policy, microeconomic sectoral restructuring and privatization (Cornia 1991).

Several commentators also add that one central economic reason for the massive negative social outcome of these reforms was a failure in their sequencing (Cornia 1991; Standing 1996). In terms of social protection, the crucial changes were the removal of guaranteed employment with obvious and direct consequences for unemployment; removal of subsidies with negative implications for prices, shortages and unemployment; and removal of work-based services (Standing 1996). The huge social problems accruing from these changes were vastly amplified by another failure: the highly inadequate welfare safety nets constructed to varying extents across the region in response to the social crisis (Standing 1996).

No doubt the lack of social protection was itself a function of economic crisis, and the relationship between these factors was, and is, a highly complex one. However, from this complex picture I would like to focus on one important contributory issue, partly because it does not receive all the attention it deserves and partly because it is important to remember that what has happened in Eastern Europe post-1989 was influenced by factors generated within the West. I refer to the role of Western capitalist institutions such as the World Bank and the International Monetary Fund (IMF).

The role of such bodies in pressurizing Eastern European countries into extreme budget squeezes with direct implications for social protection is touched on in many accounts. For instance, Gotting (1994) alludes to their role in Hungary and Bulgaria. Furthermore, Benson and Clay (1992: 144–5) provide the following account of IMF/World Bank lending packages directed at the financially desperate countries of Eastern Europe:

> The short-term stabilisation measures included in these packages have entailed sometimes large reductions in real public sector expenditure, liberalisation of prices and privatisation measures, potentially giving rise to or exacerbating economic pressures on vulnerable social groups ... In the Polish case, such pressures forced a relaxation of policies which, in turn, led to a suspension of IMF facilities. Due to failures to meet IMF targets on the size of its budget deficit, partly because of difficulties in cutting expenditure on education, health and welfare, the IMF suspended a three year US$1.6 bn extended facility to Poland in September 1991.

Standing (1996: 230) summarizes the situation thus:

> As far as the reform of social and labour market policy is concerned, it is almost correct to state that the revolution that has been taking place in Central and Eastern Europe is the first in history in which social policy has been shaped and influenced by international financial agencies.

Standing also reminds us of a newer additional influence when he asks:

> Is independent social policy in one country feasible in the 1990s, especially given [IMF and World Bank pressures and] ... the pressure from the

European Union to have the emerging social protection systems 'converge' to patterns acceptable for potential members of an enlarged European Union.
(Standing 1996: 249)

I am not suggesting that the IMF, World Bank or European Union are directly or simply responsible for the massive social dislocation which has occurred, and is occurring, in Eastern Europe. Indeed, Deacon and Hulse (1997) have recently explored the complexities and contradictions of such interventions. Nevertheless, these institutions have played a part, and it is a significant one. I leave readers to consider in whose best interests are the pressures they exert.

Turning away from the specific issue of Western institutions and having established the overall social and economic picture, let us now consider some of the elements of the crisis post-1989 in terms of social problems which form the welfare context for many families.

Social problems post-1989

Unemployment

One of the most obvious social problems in almost all countries of Eastern Europe has been unemployment. However, clearly there have been significant variations between countries in terms of both timing and extent. As Standing (1996: 235) notes, Poland led the trend, though other states such as Bulgaria have exceeded it at certain points in time. By the summer of 1996 unemployment rates in much of Eastern Europe had fallen somewhat from 1994 levels, and Poland had returned to its relatively high position. Poland recorded a rate of 14.1 per cent in July 1996 compared to Bulgaria's 10.4 (May 1996), Hungary's 10.6 (June 1996), Slovakia's 11.9 (May 1996) and Slovenia's 13.8 (April 1996) (*The European* 3–9 October 1996).

These levels are comparable with rates in a few Western European countries and higher than many others there. Moreover, two factors compound the severity of Eastern European rates compared with those in the West. First, to a large extent the high rates in Eastern Europe represent a sharp qualitative as well as a quantitative break with the past. Second, these high levels in Eastern Europe have occurred, as we have seen, in conjunction with extremely inadequate social security safety nets (Cornia 1991: 99; Ferge 1991: 82). Although it is clear from previous chapters that safety nets vary across Western Europe and are under pressure there, on the whole they tend to be more extensive than those in most Eastern European countries.

Having made these points, we need to add several qualifications to them. First, we must remember that estimation of unemployment levels is notoriously difficult on account of methodological problems which in turn can be put to political uses. This has been true of Western Europe, not least the United Kingdom. However, such difficulties magnify in relation to Eastern Europe, where the structures for adequate data collection may be less complete and where the increasing curtailment of unemployment benefit may also skew outcomes (Ferge 1991, 1993; Standing 1996).

Moreover, national statistics on unemployment can mask important differences within each country. These differences can be regional. For instance, Weclawowicz's (1996: 144–51) recent survey of Poland highlights the long-standing and massive regional variations in unemployment percentages with Northeastern and Northern voivodships being among the most seriously affected. Kemecsei (1995: 31) makes exactly the same point about regional variations in relation to Hungary. However, as we shall discuss at greater length later in this chapter, the differences in unemployment levels within states often also relate to factors such as age, gender and ethnic identity (Cornia 1991; Sipos 1991; Ferge 1993; Einhorn 1994; Kemecsei 1995; Wallace 1996; Weclawowicz 1996).

Finally, we must qualify what has gone before by underlining that not all Eastern European countries conform to the picture presented here. In this discussion of unemployment, it is significant that we have not so far mentioned the Czech Republic. In June 1996 the unemployment rate for the Republic was 2.7 per cent (*The European* 3–9 October 1996), a level of which most West European countries would be deeply envious. The explanations for the disparity between the Czech Republic and its neighbours in terms of unemployment are complex. Standing suggests some of the reasons:

> This was due in part to its split with the Slovak Republic, which is where most of the heavy industry had been based, in part to its proximity with Germany, in part to its extensive use of labour market policies.
>
> (Standing 1996: 235)

Together with other key economic indicators, the positive labour market situation in the Czech Republic led to it being the first of the former communist countries to be admitted to the Organisation for Economic Co-operation and Development (OECD). As Green (1995: 19) notes, the main reason for admittance was the relative speed of movement towards a market economy generated by the Czech Republic: 'the message to the other ex-Warsaw pact members will be that monetarism and privatisation are the keys to acceptance in the West.' This echoes our earlier discussion about the role of the World Bank and the IMF in Eastern Europe. Both Vecernik (1996) and Standing (1996) note that even more stringent neo-liberal policies are projected in the Czech Republic, but express some doubts as to how far these will be progressed. The less positive implications of such a neo-liberal approach for social welfare systems will be discussed later.

Poverty

Poverty is another related and central feature of the social and economic crisis occurring in Eastern Europe since 1989 which has a central bearing on the well-being of families. As we have already noted, it is rooted in massive price rises, loss of subsidies and reduced wage levels. Moreover, once again there are differential impacts in terms of age, gender and ethnic identity, which we also deal with later in this chapter. What we need to explore now are the implications of increased poverty on the degree and extent of inequality in the countries of Eastern Europe.

Vecernik (1996: 118) makes clear that determination of inequality levels in the states of Eastern Europe is fraught with methodological difficulties, some of which are especially characteristic of those states:

> Post-communist countries in particular are characterized by a 'portfolio of economies', meaning various degrees of legality and monetary and non-monetary forms of raising resources.

For instance, the recent work of Wallace and colleagues (Wallace 1996) on the situation of young people in Poland has re-emphasized the crucial and ongoing importance of the concept of 'social capital' in understanding the dynamics of survival there.

Bearing in mind these provisos, what seem to be the trends in inequality? One of Vecernik's main conclusions is that the relative degrees of inequality between these countries have been roughly maintained in terms of individual earnings, personal incomes and household incomes:

> Polish society is likely to be the most unequal while Slovakia appears to be still equalized. The lowest income group is much greater in Poland and Hungary than in the Czech Republic and Slovakia ... The original, very close similarity between the Czech Republic and Slovakia is disappearing.
> (Vecernik 1996: 119)

However, the extent of inequality has increased in all countries, often massively, this being especially apparent when household incomes are considered (Vecernik 1996: 106). In terms of the latter measure, Vecernik (1996: 106–8) demonstrates that the ratios of the income of the richest 20 per cent to that of the poorest 20 per cent in 1992 were already comparable with the same ratios in West European countries: 5 in Sweden compared to 5.5 in the Czech Republic, 5 in Poland and 4.7 in Slovakia; 6+ in France and 7 in the United Kingdom compared with 6.2 in Hungary.

Standing (1996: 235) provides an overview of poverty issues for Eastern Europe: 'Throughout the region, poverty rates have soared, with the sharpest increases coming between 1990 and 1992. And inequality has grown extraordinarily rapidly.'

Life expectancy

The social welfare implications of unemployment, poverty and inequality are manifold and we will shortly discuss them in specific relation to children and families. However, at this point we can make one general observation about the social impact of this state of affairs, and it relates to life expectancy. Relatively low life expectancy in Eastern Europe compared to much of Western Europe is not a new problem (Sipos 1991). However, talking about Hungary in particular, Kemecsei (1996: 33–4) underlines the fact that male life expectancy has actually been decreasing recently: by 1992 it had dropped to 64 years, having risen to 66.16 in 1988. Standing (1996: 235) provides a broader but very similar picture:

> Life expectancy has dropped almost everywhere, and morbidity rates are anything but encouraging . . . In Bulgaria, male life expectancy declined by over a year between 1988 and 1991, while female life expectancy stabilized. Similar declines took place in other countries, such as Poland, Ukraine and Slovakia.

In 1991 there were 14.0 deaths per 1000 inhabitants in Hungary compared with 12.9 in 1976–80. That 1991 figure should also be set against 8.6 in the Netherlands, 8.7 in Spain, 8.9 in Ireland and (interestingly) 11.3 in Great Britain, which is close to the Czechoslovak figure of 11.5.

Clearly the mechanisms linking death rates with social factors such as poverty and unemployment are complex. However, many commentators (Kemecsei 1995: 33; Standing 1996: 250) point to the importance of stress-related illnesses and the pressures on men, in particular, of working in second, third or even fourth economies to maintain the semblance of a living wage. Nor, in this context of death rates, should we ignore the impact of changes to the organization of health care provision. Several commentators (Cornia 1991; Ferge 1991, 1993; Einhorn 1994; Kemecsei 1995; Standing 1996) emphasize the shift from largely universal health care to systems of health insurance plus greater reliance on private insurance schemes for those who can pay for them in countries such as the Czech Republic, Slovakia and Hungary. Ferge (1991, 1993) also notes the negative impact of such changes on the lives of many children in Hungary, and Einhorn (1994) focuses on the plight of women.

Mention of health care systems in Eastern Europe draws us back to the point made earlier: that the massive social problems post-1989 have been exacerbated by the inadequacy of the social supports which have in many cases been put in place. Let us now consider the form of other social supports, particularly in relation to the social disadvantages suffered by children and their carers.

Social disadvantages, social supports and childcare

Families and social disadvantages

Cornia (1991), Ferge (1991, 1993) and more recently Standing (1996) have all outlined the growing inadequacies of unemployment benefit created in various states at the end of the 1980s and in the early 1990s: increasing restrictions in terms of length, range of coverage and monetary value. Standing notes that the fragmentation of unemployment benefits across Eastern Europe has been modelled on the most restrictive Western models of a neo-liberal nature, with, of course, highly negative welfare outcomes. The overall result has been a residualization of such benefits, often in line with the dictates of Western financial agencies, as discussed earlier (Standing 1996: 236–7).

Family allowances, once a valuable source of financial support, have become subject to similar changes. In Poland they have become income-tested since January 1995 (Standing 1996: 246) and in Hungary the real value of average family allowances fell from 41.5 per cent of the subsistence minimum for a child to 29.7 per cent in 1991 (Ferge 1993: 43). As regards Romania, Hill and Cairns-Smith (1995: 21) report that 'child benefit was "frozen" in value in 1990, so that with inflation its worth rapidly diminished to the equivalent of about 25 pence per month.'

In those countries where a minimum wage was instituted, such as Poland and the former Czechoslovakia, that minimum tended to be very low and was itself affected by the reducing level of wages. Moreover, of course, it was of no help to the growing numbers out of work (Cornia 1991: 112). As Kemecsei (1995) points out in relation to Hungary, the majority of the unemployed are 24–45 years old and so often have a relatively young family to support.

In addition we may note that unemployment has had a major impact on the job prospects of young people: 10 per cent of unemployed people in Hungary are young (Kemecsei 1995: 31). Ferge (1993: 44) mentions that at the end of the school year in 1992 one-third of young school leavers in Hungary could not find a job. Similarly, Wallace (1995: 99), writing about Poland, reports that the rate of unemployment for those under 25 years of age rose to 30 per cent in 1992. This situation is not only a function of the labour market but also of educational developments. For instance, in Hungary, Ferge (1993) describes how apprenticeship schemes have been crumbling, the age coverage of schools has further declined owing to financial stringency and there has been a parallel development of private education for those who can pay.

Youth unemployment itself has links with other worrying social phenomena. For instance, Sipos (1991) makes reference to growing youth crime across Eastern Europe, noting both unemployment and crime as being particularly associated with some children from Romany families. There are also strong indications of racism among 'dispossessed youth' in Eastern Europe, including the former GDR (Ginsburg 1992; Wilson 1993), Poland (*The Observer* 7 April 1996: 1) and Slovenia (Zorc 1994).

Partly as a result of all the restrictions on financial support, together with the massive rises in poverty and unemployment, huge numbers of people have become dependent on means-tested social assistance systems. For instance, as Standing notes, between 1990 and 1992 the number in Bulgaria increased by 340 per cent. However, he adds that in relation to social assistance systems 'nobody should be under any illusion that they could operate fairly or efficiently to provide social protection to those most in need' (Standing 1996: 246–7). Cornia (1991: 112–13) and Ferge (1991, 1993) outline some of the reasons for this: low budgetary allocations; lack of indexation in a period of high inflation; low take-up rates; high administrative costs; and last but by no means least, reliance on inadequate local authority systems leading to massive variations and gaps in financial provision. As a result, Ferge (1993) reports that some families in Hungary rely mainly on family allowances for their income, particularly Romany families – and we have already seen why family allowances are themselves generally inadequate.

One central outcome of all this is that in most countries of Eastern Europe families with children are prominent among those most affected by poverty and inequality. As early as 1991, Sipos had identified this as a major issue across Eastern Europe. The situation in Hungary has been particularly well documented. For instance, Ferge (1993: 43) notes that in 1992 'children under 15 were doubly represented in the lowest income decile, and the situation of families with several children was particularly worrying.' More recently Kemecsei, writing about the subsistence level for an average Hungarian family, said:

> one third of the population is today living under this level in Hungary. 30% of these people are under 15 years, so we have to say, that the poverty is highest among children. 42% of Hungarian children aged between 0–6 years are living in poverty.
>
> (Kemecsei 1995: 32)

Within this category of poor families and children we also need to highlight that there are particularly disadvantaged sub-categories, not least ethnic minorities, children with disabilities and lone mothers (Cornia

1991). As Kemecsei (1995: 34) notes, there is a trend towards an increase in the numbers of lone mothers, divorces and extra-marital births. We shall touch upon some of these issues again later in this chapter.

The negative situation of many poor families has been further exacerbated by the impact of subsidy withdrawal on food prices and food shortages. Both Sipos (1991) and Cornia (1991) make reference to the use of soup kitchens in Poland and Hungary as well as particular problems for young children in terms of milk shortages. Similar shortages also exist in Romania (Hill and Cairns-Smith 1995). Ferge (1993: 45) reports that a Hungarian survey in 1992 of families in the lowest income quintile found that in 34 per cent of cases the children were short of food and in 10 per cent of cases families had insufficient resources even to pay for children's school meals.

So far we have hardly mentioned an aspect of the crisis which is of crucial importance generally and to families in particular: housing. One set of commentators go as far as to suggest that:

> The key problem in Eastern Europe is related not to employment but to housing shortage. Family life is dominated by the necessity to share an apartment with older relatives, siblings, and often strangers.
>
> (McLean and Kurczewski 1994b: 14–15)

Certainly there is no doubt that such shortages, largely resulting from lack of social housing, have manifold implications for young people and for families: pressures leading to relationship problems (Corrin 1992) and divorce (Kwak 1994); homelessness (Kemecsei 1995); domestic violence (Einhorn 1994); pressure on parents of young adults remaining at home and reliance on 'social capital' (Wallace 1996); pressure on young women to marry in order to move out of the parental home; and, of course, purely financial problems owing to rising housing costs (Cornia 1991).

Ferge mentions one other potential outcome of housing shortages and homelessness which is of particular significance to our analysis:

> In 1991, out of the 1000 children in Budapest taken into state care, 100 were because of homelessness or eviction of the family . . . This phenomenon is new: eviction to the street was not a general practice in the former regime.
>
> (Ferge 1993: 45)

Child abuse

This last point raises the whole issue of child abuse and neglect in the countries of Eastern Europe. Ferge also underlines poverty as a major cause of state intervention in families:

that is why the number of children registered as 'at risk' increased in Hungary between 1989 and 1991 from 110,000 to 243,000. The category with the greatest increase is 'at risk because of financial reasons'.

(Ferge 1993: 44)

In fact, on the whole there seems to be considerable resistance to the idea of child abuse in the countries of Eastern Europe. Sobiech (1994) provides an interesting discussion about this in relation to Poland which has considerable relevance to other former communist countries. He suggests that under communism it was ideologically impossible to admit the presence of child abuse, except in a very small number of cases which were attributed to individual pathologies such as alcohol abuse or deviations from the moral order of a communist society: it was not possible to acknowledge the true extent of child abuse or its links with structural factors. He indicates that this approach still persists post-1989, even though other sensitive issues such as AIDS and drugs have reached the public agenda. My own experience of teaching student social workers in Poland about child protection in 1994 confirms Sobiech's account. The students were unable to conceive of any reasons for child maltreatment beyond the abuse of alcohol in 'alcoholic families'.

This resistance to public recognition of child abuse Sobiech (1994) attributes to those very structural factors which support abuse. He notes that corporal punishment is routine in Polish families, that violence to children is sanctioned by the penal code and that patriarchal obedience is reinforced by the powerful ideology of the Catholic Church. Sobiech goes on to suggest that child abuse is also denied because its recognition would entail more extensive state intervention in families and such intervention is anathema to the social ethos of Poland (and other former communist countries) post-1989. This arises from the fact that under communism the family frequently functioned as the only haven of personal privacy in a society which otherwise subsumed the private domain within the public. Historically in Poland, and some other countries, the family had also served as a refuge for national identity during a long series of occupations by foreign powers. In addition, state power *per se* is now treated with considerable suspicion in many former communist countries, an association being made between socialism, the social and the public (Cornia 1991). These antecedents, plus, in Poland, the sanctity of the family bestowed by the Catholic Church, assure continuing resistance to state interventions in the private sphere.

On the other hand, it is clear that a growing awareness about all forms of child abuse is occurring across Eastern Europe, including in Poland (Hanks *et al.* 1991; Bielawska-Batorowicz 1992; Solomon 1994). Moreover, there is now some acknowledgement in both Western and Eastern Europe of the sex tourism which has developed in the latter countries since 1989 to cater for men arriving from the former. This process of acknowledgement includes Poland (*The European* 28 November to 4 December 1996: 1).

However, insofar as child protective services are developing in Eastern Europe, they seem to view child abuse as very much the product of dysfunctional family systems rather than the outcome of structural dynamics within society associated with poverty and/or gender (see, for instance, Modrzejewska 1990). These comments should remind us of the debates around child abuse in the countries of Western Europe surveyed in previous chapters, debates which I will develop further in Chapter 8. At this point we need only note that, as in many Western European countries, the preference in Eastern Europe for a family dysfunction perspective on child abuse preserves the ideological and patriarchal integrity of the family as an institution. By contrast, structural explanations of child abuse would require Eastern European countries to question radically some underlying assumptions about the distribution of power both within their societies and within families. Given their recent history, it is easy to see why there would be massive resistance to such structural explanations in those countries.

Such an alternative structural perspective is provided by a minority of commentators on Eastern Europe: for instance, Makkai (1994) and Einhorn (1994), who adopt feminist approaches. Significantly, these commentators note that most forms of feminism are also subject to considerable resistance in East European countries, partly because of the discredited reputation of former state socialist women's organizations, and partly because the social agenda of many women in post-1989 Eastern Europe is rather different from that of many women in some Western European countries and the USA. While the latter have often fought for the choice of a more substantial role in the labour market, the former are now often seeking a choice to exit from that market after years of enforced inclusion (Einhorn 1994). It may well be that the lack of a strong, radical feminist movement in Eastern European countries is yet another reason why considerable denial about issues such as abuse of women and of children by men continues there. Certainly we saw in Chapter 2 that the presence of such a radical movement in the United Kingdom has been a major factor in placing those issues on public and professional agendas, in contrast to many countries on the continent.

Women and the family

Of course, there are other forces encouraging women to place more of an exclusive focus on the home in much of Eastern Europe. Some of these forces are financial. For instance, the fragmentation of benefits which we have already mentioned is paralleled by a fragmentation of childcare services. As Ferge (1991, 1993) and Cornia (1991) note, day-care provision, in the shape of nurseries and kindergarten based on the workplace, is in decline, while fees rise and private services develop. Such financial pressures on women to stay at home are partly policy inspired and in some cases the ideological drive towards pro-natalism is very obvious. For instance, Ferge writing about Hungary describes how:

> the new, relatively liberal law on the protection of the fetus ... has replaced the former lump sum maternity grant by a family allowance from the fourth month of pregnancy ... Concern with the 'health of the family' has led one Hungarian government agency to emphasise the superior psychosocial environment offered by complete (two-parent) families with three children, seen as an 'optimal model' deserving preferential treatment.
>
> (Ferge 1993: 49)

Pro-natalism is also apparent in post-1989 policies towards abortion. While it was legalized in the formerly restrictive Romania in 1991 (Hill and Cairns-Smith 1995), the trend is in the opposite direction in many other Eastern European states. For instance, in December 1992 the Hungarian Parliament passed a law which, although less narrow than an alternative proposal, is still highly restrictive (Einhorn 1994: 95). In Poland, the debate continues to swing one way and then the other (Einhorn 1994: 102; *The European* 10–16 April 1997: 7).

Hungary and Poland are both, of course, countries where the Catholic Church retains a strong ideological hold, including a powerful commitment to patriarchal 'family values'. It is therefore important to remember that policies designed to encourage women to concentrate their emotional and physical energies on the home have complex social, economic and cultural origins.

Divorce

These religious and patriarchal factors are also evident in changes to legislation regarding divorce. We have noted that in many Eastern European countries where divorce was already high under communism (Sipos 1991; Einhorn 1994) the rates have been rising further post-1989. The rising levels of divorce play a major role in creating anxieties among many people about an alleged disintegration of the family, even though it is clear that it in fact remains a highly 'popular' institution in Eastern Europe (Ferge 1993; Einhorn 1994; Kemecsei 1995). Owing to these concerns and the religious, cultural and patriarchal pressures noted above, restrictions on the ability to obtain divorces have been imposed in countries such as Hungary (Ferge 1993) and Poland (Szlezak 1994).

Heterosexism and the family

In Chapter 1 we noted that much of the literature on European social policy is rather heterosexist. In particular there is a deafening silence about family configurations and/or parenthood which involve gay or lesbian relationships (Carabine 1996). Interestingly, several comment-ators (Corrin 1992; Einhorn 1994) do discuss these issues in relation to Eastern Europe, citing the overt heterosexism of policies in these coun-tries as the product not only of their communist heritage but also of the religious and patriarchal pressures which in many states have asserted themselves further since 1989.

Having reviewed the many indications of strong tendencies towards a return to 'traditional' gendered family and parental roles, we should enter one word of caution. Although changes in the labour market and the economic situation may well tend to drive women out of employ-ment in some situations, it is clear that other financial and economic pressures may encourage the retention of women's labour outside the home, albeit in the context of even stronger socio-economic differenti-ation (Standing 1996: 245).

Social care

Let us now turn to the plight of those children and their families where the kinds of pressures we have surveyed so far in this chapter result in forms of state intervention. What are some of the main features of social care services in Eastern Europe? Once again, we need to make a plea for a recognition of diversity among these countries. For instance, there are clearly differences arising from both the past and the present between the form and extent of social care services in Hungary (Ferge 1993) and Romania (Hill and Cairns-Smith 1995). Nevertheless, it is only right to point out that there are also some broad similarities.

Development of social work services in Eastern Europe
To a large extent such services did not exist in these countries under communism. Or, if they did, it was only in an attenuated workplace form (Cornia 1991; Ferge 1993; Hill and Cairns-Smith 1995), centred on financial provision (Solomon 1994). The recognition of social problems, as understood in Western Europe, was necessarily discouraged, as we noted earlier. In some countries, such as Poland (Modrzejewska 1990; Solomon 1994; Stelmaszuck 1994), Hungary (Bodanszky 1990; Ferge 1993) and the former Czechoslovakia (Biskup 1990), there were already some real foundations for social care services in the 1980s and it is in these countries that further development occurred earliest. However, even here this development took place in the context of massive financial constraints and of weak or variable newly decentralized local authority structures (Cornia 1991; Ferge 1993; Solomon 1994). In other countries,

such as Romania (Hill and Cairns-Smith 1995), the foundations for social care services were perhaps more tenuous and their development has occurred at an even slower rate, though it is now happening.

We should also mention non-governmental organizations (NGOs), which in some of these countries have a more established tradition and may be encouraged by governments (Ferge 1993; Hill and Cairns-Smith 1995) in ways that some commentators have interpreted as demonstrating a quasi-conservative corporatist approach (Ferge 1993; Gotting 1994). However, it seems that many NGOs are too small and/or too poorly funded to play a role similar to that performed by their counterparts in Germany (see Chapter 3), thereby allowing the state simply to pull back from direct welfare provision (Cornia 1991; Gotting 1994).

Out-of-home placements

We have already mentioned several reasons why children are increasingly removed from their parents in many East European countries, including poverty and homelessness. What kinds of resources exist for such children? It is clear from several accounts (Biskup 1990; Sipos 1991; Ferge 1991; Solomon 1994; Hill and Cairns-Smith 1995) that in most communist countries residential care played a major role in provision, and to a greater or lesser extent it still does so. However, the range of provision is changing and developing in many countries. Modrzejewska (1990) describes a spectrum of provision in Poland, from residential units for diagnostic and special care services through 'replacement families' to foster care and adoption. Solomon (1994) and Stelmaszuck (1994) analyse a cooperative project between Britain and Poland to develop a shift from residential to fostering services. This project is interesting for several reasons, two of which I mention. First, the account makes clear the shift was motivated by pressing economic considerations as well as therapeutic ones. Second, the outcome is a form of family placement organization that is geared to the specific Polish cultural context rather than being a mirror-image of British practice, which might have been wholly inappropriate to that context. These are both important factors to bear in mind.

Significantly, Solomon (1994: 11) emphasizes that the residential provision he encountered in Poland was far more positive than the daunting institutions which have been reported in Romania. The account by Hill and Cairns-Smith (1995) of a cooperative Scottish–Romanian project geared to social work training suggests that those reports about Romania were often accurate. Hill and Cairns-Smith (1995: 22) note that these institutions had been grossly starved of training as well as material resources, with little personal space or stimulation for the children in them. Moreover, many of the children were not 'orphans' as often described.

Frequently they had been placed for a number of reasons: the financial deprivation of their families; the large number of births resulting from the communist regime's extreme pro-natalist policies, together with high maternal mortality rates arising from those policies; prejudice against lone parents and a resistance to fostering (p. 21). Once again, Romany children seemed to be particularly disadvantaged in terms of poverty, discrimination and an even greater unwillingness by Romanian families to foster them. As a result, a high proportion of the children in the institutions were Romany. Hill and Cairns-Smith (1995: 22) note that similar disadvantages are faced by Romany children in Hungary, where some specialist fostering schemes are being established. It seems that children with physical and/or learning disabilities were also disprortionately represented in the institutions, though Hill and Cairns-Smith (1995: 21–2) speculate that those disablities themselves may in some cases have been at least partly the outcome of the children's institutionalization. It is clear that fostering in Romania is now providing a positive resource for some children, but there is a long way to go (O'Riley 1997).

Inter-country adoption

Hill and Cairns-Smith (1995: 21) also make reference to the issue of inter-country adoption, noting that it:

> tends to assist only the healthiest and most attractive children. Whilst the motives and methods of some adopters are humane, others have engaged in various kinds of improper arrangements involving bribery, consents obtained under pressure and smuggling children out of the country ... With international help, Romania has now established formal regulations and procedures for adoption, though these are not always adhered to. According to the law, now only Romanian citizens can be considered as adopters during the first 6 months after the Adoption Committee has established that a child requires adoption.

As Ruxton (1996: 350–63) notes, the issue of inter-country adoption is complex in terms of both adopter motivations and adoptee outcomes. It seems that it is relevant to all European Union members and that some of them (for instance, Ireland, Italy and the United Kingdom) are drawing considerable numbers of children from the former communist states of Eastern Europe, particularly Romania. Ruxton (1996: 351) also states that by September 1995 only one Union member (Spain) had ratified the 1993 Hague Convention on Private International Law on Protection of Children and Co-operation in Respect of Inter-Country Adoption.

Refugee children

The topic of inter-country adoption also leads us to a consideration of children who are refugees from parts of Eastern Europe (Ruxton 1996: Chapter 16). Such movements have increased in the 1990s, of course, owing not only to the social and economic crises in these countries but also to the wars in the former Yugoslavia. Of particular concern are unaccompanied children. As Ruxton (1996: 435–50) makes clear, data collection within the European Union on this matter is highly variable and the processes faced by such children are diverse across the EU. It seems that unaccompanied children from Eastern Europe are most likely to originate in Romania, the former Yugoslavia and, to some extent, Albania. Their destinations seem most likely to be Germany, France, Sweden, Austria, United Kingdom, Finland and, in the case of Albanian children, Italy. Ruxton (1996: 440) notes that on the whole such children are not granted full refugee status but usually allowed to remain on humanitarian or other grounds. Of particular concern is the racism and the xenophobia which they, along with other asylum-seekers, may well face in their countries of destination (Ruxton 1996: 451–3). In the case of Albanian children in Italy, it seems that their involvement in sex rings has become quite a regular feature (Bini and Toselli 1997), and this highlights another, particularly insidious, threat to unaccompanied children in Western European countries more generally.

CHILDREN AND MODELS OF SOCIAL WELFARE IN EASTERN EUROPE

Having surveyed some of the main features of children and social welfare in Eastern Europe, I want now to consider how far this material conforms with, and/or contradicts, various frameworks which have been suggested for understanding welfare system development in Eastern Europe post-1989. Most of these frameworks have, once again, been based on Esping-Andersen's categorizations, though, as we have already noted, he himself did not include Eastern Europe in his analysis (Esping-Andersen 1990).

One of the earliest attempts to develop an Eastern European framework was made by Deacon (1992, 1993). Deacon acknowledges that he is dealing with welfare contexts which differ widely in many respects from the situation in the West, and that this may have a profound impact on how far Esping-Andersen's models can be fully applied. He also points out that he is suggesting tentative trends rather than definite outcomes, given that the speed of change in Eastern Europe is extremely rapid.

Deacon's (1992, 1993) framework can be summarized as follows. As far as Hungary, Croatia and Slovenia are concerned, he regards the dominant tendencies there as being neo-liberal because of the speed with which those countries have embraced market philosophies and their lack of a social democratic heritage. By contrast, the welfare system developing

in the Czech Republic is characterized as being primarily social democratic, partly because of the country's pre-Second World War history and
also because of the mass nature of the uprising against communism. In
the context of its absorption within the FRG, Deacon ascribes the former
GDR to the conservative corporatist category. Given the relative resistance to change in Bulgaria, Romania and Serbia, Deacon suggests we
should consider them to be tending towards post-communist conservative corporatism, possibly leading in the longer term to what he calls
populist authoritarianism. In these states, according to Deacon, the old
regime maintains considerable sway and a reluctant, gradualist approach
to market forces is adopted. Finally, he discerns in Poland a trend towards
populist authoritarianism.

However, the picture painted by other commentators suggests that
the situation is even more complex and indeterminate than Deacon
indicated. What is especially interesting for us is that the judgements of
these commentators draw more evidence from family policy developments than did Deacon. Ferge (1993) depicts Hungary as struggling to
adapt a combination of conservative corporatist and neo-liberal policies
to its own situation. Gotting's analysis (1994) in many ways mirrors
Ferge's approach rather than Deacon's.

In the Hungarian welfare system Gotting (1994) discerns definite, but
unstable, corporatist tendencies: a nascent though faltering attempt to
construct a tripartism of state, employers and unions; a forced attempt
to promote subsidiarity principles by devolving power (but no resources)
to the municipalities and asserting the importance of the family as a
source of care; promoting the growth of voluntary, non-profit, organizations (as in Poland) by the use of taxation support, but without the state
funding on which German voluntaries frequently depend. The establish-
ment of a health insurance scheme from 1992 (Ferge 1993) and the situation regarding divorce and abortion noted above could also be understood
within a conservative corporatist frame of reference. However, both Ferge
(1993) and Gotting (1994) recognize that there are also distinct neo-
liberal features to reforms in Hungary, most of which we have discussed
earlier in this chapter: private health and social insurance schemes,
private hospitals, private schools and private nurseries are all developing
for that section of the population with wealth; social expenditure has
decreased slightly in real terms even though unemployment and poverty
increased massively; social assistance is administered at a low level by
local authorities who often lack the funds to pay it.

Gotting (1994) believes that Slovakia has adopted rather a gradualist
approach towards marketization. The somewhat populist and national-
ist government has placed much economic and social pressure on the
Romany population of East Slovakia. Unemployment is much higher

than in the neighbouring Czech Republic and economic problems are considerable. By contrast, Gotting (1994) characterizes the Czech Republic as having so far instituted the most thoroughgoing neo-liberal reforms of any Eastern European country, benefiting also from a relatively healthy economic position prior to 1990. This analysis of the Republic is strikingly different from Deacon's (1993): a difference which underlines the problem in seeking to categorize East European countries using frameworks which are in origin Western.

In relation to Bulgaria, Gotting's (1994) analysis is closer to Deacon's (1993), since they both emphasize the rather cautious and halting 'social market' approach adopted there. Gotting points out that, unlike Hungary and the former Czechoslovakia, Bulgaria has no previous history of Bismarckian approaches to economic and social policy: as a result corporatism (let alone neo-liberalism) is comparatively alien to Bulgaria.

To the analyses of Deacon, Ferge and Gotting we should add the perspective offered more recently by Standing (1996). He regards the future trends for welfare development in Eastern Europe as being finely balanced. On the one hand he notes the widespread adoption of neo-liberal policies, to a greater or lesser extent encouraged by the IMF and World Bank. Yet he also notes the popular distaste which exists for the degrees of inequality these policies are generating. This is indeed also borne out by Vecernik's (1996) analysis of social attitudes in Eastern Europe. Regarding trends towards conservative corporatism in some countries, especially Hungary and Poland, Standing (1996: 252) acknowledges them but also points out that such a regime model seems ill-suited to an economic climate in most of these countries where industrial employment has been declining and the resources for a social insurance-based approach are insecure.

This reminds us again of the difficulty in applying Western-derived models to such different contexts as the countries of Eastern Europe. My own opinion is that future trajectories in any of the countries of Eastern Europe are unlikely to mirror directly or simply trends in the West. The situation is so complex and fast-moving, while the contexts are so different.

CONCLUSIONS

I find no evidence to indicate that future social policies in relation to children and their families across the countries of Eastern Europe will conform in any direct way to Esping-Andersen-type patterns, though there clearly are, and probably will continue to be, elements of them all present to varying extents. In this book we have seen that, when observed through the lens of children and their carers, Esping-Andersen's classifications regarding Western Europe can be seriously critiqued on a number of grounds, not least their neglect of power differentials around the themes of age, 'race', gender, disablity and sexuality. In Eastern Europe we see that recent adverse changes in all these power dynamics, as well as those of wealth, have been monumental. For that reason, and owing to the qualitative differences in context, I would argue that Esping-Andersen's framework is of even less relevance here than it is in relation to Western Europe as a meaningful analysis of children's welfare.

7

CHILDREN'S WELFARE AND PAN-EUROPEAN INSTITUTIONS

INTRODUCTION

In this book we have so far surveyed patterns of child welfare provision across most states of Europe. However, when considering provision in Europe we must also pay attention to those specifically pan-European institutions which have a bearing on childcare problems and services. In this chapter I shall concentrate on the two most significant of those institutions: the European Union and the Council of Europe. Their approaches and roles provide a degree of contrast which I expand upon in the remainder of the chapter. On the one hand, the Council of Europe has generally pursued the issue of child welfare both more broadly and more deeply than the European Union. On the other hand, by its nature the Council has far more limited resources and legislative power than the Union, even though membership of the former is much the larger. The Union potentially possesses greater legislative power than the Council, even though to a large extent that potential has not so far been fulfilled.

THE EUROPEAN UNION

The doubts expressed above about the role of the Union in terms of child welfare have two sources. The first relates to the Union's limited approach to social policy as a whole. The second concerns the low priority (and indeed virtual absence of attention) given to children within such social measures as have been enacted by the Union. I will address these issues in turn.

The role of social policy within the structures of the European Union

The limitations of the Union in relation to child welfare have initially to be viewed within the context of European Union social policy more generally. As commentators have often discussed (Hantrais 1995; Hantrais and Letablier 1996; Ruxton 1996; Swithinbank 1996), it is debatable whether social, as opposed to economic, policy has ever been a central concern of the Union and its predecessor institutions, whatever the distant intentions of the founders (Cannan *et al.* 1992; Wise and Gibb 1993). Moreover, those doubts persist to this day:

> The Commission would seem to have gathered together the necessary ingredients for a European social policy but has been held back by other political actors from creating an autonomous system. The decision to include the principle of subsidiarity in the Maastricht Treaty can be interpreted as confirmation that an overarching social policy was still not to be given an official seal of approval.
>
> (Hantrais 1995: 210–11)

There are many indications of this secondary role attached to social policy. For instance, it is surely instructive that the first White Paper on Social Policy (European Commission 1994) was issued nearly thirty years after the Treaty of Rome. Moreover, Directorate-General V (DGV), responsible for Union social affairs, is significantly designated as covering 'employment, industrial relations *and social affairs*' (author's italics), indicating perhaps the relative priority accorded to the social dimension.

Several commentators (Cannan *et al.* 1992; Swithinbank 1996) have emphasized the greater social vision evident in European Union policies during the Commission Presidency of Jacques Delors (1984–94), culminating in the 1994 White Paper. Moreover, that document does certainly make much wider claims about Union social competencies than ever before:

> social policy goes beyond employment. It affects people when they are at work but also when they are not – their family life, their health and their old age . . . The White Paper sets out a framework for Union action in the face of these challenges.
>
> (European Commission 1994: 7)

The White Paper goes on to add confidently that 'the Union's social policy cannot play second string to economic development or to the functioning of the internal market'. However before we are carried away by these grand phrases, we should consider the reasons which the White Paper itself gives for this expansion of social competency:

> If economic growth is to increase human well-being, it must also take into account social and environmental concerns. Equally, the pursuit of high

social standards should not only be seen as a cost but also as a key element
in the competitive formula.

(European Commission 1994: 10)

The suspicions raised by these comments that the 'social dimension'
is still largely secondary to economic and employment policy are reinforced by the remainder of the document, which makes frequent references to the crucial importance of economic success. In fact, there are
many different discourses around social policy in the White Paper, discourses which are often in disharmony. They reflect uncertainty about
not only the future role of social policy but also the kind of welfare
approach which is favoured. The following are some of the discourses to
be discovered within the White Paper:

1 The growth in unemployment, numbers of older people, extent of cri-
   minality, demands on health care and the size of an alleged 'underclass'
   all place a drain on resources which must be reduced.
2 The United States and Japan have less unemployment and utilize
   women in the labour market more effectively than the European
   Union. The latter must emulate them to be competitive.
3 Economic and social policy are mutually dependent: social progress
   requires economic success and high employment; economic success
   also depends on social harmony and a socially protected workforce.
4 Human well-being involves not only economic growth but also social
   and environmental concerns.
5 Minimum standards in social protection must be laid down for the
   cohesion of the Union, so that some countries cannot undercut other
   member states in attracting business by offering lower wages.

Clearly some of these discourses, such as 1 and 2, are more in line with
Esping-Andersen's (1990) concept of neo-liberal welfare regimes, while
others are inimical to them and closer to his conservative corporatist or
even social democratic configurations: for instance, discourses 3, 4 and 5.

Thus the White Paper on closer inspection provides a highly confused
and confusing 'steer' on the extent of Union social competencies, which
no doubt partly reflects the play of political and economic forces among
its members and, as we have seen in previous chapters, the uncertainties
about the future of social policy within the individual states themselves.

It is clear that, as Swithinbank (1996: 72, 73) indicates, the White
Paper offers relatively few concrete proposals about Union social policy
implementation – and the principle of subsidiarity to which the European Union seems committed limits its willingness significantly to extend social competencies. Moreover, since the publication of the White
Paper the Union has in fact continued to be relatively inactive on the

social policy front (Falkner 1996; Pochet *et al.* 1996b). To some extent this no doubt reflects a policy inertia arising from the proceedings of the Inter-Governmental Conference (IGC) (Falkner 1996: 13). However, Falkner suggests that longer term factors than the IGC also limit social welfare activity. These factors do not relate to a lack of legislative capacity: such capacity has existed at least since Maastricht and probably long before (p. 4). Instead Falkner attributes past, and probably future, inertia about the extension of social policy to the absence of 'a consensus between governments on the desirability and specifics of doing so' (p. 4). This inertia also derives from:

> the often antagonistic interests within the EC Social Council (even if only composed of 14 members), and ... the general political trend towards flexibilization and lowering of social and labour standards which is due to ever-increased economic pressures within the internationalized economy.
>
> (Falkner 1994: 13)

Official pronouncements from the Commission since the White Paper on social policy confirm the secondary role of such policy. For instance, in its communication on the future of social protection, issued in 1995:

> the Commission proposes that Community institutions and the Member states should embark together on a process of cooperative reflection on the future measures which should be taken to make social protection systems more efficient and more conducive to employment growth.
>
> (Pochet *et al.* 1996a: 65)

Having said all this, and bearing in mind the limitations we have so far noted, it of course remains true that the Commission and the Union have engaged in a large number of measures which can be described as in some sense 'social'. These measures include legislative instruments (involving various degrees of compulsion or non-compulsion), social care programmes, training initiatives, data-gathering agencies and focused transnational networks (Swithinbank 1996).

Even the United Kingdom, which famously 'opted out' from the 'Protocol on Social Policy' in the 1993 Treaty of European Union, has to some extent been influenced by the Union's social dimension. This influence partly arises from the impact of the Single European Act 1985, to which the UK remains a signatory (Swithinbank 1996: 75–9). However, the social dimension also impacts on the United Kingdom in more indirect ways. The corporatist mechanisms of the European Union include the involvement of labour and employer organizations in debates on social provision. Although this involvement contrasts starkly with the anti-labour union practices of the 1979–97 British government (Sperling and Bretherton 1996: 310), it has relevance to the United Kingdom. British labour and employer organizations have taken part in those European Union debates. As a result, many businesses in the United Kingdom have *de facto* adopted the European Works Council Directive either because they have subsidiaries elsewhere in the Union or because they themselves are subsidiaries of companies with headquarters in other member states (Falkner 1996: 10–11).

However, we need to recognize that the limitations of the European Union from the perspective of child welfare also arise from the relatively low priority accorded to children as objects of those Union social measures which have been implemented – and it is this issue that I now address.

The place of children within European Union social policies

Ruxton (1996: 15–9) makes the point that children are accorded a very low priority in terms of Union social policies: no consideration has been given to their interests; neither children themselves nor child welfare agencies have much say in the Union's elaborate policy consultation procedures; there is no mention of children in the Treaties of the European Union; and Union statistics on children and childhood are often inadequate compared to data-gathering on other issues (Ruxton 1996: 16–17). To a large extent this low priority accorded to children arises from the subservience of Union social policy to economic and employment policies, which we discussed more generally in the last section (Ruxton 1996: 16). Put simply, children are not workers and are therefore not a primary focus for European Union attention.

In her recent work Hantrais (Hantrais 1995: Chapter 5; Hantrais and Letablier 1996: Chapter 8) has expanded this point by emphasizing the limitations of Union family policy as a whole. Hantrais and Letablier (1996: 140) note that in 1983 the European Parliament passed a nonbinding resolution calling on the Commission to introduce a comprehensive family policy and appropriate harmonization of national policies. Yet by 'the mid-1990s, it could be argued that the Union had still not developed a clearly defined or "comprehensive" family policy' (Hantrais and Letablier 1996: 141).

Hantrais (1995: 79) attributes this state of affairs to three factors. First, as we have observed in the course of this study, 'the family' issue raises deep ideological divergences both within and between member states, divergences with which the European Union has no desire to grapple. Second, in some member states (as again we have seen) 'the family' is regarded as being largely outside the ambit of state intervention and the Union has not been eager to challenge such national attitudes. Finally, echoing Ruxton's earlier point about children, Hantrais (1995: 79) notes that children's welfare is a marginal consideration for the European Union, since it concentrates on workers' rather than citizens' rights as far as social protection is concerned. She demonstrates this point by surveying most of the major 'landmarks' in Union social policy. For instance, Hantrais notes that the non-binding 1989 Charter of the Fundamental Social Rights of Workers (often known as the Social Charter) took:

> some account of the status of women as mothers by recognising that parents needed support to enable them to reconcile family and employment responsibilities, but again on the understanding that employment status was paramount.
>
> (Hantrais 1995: 79)

She goes on to describe how the Agreement on Social Policy, underpinned by the Protocol on Social Policy, also referred to family issues only obliquely. While the non-binding 1992 Council Recommendation on the convergence of social protection objectives and policies went further by advocating targeted benefits for categories of families in need, Hantrais (1995: 81–2) notes that the social policy White Paper which followed in 1994 made no concrete proposals for a European family policy by the year 2000 – though it did emphasize the requirement for 'a broadly based social policy which took account of family life'.

Where substantial Union developments have occurred in relation to family issues, these tend not to have been prompted by a recognition of the need for a comprehensive European family policy *per se*. For instance, in 1989 the Commission produced a draft Communication on family policies which was largely reiterated by the Council of Ministers. The foundation of the European Observatory on National Family Policies followed from this, a network which has produced highly valuable data over the years on family issues. Nevertheless, Hantrais (1995: 80–1) notes that these developments were initially prompted by several worrying reports on demographic trends and the Commission draft Communication advocated action based not on ideological considerations, but on the grounds that the family played an important economic role, serving as a 'touchstone between the generations' and as a route to equality between men and women.

Moreover, within families, just as the rights of children have been largely overlooked due to their lack of status as non-workers (Ruxton 1996: 16), so too has the specific situation of women been ignored (Sperling and Bretherton 1996: 310). Hantrais (1995: 104) notes that the 'attention paid to women in the Union has been primarily and almost exclusively in their capacity as workers'. Although it is true that women's rights (unlike family issues) have been the object of considerable, and early, European legislative attention, Hantrais (1995: 102) suggests that this attention may well have originated not 'from a desire to ensure equality between the sexes but as a means of promoting equal competition between member states'. Within the specific context of member states' economic and employment needs, and addressing women primarily as workers, the Union has sought to 'promote women's labour market rights and equal opportunities at the European level' (Hantrais 1995: 104).

These measures have of course had an impact on family issues and on the welfare of children in families. Hantrais (1995: Chapter 6) describes in detail how those measures have included the following elements: sections of the original 1957 EEC Treaty; a series of Directives in the 1970s and 1980s; several specific initiatives in the field of childcare; clauses within the Social Charter, the Agreement on Social Policy and the 1994 White Paper on social policy; the four medium-term Community Action Programmes on equal opportunities for men and women (the latest running from 1996 until 2000); and finally projects associated with those programmes and with the European Union's structural Funds, such as the New Opportunities for Women (NOW) initiative.

Rather than simply replicate Hantrais's comprehensive account of all these measures, I want to go on here to focus on those issues which have specific and direct salience for the social welfare of children.

The European Union and the social welfare of children

As we noted earlier and as Sandy Ruxton (Ruxton 1996: Chapters 1 and 2) has pointed out, children seem to be afforded a rather low priority in terms of the Union's direct concerns, largely because of their non-participation in the labour market: 'The position of children in their own right is not within the competence of the European Union, and therefore children's issues are not dealt with separately by the Community' (Ruxton 1996: 27–8). Nevertheless, in various ways the interests of children have been addressed by the Union, albeit as an adjunct to other issues of more direct concern to it.

Child and family welfare in EU legislation
Perhaps not surprisingly in view of what we have already said, very little purely legislative Union attention has been paid to children. As early as 1977 a relatively wide-ranging Directive was issued concerning the education of children of migrant workers (Ruxton 1996: 433). This was aimed at the children of workers who are nationals of a member state but resident in a different one. It included an obligation on member states to promote the teaching of the children's language and culture of origin. However, Ruxton (1996: 433) notes that this Directive has been

ignored or had little attention paid to it in many member states, and that consequently the Commission has adopted a more gradualist approach – which says much about the limitations of the Union in implementing its social policies.

At a more general level, Ruxton (1996: 23–4) notes that in 1990 the European Parliament 'called on the Commission to consider how to adopt the [1989 United Nations Convention on the Rights of the Child] to the European context' by designing a European Charter. This call was echoed in 1992 by the Parliament's Committee on Legal Affairs and Citizen's Rights, although Ruxton (1996: 24) adds that the committee's proposals are in many respects a watered down version of the United Nations Charter.

In 1991 the Parliament's Committee on Youth, Culture, Education, the Media and Sport produced a report on the problems of children within the European Community, calling for a legally based Community policy on children, albeit respecting principles of subsidiarity (Ruxton 1996: 25). Ruxton outlines the twenty-eight recommendations of that report directed at both European institutions and member state governments, addressing such issues as the requirement for a children's ombudsperson, the urgent need for more detailed data on children in the Community and harmonization of member state legislation on child abduction.

One recommendation is especially striking in view of the lack of attention paid to this particular issue by the Union generally. The report advocates 'a raising of public awareness of all forms of violence against children' (Ruxton 1996: 25). The European Union has been remarkably silent about this topic, which our study has identified as a major social problem throughout Europe. As we shall see later, even when the Union has taken measures where the subject of child abuse ought clearly to have been high on its agenda, scant attention has actually been paid to it. Swithinbank implies that this may reflect wide variations in approach to the issue across member states:

> There is no European-wide definition of the concepts of child abuse and neglect . . . The level of identification and recognition of the problem varies enormously throughout Europe with taboos ensuring that abuse, particularly sexual abuse, is not revealed.
>
> (Swithinbank 1996: 77)

That point is well made (Harder and Pringle 1997; Jonsson 1997; Chapter 8, this volume). I shall demonstrate in the following chapter that awareness of the extent of sexual abuse, and the urgency adopted to counter it, is much greater in the United Kingdom than in other member states of the Union – even if the actual measures instituted against child abuse in Britain still leave much to be desired. The lack of attention paid by the Union to child abuse may partly be related to the fact that the United Kingdom has historically played (and indeed is still playing) a relatively minor role in shaping European Union institutions and policies, compared to countries such as France and Germany (see Chapter 3). This is reinforced by the findings of Sperling and Bretherton (1996), who compared the issues focused upon by women's networks in the United Kingdom with those in the European Union. Employment/training held the top place in both sets of networks. However, violence/harassment ranked second for the British networks but only eighth for their European Union counterparts. As we shall also see later in this chapter, the relatively passive approach adopted towards child abuse by the European Union to some extent contrasts with the more active response by the Council of Europe.

However, returning to the more general question of the limited legislative interest taken by the Union in children's issues, Ruxton (1996: 17–18) discerns some indications that the European Union may become more proactive legislatively in the future. For instance, he cites the fact that in 1995 the Parliament called for more attention being given to policies affecting children. In addition, he notes that the Reflection Group considering the issues to be addressed by the Inter-Governmental Conference (IGC) has suggested the possibility of prohibiting discrimination on the grounds of age – as well as the grounds of gender, 'race', religion, disability and sexual orientation. In view of our analysis in the previous chapters of this study, it is clear that such a move ought to be highly welcomed and urgently encouraged in terms of children's rights.

As regards the wider question of whether the Union will be more proactive regarding children and family issues in the future, there may still be cause for a lack of optimism. These doubts have several sources: the view of some commentators such as Falkner (1996), cited above, that social policy in general is unlikely to hold anything approaching centre stage now after the IGC; and the more specific fact that Hantrais's analysis (Hantrais 1995; Hantrais and Letablier 1996) suggests that the Union continues to avoid developing a coherent set of family policies.

Ruxton's (1996) study, which was itself part funded by the European Commission, contains a foreword by Padraig Flynn, Commissioner for employment and social affairs, in which he says:

> while the contents of this document represent the views of NCH Action For Children alone, it will provide a much-needed focus for constructive debate about the future for children in the European Union.
>
> (Ruxton 1996: x)

How far this guarded statement suggests any major change in the approach of the Union towards children and families is rather hard to say. However,

Commissioner Flynn, and Ruxton (1996) himself, make the point that the Union has passed at least one major piece of legislation relating very specifically to the issue of childcare, the 1996 Directive relating to leave for parents, and it is to this topic that we now turn.

The European Union and the issue of parental leave

In 1992, the Council of Ministers had adopted a Pregnancy Directive, which included a stipulation regarding an entitlement to fourteen weeks' maternity leave with some financial support. Despite United Kingdom opposition, this measure was adopted because it was put forward as a health and safety measure and thereby did not require unanimous agreement by members (Hantrais and Letablier 1996: 122–3; Ruxton 1996: 139). In 1996, the Union finally issued a Directive, under the Social Agreement of the Treaty of Union (excluding the United Kingdom), giving parents the right to a three-month period of leave from employment to care for their children (Pochet *et al.* 1996a, b; Ruxton 1996: 139–40). The process by which this measure came into being, and its present scope, illustrates several major issues dealt with in this study.

Let us take first the process leading up to the measure. Pochet *et al.* (1996b: 163), reviewing that process, note somewhat wryly:

> The Commission proposal for a Directive on the right to parental leave, was first issued in 1983. However the British Government had constantly vetoed this proposal since it granted the right to leave for women *and* for men. In 1995, the Commission, in order to bypass this veto, started the procedure according to the Agreement on Social Policy.

In view of the analysis presented in previous chapters of this study (especially Chapter 2), it is probably unnecessary to make much further comment as to what this says about the negative attitudes of the 1979–97 British government towards both child welfare and gender issues (Hantrais and Letablier 1996: 132). The British resistance to a parental leave Directive was allegedly based on a concern about the potential costs for the business sector. Yet we should note that recent research has demonstrated that this concern was in fact wholly unfounded (Ruxton 1997: 19). The following quotation from Michael Portillo, Defence Secretary in the Conservative administration of 1992–7 and a leading Conservative Party figure, suggests that opposition to parental leave may well have been only part of a much broader government hostility to the European Union. It also indicates a considerable misunderstanding about actual Union policies:

> We will not allow Brussels to control our defence policy ... Britain is blessed with very brave soldiers, sailors and airmen, willing to give their lives – for Britain, not for Brussels ... the European Court would probably

want to stop our men fighting for more than 40 hours a week. They would probably have sent half of them home on paternity leave.

(*The Guardian* 11 October 1995)

Regarding the scope of the actual Directive as it was eventually passed in 1996, there are two points to be made. The first is, of course, that it held no sway in the United Kingdom owing to the latter's 'opt-out' from the Social Agreement. However, the Labour government which came to power in 1997 committed itself soon after its election to a full involvement in the Union's social affairs, including adoption of the Social Agreement. The second point is that the measure did not go as far as some parties would have wished. In particular, the social partners who were (as is customary in the corporatist approach of the European Commission) closely involved in the creation of the measure could not agree on the payment question regarding parental leave (Pochet *et al.* 1996a). Consequently, during that leave 'the worker must remain covered by social security benefits, such as health care, for at least a period of three months' (Pochet *et al.* 1996b). Thus, even without the loudly dissenting voice of the United Kingdom, it is clear that the mechanisms of the Union had still to grapple with considerable differences of approach between member states and social partners, underlining once again the barriers limiting the scope of Union social policy-making.

Another reason for paying attention to the 1996 Directive is because it brings into focus the ongoing efforts of one specific European Commission structure which has genuinely had an important impact on childcare policy issues at both the European Union level and the member states' level: the European Network on Childcare and Other Measures to Reconcile Employment and Family Responsibilities (the Childcare Network). Owing to the positive contribution of the Childcare Network in the context of the Union's overall neglect of childcare issues, I will now consider it in some detail.

The European Network on Childcare and Other Measures to Reconcile Employment and Family Responsibilities

The actual title of the Network emphasizes again a point made throughout this chapter: the dependence of Union social policy as a whole, and of Union child and family measures specifically, on employment and economic considerations. Nevertheless, bearing in mind this policy limitation, there is no doubt that the Network has played a tireless and influential role, not least in disseminating data on childcare practice throughout the member states (European Commission 1990, 1996a, b, c;

Ruxton 1996: 30). However, its activities have gone well beyond data dissemination, and I want to discuss several of those activities now.

One activity has been lobbying for a policy on leave arrangements which contributed so crucially to the adoption of the Union Directive outlined above. It is deeply ironic in view of the British Conservative government's attitude to these measures that the central figure in this process, as in many of the Network's activities, has been its coordinator Peter Moss – himself based at the Thomas Coram Research Unit in London. The part played by Moss and the Network in achieving progress in this area cannot be overestimated.

In its annual reports and publications (for instance, European Commission 1996a, c), the Network has advocated on behalf of good practice in childcare. Given the importance which our study has attached to the issue of racism and child welfare in Europe, it is particularly important to mention the coordinating role played by the Network in the 'Challenging Racism in Childcare Provision' project which the European Commission has funded in the 1990s (Children in Scotland 1994).

There is another specific area in which the Network has been active since the late 1980s and which has become the focus of considerable controversy in recent years. Because of this controversy and because the area in question is so central to the anti-oppressive issues which underpin our analysis of child welfare, I will now discuss it in detail. That area is the topic of men as carers and in particular as professional workers in child welfare settings (European Commission 1993, 1996b).

Men as professional carers
In the 1992 Council Recommendation on Child Care (European Commisssion 1992) it is made clear that member states should promote and encourage increased participation by men in the care and upbringing of children. The 1994 White Paper on European social policy (European Commission 1994) re-emphasizes the importance of this theme. As I have noted, the Childcare Network has carried it forward with great energy. Indeed, the Network proposed a target for the next ten years of men constituting 20 per cent of workers in childcare services across the European Union (European Commission 1996b: 6). By contrast, the figures from the 1991 census suggest that men account for 2 per cent of staff in 'childcare and related occupations' within the United Kingdom (European Commission 1996b: 31).

The Network in many of its publications (European Commission 1993, 1996b) recognizes the need for greater inclusion of men in childcare in relation to both informal and professional childcare settings such as nurseries and family centres: indeed, it regards men working in the latter as also being able to promote men's participation in the former.

The motives of the Network in advocating the greater inclusion of men in childcare are several-fold but, not surprisingly in terms of European Union social policy, with a considerable emphasis placed on employment issues (European Commission 1992: Article 6; European Commission 1993: 12). However, some Network documents (European Commission 1996b: 15–18) place more importance on the advantages to children, particularly in relation to men as workers in formal childcare settings. It is argued that a movement of men into those sectors will benefit children by providing them (boys and girls) with positive male role models who are important for their identity formation and who may help them realize that some men are safe. It is also said that men as professional carers can meet children's need to be held and receive physical contact from men (Chandler 1993).

I want to review critically these arguments in relation to men as professional childcare workers. My main contention is that while there is considerable value in many of these arguments, two important qualifications need to be placed upon them. First, the Childcare Network's analysis is over-simplistic. Second, the value promised by men's increased involvement can only be achieved by placing that involvement within a broader model of men's practices: a model which centres on issues of men's power and is grounded in the materiality of women's and men's lived experience (Pringle 1997b).

That men on the whole can indeed provide successful nurturance to children is borne out by recent research in both Britain (Barker 1994; Pringle 1997d) and the United States (Marsiglio 1995). Moreover, there is every reason to believe that the potential capacity of men to nurture very successfully is also applicable to those who work in formal childcare settings (Ruxton 1991; Chandler 1993). However, the analysis of men as childcarers becomes oversimplistic when claims are made that men's presence in formal (and informal) settings is a necessity. We can begin to deconstruct such deterministic claims by referring to studies on the developmental progress of children in lesbian households (Golombok *et al.* 1983; Patterson 1992). No one would deny that more research on this issue is required both to broaden the evidence and to deepen it longitudinally. However, there is an impressive consistency in the data we do possess: the children in these households seem to develop emotionally and physically just as well as children brought up in heterosexual ones.

A theme which sometimes occurs in arguments for men being more engaged in childcare is that boys will not be able to learn how to be fathers themselves unless they too have male nurturance models. While one would not deny that children may well benefit from emotional proximity to adults of both genders, there is a danger of being too crude and prescriptive in analysing this. For instance, it is increasingly apparent from research in the United States (Daly 1994) and in the United Kingdom (Heward 1996; Pringle 1997e) that men's construction of their masculinity, and in particular those aspects related to fatherhood, are heavily influenced in complex ways by significant female figures, including their mothers. Of course, many men will have much to offer as workers in childcare services. However, there seems to be no valid argument to support the contention that male workers must always be present in formal childcare settings for the benefit of children (Pringle 1992, 1993).

At this point we must introduce perhaps the most contentious issue to the debate: the violence of some men towards children. I would argue that in fact this issue has not been sufficiently taken into account by the Childcare Network. For instance, the report entitled 'Men as Workers in Childcare Services' (European Commission 1996b), which focuses wholly on the issue of men working in professional childcare, devotes only one and a half pages to the topic of men and sexual abuse in a document which is fifty-five pages long. Elsewhere I have reviewed in detail the place of men in social welfare, including childcare (Pringle 1995, 1997a, b). While I do not deny the abuse of power which women may exercise over children (Hanks and Saradjian 1991; Elliott 1993; Kelly 1991, 1996), men's violences present a considerably larger threat in many respects. This is particularly true in relation to sexual violence both inside and outside the home (Pringle 1995: 39–52, 169–203). With specific reference to day-care, it is of course true that women seem to constitute about 40–50 per cent of sexual abuse perpetrators there (Finkelhor *et al.* 1988). However, this figure reflects the massive majority of females working in such settings. When allowance is made for the very small proportion of men involved in day-care, they account for a huge amount of the sexual abuse committed there relative to their numbers (Pringle 1994).

In view of the lack of awareness regarding child sexual abuse in continental Europe compared to Britain which we have noted throughout this book, it is hardly surprising to find that most European discussion about the abuse of children in welfare settings has also occurred in the United Kingdom (Pringle 1993, 1994, 1995, 1997a, b, e). Indeed, British concern over the sexual abuse of children in the welfare services is probably higher now than it has ever been in both public and professional circles. In 1996 the British government established the setting up of a national Children's Safeguards Review covering out-of-home placements, including residential care, boarding schools and foster care (see *Community Care* 20–26 June 1996: 1). In announcing this review, the British Health Secretary said that it had 'become clear from court cases and criminal justice investigations that the scale of abuse and of abuse risks was higher than generally appreciated' (*ibid.*). A judgement now fully vindicated by the Review report which was published in November 1997 (Brindle 1997).

I have not introduced the question of men's violences towards children in order to argue against men's presence in the provision of professional childcare. I make this point strongly because there appears to be an implication in some work produced by the Childcare Network that I do take such a negative position (European Commission 1996b: 23). The truth is quite to the contrary. I accept that men can often provide a useful service and I welcome their greater participation in the vast majority of welfare settings, mainly because I believe they potentially have a massive role to play in challenging manifestations of oppression associated with hegemonic forms of masculinity (Pringle 1997b, e).

The issue of men's violence towards children is instead raised here for a different purpose: to point out that men's potentially valuable professional contribution has to be framed within a set of positive practices which guard against the negative impact that some men may have on children's welfare, including abuse. Elsewhere I have outlined a framework for the development of those positive professional practices (Pringle 1995, 1997b, c, d), and I refer readers to that material rather than repeating it here. Some discussion of the framework also occurs in the next chapter, which reviews responses to child sexual abuse across Europe. My focus in this present chapter remains on the work of the Childcare Network.

As far as the Network is concerned, its relative lack of focus on men's sexual violence may well partly relate to a wider phenomenon which we have already commented upon above: the comparative passivity of the European Union in relation to the subject of child abuse and, in particular, child sexual abuse. Earlier I made some links between that passivity and the relative lack of awareness about the issue in continental countries such as France and Germany – countries which have clearly played a central role in the formation of European Union social policies and approaches. However, the attitudes of the Childcare Network to child sexual abuse in welfare settings also remind us that a similarly limited awareness of child sexual abuse and its connection with matters of gender seems to exist in the Nordic member states of the Union (see Chapter 5). The participation of the Nordic states has had an important impact on the direction of the Childcare Network regarding the issue of men in professional childcare, as Peter Moss himself recognizes in his foreword to one of its most forthright and influential documents (European Commission 1996b: 5–6). In the next chapter I will address in detail why awareness of child sexual abuse and gendered violence seems to be lower in most of Western and Northern Europe than in Britain. The explanation I provide there also has implications for the approach to the problem adopted by the European Union, heavily influenced as it is by practices in Western and Northern Europe. Moreover, the analysis in the next chapter about how to counter child sexual abuse effectively by comparing European experiences has relevance to the Union's future response to child sexual abuse.

The Childcare Network: a summary

The overall impact of the Childcare Network presents a slightly mixed picture. For the most part we may judge that it has been one of the most proactive and positive initiatives to have emerged from the European Union in relation to child welfare. The nature of its contribution to a large extent reflects the contours of Union social policy more generally: it has relied primarily on data collection and stimulation of debate to progress good practice in child welfare. Given that limitation, its achievements are mainly impressive, even managing to lobby successfully for European Union legislation. However, on the debit side, the Childcare Network has devoted much energy to increasing men's participation as professional childcarers in a way which has perhaps not taken sufficient account of the British experience. This gap reflects what may be a considerable degree of denial regarding the extent and dynamics of men's violence across the Nordic and 'continental' member states which are so influential within the Childcare Network.

As a coda to this section, we should note that at the end of 1996 the Childcare Network was 'wound up' and its activities were absorbed into the mainstream Union machinery. Despite my doubts about some aspects of its approach to the specific area of men in professional childcare services, I think we have to recognize that in general the Childcare Network represented one of the most proactive and energetic initiatives within the European Union regarding the welfare of children. Its departure as a discrete entity is to be regretted and may, or may not, indicate once again the extent of the Union's commitment to children's issues.

Children, young people and European Union action programmes

Having surveyed in detail the activities of the Childcare Network, I now want to end this part of the chapter devoted to the European Union by considering several of its other initiatives aimed at young people, in particular those arising from action programmes associated with the European Social Fund (ESF). Earlier in the chapter we noted the presence of such action programmes and the indirect implications which some of them have for issues of family welfare. The ESF and the action programmes are centrally concerned with the objective of helping various categories of people to gain a more secure hold on employment and access to the labour market. Their keynote is the promotion of social inclusion and the reduction of social exclusion (Swithinbank 1996: 81). We have, of course, encountered these concepts of social inclusion and exclusion earlier in this study, not least in our survey of child welfare in France and Germany (Chapter 3). That reminds us once again how heavily influenced are the social policies of the European Union by approaches within those countries which founded it.

One sector of the population repeatedly identified as requiring assistance to achieve social inclusion within formal European Union statements is young people (European Commission 1994). This is not surprising given the fact that in previous chapters our study has highlighted youth unemployment as an important problem in almost all member states (Ruxton 1996:181). Swithinbank (1996: 85–6) usefully summarizes some of the most recent Union programme initiatives relating to young people, including 'Youthstart' and 'Youth for Europe'.

Racism and European Union initiatives

We should note that the third instalment of the 'Youth for Europe' initiative supports projects to counter racism and xenophobia (Ruxton 1996: 435). It follows on from increasing concern about this issue within some sections of the European Union over the past few years. For instance, Ruxton (1996: 434–5) notes that in 1990 the European Parliament's Committee of Inquiry into Racism and Xenophobia produced a report highlighting this issue across member states and making a series of recommendations to counter it. In previous chapters of this study we have emphasized that across the Union racism is a major social problem which has not been adequately addressed by most countries. Consequently the Parliament's recognition of it was not before time – indeed, it seems to have been rather belated. Moreover, Ruxton (1996: 434) adds, significantly, that few of the Committee's recommendations have actually been taken up.

In fact, the overall response of the Union to racism (including that against children and their families) has been, and continues to be, open to criticism. I am conscious that 1997 was designated by the Union as the 'European Year Against Racism' (EYAR). There is no doubt that this represented a step forward for the Union (*Social Work in Europe* 4(1), 1997: 40–1). However, there are reservations which need to be expressed about EYAR, reservations which apply to many Union initiatives. For instance, in line with principles of subsidiarity, EYAR explicitly leaves the main responsibility for combating racism with the different member governments – whose responses, we can be sure, will be variable. In addition, the budget of 4.7 million ECUs will be confined largely to local or national information exchange and communication projects, which, though of course valuable, may be regarded as extremely limited compared to the serious extent and depth of European racism. Admittedly, more concrete measures are also being considered. The White Paper on Social Policy (European Commission 1994) does encourage implementation of Union legislation against discrimination on grounds of 'race', religion, age and disability. Moreover, Padraig Flynn, Commissioner for Employment and Social Affairs, has gone on record as hoping that EYAR may result in a ban on racial discrimination in the new European Treaty by the end of 1997 (*Social Work in Europe*, 4(1), 1997: 41). However, these anti-discriminatory initiatives do not really impress as much as perhaps they should. The original Community Treaty was signed forty years ago. It contained, even then, clauses on gender discrimination (albeit for primarily economic and political reasons). Why has it taken forty years simply to consider an extension of legislation to other forms of discrimination, including racism? Moreover, even now there is still no mention at all in the White Paper of anti-discrimination in relation to heterosexism. Why?

The answers to these questions are no doubt complex. However, our survey in previous chapters suggests one important element of the explanation. We have seen that across much of the Union relatively little attention has been paid by member states to issues of structural oppression. The country which has recognized most clearly the impact of a wide range of such issues and has, to an extent, sought to address them by legislation and by welfare practice is the United Kingdom.

This statement has of course to be carefully qualified on a number of counts. First, I fully acknowledge that the British legislative action in relation to 'race', gender and disability has massive limitations (Lavalette and Pratt 1996). Second, other member states have probably moved further regarding some forms of discrimination: for instance, Germany in relation to disability (Wilson 1996: 170). Moreover, there is no doubt that, in terms of action programme activity and data collection, the Union has itself played a relatively positive role in the area of disability issues in relation to adults and children (Ruxton 1996: 377–8; Wilson 1996: 167). Finally, it has to be acknowledged that the UK has made little legislative progress regarding ageism (in relation to both children and elders) or heterosexism. Nevertheless, on the whole I believe that my generalization above, about the greater awareness in Britain regarding the range of social oppressions compared to most other member states, holds true.

As we have noted earlier in this study, Mitchell and Russell (1994: 142) make very much the same point as myself in relation to the specific issue of racism:

> Britain . . . is unable to look to Europe for a positive lead in progressing race equality. For once Britain does not seem to be dragging its feet in comparison to the rest of Europe, even though it has little reason to be complacent over the results of its race equality initiatives.

Their work is also important because they point out that the European Union and its members are actively constructing a 'Fortress Europe' which is itself hostile to people from outside the Union perimeter. There are many manifestations of this fortress construction. For instance, where the Union does address the situation of migrants it is often in the context of some form of alleged threat to the social fabric of the member states, rather than regarding their presence as a positive opportunity for social enrichment. The concerns of the Trevi Group and the conditions of the Schengen Agreement are two prime examples of this negative Union approach (Mitchell and Russell 1994: 146; Ruxton 1996: 432–4). Thus, while the Union implements some limited measures to counter racism in relation to young people and declares a European Year Against Racism, it still lacks any real legislative commitment to challenge such oppression. Moreover, the Union actually engages in policy-making which, at the very least, can be regarded as hostile to some people outside the member states and, at worst, might be defined as colluding with racism. It is in this largely negative context that we have to view the alleged opportunities made available by Union structures to children and young people who are black and/or migrants.

However, the relative neglect of racism by European Union structures should come as no surprise. As we have seen, there is clearly a strong link between European Union social policies and the approaches adopted in those member states most influential within the Union. In Chapter 3 we reviewed social approaches to racism in France and Germany. In both of them we suggested there was cause for concern. In Chapter 5 we similarly examined attitudes to racism in the Nordic states which now represent an important power bloc within the Union. Once again, we discovered that all was not well: there was indeed 'trouble in paradise'. Given this overall context, the tardiness of the Union in relation to anti-racism is scarcely surprising.

I want to link the analysis presented above concerning British and continental responses to racism with my earlier comments about differential responses across Europe to child sexual abuse and its association with gender oppresssion. The latter issue is the subject of detailed analysis in Chapter 8. However, I believe we are already in a position to recognize the similarities between racism and child sexual abuse in this particular context. Why should there be a higher degree of anti-oppressive challenge to both child sexual abuse and racism in the United Kingdom than in the remainder of the European Union? As far as racism is concerned,

Mitchell and Russell (1994: 142) offer some important clues as to the answer, including the different historical way in which Britain's present black population has come to experience citizenship. Another important clue is also provided by them:

> in comparison with most other EC countries, it has been the relative strength of black political mobilization in the UK that has helped to advance the claims of black people to citizenship rights and to ensure that services are more accessible, more adequate, and more available to their communities.
>
> (Mitchell and Russell 1994: 142)

This comment is very helpful but itself begs some questions. Why has there been that mobilization in Britain? Are the reasons only related to the historical experience of black people in Britain, or are there also factors relating to the nature of British social institutions? In Chapter 8 I shall suggest that in relation to child sexual abuse, and men's sexual violence more generally, a crucial difference between Britain and its continental neighbours is that a similar mobilizing force has been active in the former but largely absent in the latter. Once again I will ask why this difference exists. I will suggest that the answer to that question in relation to child sexual abuse has wider relevance to a broad range of social oppressions, including racism. In Chapter 9 I will address that broader picture in considering why anti-oppressive welfare practice has developed further, albeit hesitantly, in Britain than elsewhere in Europe. How has this happened given the heavily right-wing social policy context which prevailed in the United Kingdom from 1979 to 1997? How has this occurred given Britain's relative lack of commitment to principles of social cohesion, consensus and solidarity compared to its neighbours in North, West and South Europe? For the time-being I leave readers to ponder these questions while I return to the main subject of this chapter, the European Union and other pan-European institutions.

Conclusion: the European Union and child welfare

We have now explored the considerable limitations which exist in relation to European Union social policy as a whole, family policy more specifically and the welfare of children most particularly. Despite these limitations, the Union does have some impact, both direct and indirect, on the social situation of children in Europe, via instruments such as legislation, observatories, networks and programmes. We have focused on the most significant features of these structures, noting both positive outcomes and some far less desirable phenomena. Among the latter, we included the Union's relative neglect of child abuse as a major social issue and its ambiguous response to other social oppressions which bear down on children and their families, including racism. We observed that in many respects the positives and negatives of Union measures in relation to children reflected features which we have surveyed in previous chapters: in particular the data on France, Germany and the Nordic states.

We noted that many of the approaches of the Union in the social field regarding child welfare contrasted quite strongly with those in Britain. Often this contrast served to highlight welfare progress in the other member states compared to Britain's more negative childcare policies in the period 1979–97: for instance, in relation to parental leave and daycare. However, in a few important respects we suggested that those other states within the Union, and the Union itself, might be lagging behind British welfare practice: for instance, in levels of awareness and response towards child abuse, racism and some other forms of structural social oppression. We began the process of analysing why these contrasts should occur and highlighted the crucial paradox of these positive British anti-oppressive approaches developing in a welfare context which for eighteen years was extremely hostile to them.

THE COUNCIL OF EUROPE AND CHILD WELFARE

The Council of Europe is a very different institution from the European Union (Lane and Ersson 1996: 64–73), in terms of longevity (it was founded in 1949), size (in 1996 it had thirty-nine members, including many of the former Eastern bloc countries), remit (over time it has come to focus on human rights, while economic and political concerns have tended to be split off from it) and legislative power (its decisions and declarations are recommendations and non-binding on member states). It is therefore in several ways far more limited than the European Union in what it can potentially achieve. This is probably an important qualification to bear in mind as we review its activities in the field of child welfare.

In terms of the attention which the Council has devoted to the welfare of children and their carers, it has far outstripped the European Union. This is plain at a number of different levels. At a general level, the European Convention for the Protection of Human Rights and Fundamental Freedoms 1950, the core document of the Council, sets out an important framework for preserving the rights of adults and children. In recent years, the Council has been more explicit in supporting the rights of children in the form of the 1994 European Convention on the Exercise of Children's Rights and the European Strategy for Children, adopted in January 1996 (Ruxton 1996: 21–9). The latter document gives a particularly useful idea of the wide range of the Council's concerns regarding childcare, since it embraces education, children's rights, use of the media in relation to children, training for childcare professionals, citizenship, anti-racism and migration, the responsibilities of adults to children and, last, but in terms of my analysis by no means least, child abuse (Ruxton 1996: 26–7).

In terms of developing good practice in relation to childcare, disseminating information about such practice and lobbying on behalf of it, we should note the Council's broadly based 'Childhood Policies Project', which ran from 1992 until 1996, producing a series of important conferences, a mass of data and policy recommendations (Council of Europe 1996a). The range of the project was impressive, covering many of the same issues as the strategy: mass media, residential care, street children, children's participation in family and social life, children's rights, social protection and family policies, migration, legal affairs, health, education, day-care and, again, violence within the family. The range of working groups reporting back at the closing conference of the project in May 1996 demonstrates the scope of the project. They included: family life participation; social life participation; children's interests in day-care facilities and in the family; the life of children in residential care and their rights; how children experience violence in contemporary society; children and the challenge of new technologies; children in urban contexts (Council of Europe 1996a). By means of both the strategy and the project, the Council has produced a more coherent and thorough child welfare framework than the Union. Similarly, it is apparent that the Council has been far more ready to address 'difficult' and controversial issues, such as child abuse, family violence and racism.

Given the European Union's marked silence about the issue, let us see what the Council has said about child abuse. In fact, not only have Council initiatives embraced this issue but they have also done so in a rather sophisticated manner. For instance, at the closing conference of the Childhood Policies Project, the workshop on this topic noted the dangers of violence to children within welfare settings (Council of Europe 1996a: 133). A meaningful awareness of this problem has been relatively absent in many European countries, although such an awareness seems to have developed in recent years in Britain (Pringle 1997a, b). It is therefore heartening to see the issue highlighted by one of the pan-European institutions. Similarly, the paper presented on child abuse in the same document focuses on the subject of 'violence against children with a mental disability' (Council of Europe 1996a: 137–42). This is yet another issue which has failed to receive its fair share of attention in many European countries and has been accorded a limited degree of recognition in Britain (Kennedy and Kelly 1992). On the other hand, some important topics are significant by their absence from the Council's main literature. For example, the workshop mentioned above signally failed to address the subject of gender in discussing the factors relevant to perpetrators of abuse, especially sexual abuse. Similarly, a recent project position paper on 'Child Day Care and Family Policies' (Council of Europe 1996b) fails just as much as the Union's Childcare Network to address issues of maltreatment in day-care. It also advocates the greater inclusion of men in day-care work without any acknowledgement of the problems this may sometimes entail (Council of Europe 1996b: 8).

However, on the whole the Council of Europe has provided an invaluable forum in which a broad range of child welfare topics across Europe have been highlighted, often embracing a wide spectrum of opinion and including some relatively radical voices. This contrasts with the more limited remit of most European Union initiatives relating to child welfare. In concluding this chapter, it may be worth considering why there continues to be such a difference in emphasis between the two institutions.

OVERVIEW

One reason for the difference must surely lie in the more specific role which the Council has come to develop for itself compared to the Union. As we have seen, the welfare of children is still a peripheral, rather than core, interest of the Union in comparison with the Council. The contrast in memberships of the Council and the Union is probably also a factor. The social policies of the European Union, including those impinging on child welfare, often seem to be heavily influenced by corresponding approaches in some important member states, not least France and Germany. The Council's membership has always been broader from its inception in the immediate aftermath of the Second World War. We might on this count also expect a wider spectrum of opinion to hold sway in the Council than in the Union.

However, the most important reason for the wider scope of the Council may paradoxically lie in its relative lack of formal power compared to the Union. It may be that breadth and radicalism are luxuries which national power-brokers and policy-makers feel they can afford only when no concrete legislative outcome is possible. I do not intend to belittle the impact of Council initiatives in terms of data gathering, providing a forum for debate and acting as a pan-European pressure group for best practice. Nevertheless, it is important to be realistic about the limits of Council of Europe influence and power.

In this chapter we have reviewed the role of two of the most important pan-European institutions as regards matters of child welfare: the

Council of Europe and the European Union. It is important to emphasize that there are other European institutions and agencies which are playing a vital role in advocating the rights of children in Europe: for instance, the European Forum for Child Welfare and the Confederation of Family Organisations in the European Communities (Ruxton 1996: 31–3). Both agencies are collaborating with the European Parliament's Committee on Social Affairs and Employment and Institutional Affairs to lobby for an increase in the Union's legislative capacity in the area of family policy and child welfare via the 'Coalition for Children and Young People in the EU Treaty' (M. George 1996: 25; Ruxton 1997: 22). Given our earlier analysis of the European Union in this field, we may feel a degree of scepticism about the eventual outcome of these efforts. Nevertheless, they are significant in themselves for pointing out that active lobbying on behalf of children in Europe is occurring on rather a broad front.

CONCLUSIONS

First, the mass of child welfare initiatives across Europe, whether they be statutory, charitable, voluntary, self-help or family-based, occur within primarily national frameworks rather than pan-European ones. The role of pan-European institutions remains largely secondary in relation to child welfare.

Second, approaches to child welfare adopted by European Union initiatives often seem to mirror divergences, debates and differences which are also occuring in the member states: hence the diversity of perspectives, sometimes contradictory, which we discovered in the social policy White Paper (European Commission 1994).

For the future there seems every reason to believe that the Council of Europe will continue fulfilling the highly valuable role which we have reviewed above. As for the European Union, it is harder to foresee the way ahead in terms of its social policies and their impact on child welfare. Given the uncertain long-term economic trajectories of the existing (and prospective) member states within the global economy (Falkner 1996), it may be that a complex multispeed and multidimensional Union (Leibfried 1994) awaits us in the future. Such a scenario is hardly conducive to the idea of an overarching European Union social policy for children and their carers.

8

A CHILD WELFARE CASE STUDY: CHILD SEXUAL ABUSE IN EUROPE

INTRODUCTION

In previous chapters we have surveyed the nature of child welfare in terms of individual countries or regions, classifications of welfare regime and some 'pan-European' institutions. The analysis built up can also be used to explore specific child welfare issues. In this chapter I therefore want to focus on one such issue in a European context as a form of case study. As we shall see, this focused discussion will also assist us to take our general analysis further forward.

For the following reasons I have chosen the issue of child sexual abuse as my example in this chapter. First, my means of assessing different welfare systems in this book has placed an emphasis on how far they positively challenge oppressive relations of power, including racism, heterosexism, disablism, classism, ageism and sexism. For, along with many other comparative commentators (Cannan *et al.* 1992; Cochrane and Clarke 1993; Lorenz 1994; Aluffi-Pentini and Lorenz 1996), I believe that this anti-oppressive objective is a hallmark of an effective welfare system (see Chapter 1). Consequently, the case study for this chapter needs to be a social problem which can effectively open out for analysis oppressive relations of power across the different societies of Europe. In previous texts (Kidd and Pringle 1988; Pringle 1995, 1997a) I have suggested that the issue of child sexual abuse has a particular salience when it comes to making links between forms of structural oppression within society and the social problems generated from them. The relevance of sexual abuse for our purposes derives from the fact that its causation seems to arise from the complex interaction between a wide range of oppressive power relations, of which those associated with g⟨ stitute a part. It can be argued that ageism, racism, disabilis⟨ sexism and classism, as well as sexism, enter crucially into th⟨ by which sexual violence is generated (Pringle 1995: Chapter 8). Thus an analysis of child sexual abuse as a social problem offers the possibility of examining the range of structural fissures which may exist in the different welfare systems across Europe.

My second reason for choosing child sexual abuse is that it has been the subject of much less comparative European study than many other child welfare issues, which is, of course, an interesting fact in itself. It is true that some comparative study of child abuse as a general concept has taken place (Sale and Davies 1990; Armstrong and Hollows 1991; Birks 1995; Cooper *et al.* 1995; Davies and Davies 1997; Harder and Pringle 1997; Hetherington *et al.* 1997). However, as I have argued elsewhere (Pringle 1992, 1993, 1995, 1997a), it is vital to consider the dynamics of sexual abuse separately from those which pertain to physical abuse, because those dynamics are often so very different. There is a growing recognition in this field that any sensible analysis about causation or positive action requires us to disaggregate conceptually physical, sexual and emotional maltreatment, even if in the reality of people's lives they do sometimes overlap (Hallett 1995: 44–9). Such disaggregation still occurs infrequently in the literature as a whole, including comparative European texts. The only full-length European comparative text on child sexual abuse of which I am aware is the path-breaking volume by Elke Jonsson (1997). This chapter therefore enables me to continue that initial process of opening up the issue of child sexual abuse within a European framework.

My third and final reason for addressing child sexual abuse in this chapter is that I believe it constitutes a major European social problem. There are significant indications that the prevalence of sexual abuse in other European countries may well be similar to that in Britain, even though far more research attention has been paid to the subject in the United Kingdom. A research review was conducted by Finkelhor (1991) of child sexual abuse prevalence studies around the world, including a number carried out in European countries. Some of the continental European studies produced considerably lower rates than those found in most British studies. Finkelhor concluded that the wide statistical variations in the studies he reviewed related primarily to the different methodologies which they had adopted rather than their geographical location. Crucially, he also discovered that the most sophisticated and reliable research methodologies usually produced the highest prevalence rates, regardless of location. To this evidence we may add a newly developing awareness of child sexual abuse in some European countries such as

Belgium and Ireland, an awareness which I will discuss later in this chapter. So we have here the opportunity to explore an issue which in itself has considerable European significance and may also act as a form of case study for other manifestations of oppression against children.

Having justified the choice of child sexual abuse as the European case study, I will now begin the analysis by placing child sexual abuse within an English welfare context. In later sections of the chapter I compare that context with others in various European countries, particularly those in Western and Northern Europe. I want to argue that the English child protection system is deeply flawed, although not primarily in the way that some commentators have indicated. I will suggest that continental family support approaches are equally, though differently, inadequate. I then broaden the discussion to explain the contrast which is apparent between the English and continental welfare contexts and extend that explanation further to analyse why anti-oppressive welfare practice as a whole seems to have gained a higher profile in Britain than elsewhere. Finally, I focus back down on to child sexual abuse and seek to draw conclusions about what our wide-ranging analysis may tell us about ways forward in Europe for the protection of children against sexual abuse.

CHILD SEXUAL ABUSE IN AN ENGLISH CONTEXT

First, I must acknowledge that in this chapter, where I discuss welfare practice in relation to child sexual abuse, I explicitly confine my analysis to the English experience rather than the British one. This is owing to the large legislative differences which exist between various parts of the United Kingdom in relation to child abuse, most especially between England and Scotland. In later sections of the chapter, where I extend discussion beyond child sexual abuse to wider issues of anti-oppressive practice, I do refer to Britain and the United Kingdom where appropriate.

Over the past fifteen years probably no welfare issue has attracted more attention in England from the public, the media and professionals than child abuse and the child protection model (Franklin and Parton 1991; Pringle 1997a; Chapter 2, this volume). Recently there has been widespread recognition across a spectrum of commentators (Thorpe 1994; Campbell 1995; Department of Health 1995; Pringle 1995; Parton 1996c; Gray *et al.* 1996, 1997) that this model is in a state of profound crisis. Some of these commentators, and indeed the government itself, now seem to have advocated a shift of emphasis in services provided, away from investigation of abuse incidents and towards support for families. In the context of our present study it is particularly important to note that this family support model appears to be close in outline to the models which dominate services for protecting children in many continental countries (Hetherington *et al.* 1997; Pringle 1997a; Pringle and Harder 1997).

In terms of child sexual abuse cases, two very different critiques of the English child protection system can be offered. The first, adopted by the British government in 1995, leads directly to advocacy of the alternative, continental family support model. The second critique, to which I adhere, suggests that neither the child protection nor the family support model offers an effective answer to child sexual abuse.

Two critiques of English child protection

I turn now to the first of these critiques, which has been summarized as follows:

> In accepting the new ideology of child protection and its representations of private social events, it seems that social work has bought another 'lemon'. In response to a moral panic it has obtained new resources, changed laws, and agency procedures and introduced new technologies of intervention in order to secure the safety of a small number of children.
>
> (Thorpe 1994: 201–2)

David Thorpe outlines the now standard case against the child protection model in tems of child abuse as a whole: it allegedly suceeds in picking up the relatively small numbers of 'serious' child abuse cases but at the massive expense of drawing into the bureaucratic net a much larger number of cases for which it is not appropriate. That analysis has been more or less echoed in a series of research studies commissioned by the British government and summarized in the important Department of Health document *Messages from Research* (Department of Health 1995: 31–2). Several comparative European texts adopt a similar perspective about the English system (Cooper *et al.* 1995; Hetherington *et al.* 1997).

We should note that all these studies focus on child abuse as an aggregated whole. I argued above that it is vital to disaggregate the various forms of child abuse for the purposes of analysis. I believe the failure of those studies to do so is one reason why their analysis is flawed. I shall of course disaggregate and concentrate on child sexual abuse. As far as child sexual abuse is concerned, my view is that the Thorpe/Department of Health critique of the child protection model is not adequate and that the very real problems of that model lie elsewhere. My doubts about the critique are several-fold, and themselves constitute a second alternative critique of English child protection which is more convincing than the first.

The elements of this alternative critique are as follows. First, we need to challenge what Thorpe refers to above as the 'small number' of children for whom the term 'child abuse' is supposed to be appropriate. As we have seen in previous chapters, it is now quite apparent from large-scale sample surveys of the general population in the United States and the United Kingdom that prevalence levels for child sexual abuse are massive, perhaps 1 in 5 or even 1 in 3 (Finkelhor *et al.* 1990; Kelly *et al.* 1991). Of course there will always be debates about the precise prevalence in relation to different definitions of child sexual abuse. However, the fact remains that even when so-called 'less serious' forms of sexual violence are discounted from Kelly *et al.*'s survey, the prevalence ratio for girls remains 1 in 5 and for boys 1 in 14 (Fisher 1994: 4). These are still massive numbers.

Furthermore, the confidence expressed by Thorpe and the Department of Health that most serious abuse is caught within the net of the child protection system seems grossly misplaced as far as child sexual abuse is concerned. In 1992 the prevalence rate in England for all forms of child abuse, *calculated from child abuse registers*, was 3.54 per 1000 population aged under 18: and sexual abuse accounted for 17 per cent of this number (Hallett 1995: 33–7). The gap between that rate (based on cases picked up by statutory authorities) and the general survey prevalence rates noted above is clearly immense. The mass of child sexual abuse in England fails to be detected by statutory agencies (see Wattam 1997).

Moreover, even when child sexual abuse is detected by the English child protection services, they still often fail to act positively in terms of either prosecuting perpetrators or providing therapeutic help to survivors. As regards prosecutions, government-sponsored research (Davies *et al.* 1994) has demonstrated that the vast majority of the huge number of evidential interviews with abused children, video-taped in accordance with official government guidelines, are never even presented to the Crown Prosecution Service, which decides whether cases will go to court. Regarding therapeutic responses, as we have already seen in Chapter 2, statutory agencies frequently fail to provide adequate helping services either to children who have been sexually abused or to their non-abusing parents (Gray *et al.* 1996, 1997). Taken together, these facts constitute the second critique of child protection, which is far more convincing than the first one posited by Thorpe (1994) and the British government (Department of Health 1995).

Put bluntly, this second critique concludes quite correctly that the English child protection model often fails both to protect children from perpetrators and to offer them the therapeutic help they need. Yet it is the first critique which has been used to justify the new shift of policy in England towards a continental-style family support model, and in the next section I address this shift of policy.

From child protection to family support

The true motives for the British Conservative government's espousal of the family support model from 1995 can only be matters for speculation. Elsewhere (Pringle 1997a) I have suggested that they probably include factors which are both ideological and pragmatic: ideological in that the model reinforces Thatcherite/Majorite assumptions about the dangers of state interference in family life; pragmatic in that the child protection apparatus had become massively expensive. However, those were certainly not the arguments which the Conservative government offered in public for advocating a greater emphasis on family support. Instead, as we have seen, they turned to the analyses of commentators such as Thorpe (1994) and the research sponsored by the Department of Health summarized in *Messages from Research*:

> The research studies suggest that too much of the work undertaken comes under the banner of child protection . . . A more balanced service for vulnerable children would encourage professionals to take a wider view. There would be efforts to work alongside families rather than disempower them.
> (Department of Health 1995: 54–5)

While I fully acknowledge that it is important to make more services available, I nevertheless want to argue that there are considerable problems with the new family support emphasis. Some of the difficulties with that approach are already apparent; others are potential rather than actual. Let us first briefly mention the problems which are already apparent.

Parton (1996c: 6–11) points out that the government-sponsored studies on which *Messages from Research* (Department of Health 1995) is based crucially failed to examine the manner by which social workers and their agencies label cases as being child protection ones at the point of referral. In particular, he emphasizes that no attempt was made in those studies to consider the economic, political and societal contexts within which agencies have to make such decisions. The result is that social workers and their agencies are simply admonished by the government to shift their perspective towards family support without any reference to the structural context which prevents them from doing so. He ruefully concludes that as a result the policy shift is unlikely to suceed.

Another crucial problem associated with the shift to family support which is already apparent can be seen in the language which *Messages from Research* adopts. It talks broadly about support to 'families' or 'parents' without any recognition of the structural power imbalances within two-parent heterosexual families. This latter consideration is especially crucial in cases of sexual abuse, where the services provided to non-abusing and abusing parents will almost always demand clear differentiation (Campbell 1995: 19; Pringle 1995: 195–8). Support to non-abusing parents in sexual abuse cases is now recognized as being critical in determining outcomes for children (Hooper 1992; Smith 1994, 1995). This lack of differentiation between parents in the summary report mirrors the similarly inadequate guidance to welfare professionals in other crucial British government or government-inspired documents (HMSO 1989; Department of Health 1988, 1989). As a result, service provision to non-abusing parents in England has been massively jeopardized.

However, these problems of the family support model which are already apparent in England are perhaps the least of that model's difficulties in relation to child sexual abuse. Far deeper problems can be discovered if we review the systems for protecting children against child sexual abuse in some other European countries which operate on a largely family support model basis. For their experience can alert us as to what may occur in England if the family support model is fully implemented. We do not know yet whether the election of a Labour administration will make any difference to this policy shift. My own guess is that it will make little difference and that a greater emphasis on family support will continue in England.

THE FAMILY SUPPORT MODEL AND CHILD SEXUAL ABUSE IN WESTERN AND NORTHERN EUROPE

First, I need to emphasize that it would be utterly wrong to suggest that there is a unified approach to child abuse in the welfare systems of Western and Northern Europe. As we have previously seen, heterogeneity exists in the detailed operation of the way systems protect children in different countries (Sale and Davies 1990; Armstrong and Hollows 1991; Lorenz 1994; Harder and Pringle 1997; Hetherington *et al.* 1997).

Nevertheless, I believe it is possible to argue that in a cluster of European countries such systems do share a significant degree of similarity in the ways they explain why abuse happens and in the principles which underpin their various forms of intervention. In particular, these systems all seem to place a relatively heavy emphasis on working cooperatively with families and avoiding criminal action wherever possible. I will now expand upon this.

Principles underpinning protective intervention: a selective European survey

The most well known example of such a family support model is the confidential doctor service which operates in the Netherlands and constitutes a portion of the protective services there (de Ruyter 1990: 33–4; Armstrong and Hollows 1991: 146–8; Van Montfoort 1993; Hetherington *et al.* 1997: 74). As Armstrong and Hollows (1991: 147) note, the underlying theory of the service 'is that where abuse occurs, families need help rather than coercion if they are to change damaging modes of behaviour.' Confidential doctor centres have also developed as an important specialist part of the services available in nearby Belgium, particularly in Wallonia (Marneffe *et al.* 1990: 7–10; Armstrong and Hollows 1991: 148; Hetherington *et al.* 1997: 59). The approach is similar to that in the Netherlands. The centres will:

> accept and follow up referrals from other agencies and from individuals, while preserving their anonymity, but will only intervene with the agreement of the parents and children. It is not impossible for referral to be made to the legal system but it is very unusual.
>
> (Hetherington *et al.* 1997: 59)

Influenced partly by developments in the Netherlands, Reinhard Wolff was instrumental in establishing child protection centres from the mid-1970s in the (then) Federal Republic of Germany (Hutz 1990: 60; Armstrong and Hollows 1991: 152–4). They now provide a significant form of service in many German cities, particularly the centres run by the German Child Protection Society (der Deutsche Kinderschutzbund) and have distinctive principles:

> the decisive duty is to help the affected family and to work together with the family to solve existing problems and hence to solve the conflicts which are the root cause of violence . . . offers of assistance are based on the fact that the affected family itself is at liberty to decide if and to what extent these offers may be taken up. Confidentiality is strictly observed and the intervention of a third party only takes place with the agreement of the family and as a rule with the family itself present.
>
> (Wustendorfer 1995: 241)

In turn, Wolff's work has influenced practice in Austria (Paulischin 1990: 5–6), where, as Planicka (1995: 66) notes, the child protection centres are regarded as 'model institutions whose work also has an effect on the public sector'. She goes on to describe their underlying principles, which by now will sound familiar to readers:

> The aim of the help or care is defined in consultation with the family, and this aim should be to provide the best possible support for all members of

the family. Arriving at a decision in consultation with the family is of particular importance when a child is in grave danger. Following this procedure means that the question of separating the child from his parents without his or their agreement can almost always be avoided. In addition to this focus on situation-specific help rather than imposed measures, this approach also dispenses in principle with punishing the abuser. Child protection centres operate without the threat of punishment (prosecution) . . . it is possible to guarantee the families strict confidentiality. Contact with third parties only takes place with the agreement, and as a rule in the presence, of the family. Anonymity is possible.

(Planicka 1995: 68)

Systems in France, though differently structured, seem to share a philosophy not far removed from that which we have already outlined (Girodet 1990: 20–1; Cooper *et al.* 1995: Chapters 1 and 11).

Turning to the Nordic states, the clearest example of a family support model for protecting children occurs in Finland:

The child welfare legislation reforms of 1990 emphasise preventive, non-stigmatising, and supportive measures and services. One of the central objectives of the reform was to shift the emphasis of child welfare from extrafamilial care to measures that encourage and support the maintenance of children in their own home.

(Tuomisto and Vuori-Karvia 1997: 90)

Although Pringle and Harder (1997) emphasize that it is important not to aggregate the Nordic states excessively, they also note some degree of commonality between Denmark and Finland in terms of:

the relative extent to which child maltreatment is defined within the context of positive models of childcare policy in both countries. Moreover, such a definitional perspective is paralleled in both countries by a practice approach which places provision for maltreated children within much broader services designed to positively promote the well-being of all children . . . i.e. there is relatively little tendency to separate child abuse as a wholly distinct and different phenomenon from the wider context of childcare generally. This approach contrasts with the highly differentiated one in England and Wales where child abuse has almost been reified into a separate entity with virtually no connection to wider concerns about promoting positive childcare.

(Pringle and Harder 1997: 153)

It seems clear from this survey that the approaches in the countries outlined above have a degree of commonality and possess similarities to the pronouncements about family support recently endorsed by the English Department of Health in its document *Messages from Research* (Department of Health 1995). Hetherington *et al.* (1997) come to an almost identical conclusion following their detailed survey of systems for protecting children in eight European countries (which, by the way, did not include any Nordic states):

> The evidence of this comparative research has shown that most of the systems under scrutiny abroad . . . stressed family support and diversity in services along the lines of the main conclusions in *Messages from Research*.
> (Hetherington *et al.* 1997: 158)

However, the study by Hetherington *et al.*, like its companion volume by the Brunel University College research team (Cooper *et al.* 1995), goes on to imply that these continental approaches are superior to the English child protection model and that they may therefore offer potentially creative lessons to English welfare policy-makers. Nor are the Brunel group alone among British commentators in their advocacy of ideas drawn from continental family support models. A report from the National Society for the Protection of Children (NSPCC) refers positively to several innovatory approaches:

> such as the Confidential Doctor Bureau in the Netherlands, the work of the Berlin Child Protection Centre and the Judge for Children in France. The Dutch and German models have already inspired similar initiatives in Belgium and Austria respectively.
> (Davies and Davies 1997: 32)

On a Europe-wide basis, the report then advocates the creation of: 'non-punitive and non-coercive climates, wherever possible, which combine family support with a therapeutic approach to problems of abuse' (Davies and Davies 1997: 33).

Given such strong endorsements for these continental family support systems, I will now explore whether they are in fact effective in dealing with child sexual abuse.

European family support systems: do they adequately address child sexual abuse?

In fact, there are strong indications in the literature that all is not well from this point of view. For instance, in surveying child protection centres and public attitudes which underpin them in Germany, Armstrong and Hollows (1991: 152) note that:

> These developments have . . . been recently challenged as the issue of sexual abuse (with its impact on such personal and volatile areas as the family, gender and power issues, and sexuality) has caused a re-appraisal of the need for legal controls on the family.

Similarly, Wustendorfer (1995: 243) points out that in terms of child abuse and the child protection centres generally:

> the feasability of an approach based on voluntary referral, confidentiality and anonymity is still being questioned. The tendency to adhere too long to these principles even when it becomes clear they have failed is also being questioned, as some people believe this may harm the children or the families more than if the local authorities had been involved at an earlier stage.

These qualifications are echoed by the comment of Armstrong and Hollows (1991: 150) that in France there has been 'increasing concern that the child's perspective is often poorly represented or unheard by the Juge [des enfants].' Moreover, in his very balanced appreciation of the welfare and justice systems in the Netherlands, Van Montfoort (1993: 62) touches upon a similar concern: 'By not clearly defining individual positions, the welfare approach involves the risk of overlooking power relationships inside the family.' More specifically, he also notes that:

> public interest in child sexual abuse has put the role of the criminal justice system in protecting children back on the agenda ... the medical and social welfare models of handling child sexual abuse were criticised by both survivors of child sexual abuse and the women's movement. This resulted in closer cooperation between the Confidential Doctor and the police ... it removes the Confidential Doctor's Office from its initial non-judicial principles and makes it look more like other agencies.
>
> (Van Montfoort 1993: 60)

It seems that family support approaches on the continent frequently manifest problems when they encounter sexual abuse. Why should this be? The answer lies in the theoretical explanations of sexual abuse which the continental and Nordic models adopt. Those models generally conflate sexual abuse with other forms of abuse in the manner that I criticized so heavily at the beginning of this chapter. As a result, they explain sexual abuse in exactly the same way as they do all forms of child abuse: as a product of dysfunctional family interactions. In other words, their dominant causative model for child abuse is a family systems one.

Family support and family systems explanations of child sexual abuse in Europe

In the Belgian protective system we are told that 'child abuse and neglect is interpreted as a signal, a symptom of a serious family dysfunction' (Marneffe *et al.* 1990: 9). The same is true in the Child Protection Centres of Austria (Paulischin 1990: 6) and of Germany (Hutz 1990: 60). In the case of Germany, Wustendorfer (1995: 244) also notes a feminist critique of the child protection centres:

The approach based on family therapy, is accused of being interested above all in the ability of the family to function as such and of trying to solve the sexual conflict between the parents as a matter of priority. The recurrence of sexual abuse cannot be prevented in this way. Accordingly working together with the abuser is not possible.

Similarly, Cooper *et al.* (1995: 6) note that:

Child protection work in France is first and foremost a family affair. It is not the individual child who is the primary focus of concern and intervention but the child-as-part-of-the-family and the whole thrust of the French system is towards maintaining children as part of their families of origin.

As for Finland, Tuomisto and Vuori-Karvia (1997: 89) suggest that family systems approaches are regarded as the way forward there:

Traditional, individual-oriented forms of care have been criticised for being expert dominated, time-consuming and apparently ineffective. These traditional forms of care have been widely replaced by approaches based on systems theory.

Moreover, Pringle and Harder (1997: 154) note that 'it seems that the predominant theoretical model for explaining sexual abuse in both Denmark and Finland is a systemic one.'

In Britain there is still considerable dispute about the causation of most forms of abuse (Hallett 1995: 44–9). However, a limited resolution of the issues surrounding sexual abuse seems to have been achieved after a long debate, the details of which have been chronicled adequately elsewhere (MacLeod and Saraga 1988, 1991; Kidd and Pringle 1988; Will 1989; Pringle 1993, 1995: 171–80). In contrast to their continental counterparts, relatively few British commentators and welfare practitioners would now regard the family systems explanation of sexual abuse as being of overriding importance. Most British commentators and many welfare practitioners seem to believe that a multifactoral approach is essential. The majority would probably now at least include feminist perspectives within such a multifactoral framework. A considerable number of them would go further and identify feminist or pro-feminist perspectives as being the most critical element of that framework. As already stated, I certainly count myself among this latter group, even though I regard child sexual abuse as being the outcome of complex power relations focused around issues of age, 'race', disability, sexuality and class as well as gender (Pringle 1995: Chapter 8).

Family systems and child sexual abuse: a critique

I will now summarize why the family systems perspective of sexual abuse has been so heavily critiqued in Britain. In the process I will also discuss

of the reasons why the continental family support services, which
use ⌐hat perspective, seem inadequate in the face of child sexual abuse.

The critique, developed in Britain, of the family systems perspective
on child sexual abuse has several elements:

1 The family systems explanation has no relevance to the majority of
child sexual abuse cases which we now know occur outside the
immediate 'nuclear family' (Kelly *et al.* 1991).

2 It fails to confront power issues relating to masculinity which are
central when working with the majority of sexual abuse cases (Pringle
1995: 170–80).

3 It tends to 'fudge' the exclusive responsibility borne by the perpetrator
for the abuse and can thereby result in non-abusing parents being dis-
empowered as well as unsupported, and the child being left insufficiently protected (MacLeod and Saraga 1988, 1991; Pringle 1990, 1995).

When we consider that the continental family support services which
we reviewed are largely underpinned by this family systems perspective,
we can begin to understand more clearly some of the problems about
those services which commentators such as Van Montfoort (1993) and
Armstrong and Hollows (1991) identified earlier. There is consequently
considerable doubt about how far family support services do effectively
protect children who have been sexually abused. In many cases the suspicion must be that they are far more effective in protecting the adults
who are the perpetrators of the abuse rather than the children themselves.
The shift of social work policy and practice in England towards a similar
family support perspective on child sexual abuse cases means that I have
precisely the same doubts about what will now happen to children who
have been sexually abused in England.

To summarize so far: in relation to professional services for children
who have been sexually abused we have critiqued the English child protection model, as well as the continental family support model which was
officially promoted in England by the Conservative government.

In the next segment of this chapter I want to discuss more broadly
why the critique of a family systems explanation for child sexual abuse
was developed in Britain rather than in continental Europe – and why
more radical, anti-oppressive perspectives have come to hold greater
sway in England about the extent and nature of child sexual abuse. I
will suggest that, paradoxically, a key element in these developments
has actually been the lack of a commitment to solidaristic principles
within England's welfare context. This discussion will then be extended
to consider why it is that anti-oppressive welfare practice generally has
developed to a greater extent in Britain than elsewhere in Europe, despite

the right-wing political context in which that development occurred during the period 1979–97.

DEVELOPMENT OF ANTI-OPPRESSIVE PRACTICE AND THE BARRIER OF SOCIAL SOLIDARITY

In Chapter 2 we discussed the relative lack of a historical commitment to principles of social solidarity in many English social institutions. The cultural absence of a sense of social solidarity helped to explain the markedly residual nature of England's welfare provision compared to many of its neighbours in Northern and Western Europe, and we explored this comparison further in Chapter 3. More specifically, we related this lack of solidaristic commitment to the individualistic and negative aspects of state interventionism which characterized England's child protection model. I now want to examine the issue of social solidarity more closely and to suggest that a commitment to it may have negative as well as positive welfare outcomes.

The nature of social solidarity

I have addressed the issue of social solidarity and the problems of English child protection at more length elsewhere (Pringle 1997a). A similar analysis has recently been offered by Hetherington *et al.* (1997). Noting the different social context existing in England compared to many continental countries, they comment:

> Where services for children are enshrined by the principles of social solidarity, subsidiarity and citizenship, one consequence is that the institutions which organise, deliver, and shape local responses to child protection are structured into, and derive their authority from a total conception of society.
> (Hetherington *et al.* 1997: 34)

The lack of those principles in England they attribute to a combination of historical tradition and more recent political action:

> The concept of *rights* in matters involving the family and the state is different in many continental countries when compared with the Anglo-American tradition. The last fifteen years have witnessed a consolidation of ideologies of individual rights in Britain, and a general decline in ideas of collective responsibility. However the differences between Britain and

other European countries have much deeper historical roots than this, and are not simply a by-product of Thatcherism-cum-Majorism. Republican-ism, solidarity and subsidiarity are grounded in a set of assumptions about the relationship of the individual to society and government.

(Hetherington *et al*. 1997: 85)

We should also notice that Hetherington *et al*. refer to the cultural importance of Catholicism in the historical development of a solidaristic approach largely alien to the English welfare context:

> *Subsidiarity* is an important principle of political life in many northern European countries, particularly Germany, the Netherlands and Belgium. The principle is strongly influenced by catholic social teaching which in turn has played a powerful shaping role in social life in many continental states.
>
> (Hetherington *et al*. 1997: 83)

In terms of explaining the roots of social solidarity in other countries than England, we need to remember that Hetherington *et al*. largely limit their analysis to welfare systems which, typologically, have been described as 'conservative corporatist' or 'Catholic corporatist'. This is fine as far as it goes. However, in Chapter 5 we saw that a very strong commitment to a solidaristic welfare approach also characterized the Nordic countries, most of which have their historical roots in neither republicanism nor Catholicism. So, the analysis of Hetherington *et al*. (1997) needs to be supplemented to explain the phenomenon of Nordic solidarity.

There is not space here to explore in depth its foundations. However, it seems clear enough (Ginsburg 1992, 1993; Gould 1993, 1996) that Nordic forms of social solidarity relate to the following factors: long-developed political and social traditions centred on consensus; a specific history of twentieth-century corporatist labour–employment–state relations; and finally the characteristically Scandinavian gender equality deal struck between men and women – a deal which, however, often seems to dis-guise important underlying gender oppressions, as we saw in Chapter 5.

Moreover, the analysis of Hetherington *et al*. (1997) regarding the con-cept of social solidarity also requires adaption when we recall (see Chapter 6) that it has historically manifested itself in Eastern Europe and continues to do so in some countries there. In Chapter 6 we noted the heterogen-eity of those countries. This heterogeneity extends itself to the historical foundations which underpin the commitment to solidaristic principles. For instance, we saw that in Poland there was a particularly long and important social contribution made by the Catholic Church (Millard 1997): the same applied, though less clearly, in relation to Hungary and the Czech Republic. Similarly, we discussed the fact that evolving social welfare responses in the latter two countries might owe something to their historical and cultural links via the Holy Roman and Austrian Empires with countries such as Austria and Germany. Finally, we explored the historical influence of the communist past which had a variable impact on the emerging societies of the region.

Thus a commitment to principles of social solidarity as it is currently manifested across Europe must be viewed as specific to its particular geographic, historical and cultural context. Having said that, it certainly seems to remain true that, as Hetherington *et al.* (1997) suggest, England stands out from much of Europe in its relative lack of commitment to those principles. It is largely to this contrast in social contexts that both Hetherington *et al.* (1997) and I (Pringle 1997a) attribute the negativity and diviseness of the English child protection model.

Social solidarity: a potential barrier to the recognition of social problems?

However, I believe that Hetherington *et al.* (1997) tell only half the story as far as child sexual abuse and Europe is concerned. We have seen in earlier parts of this chapter that societal and professional awareness concerning the extent and causes of child sexual abuse may be more developed in England than in virtually any other European country. Previous chapters of this study have also underlined the fact that, compared to England, awareness of child sexual abuse seems limited to varying degrees across the whole of continental Europe. This remains true even though the procedural structures which exist in England and within which welfare professionals have to operate are, as we have seen, deeply flawed. Indeed, a colleague and I have suggested elsewhere that perhaps:

> the real tragedy of the situation in England and Wales is that the enormity of the problem has been more fully realised there than anywhere else in Western Europe but the system designed to deal with it is wholly inadequate.
> (Pringle and Harder 1997: 168)

In this section of the chapter I want to concentrate on how far awareness about the *extent* of sexual abuse across Europe may be restricted by a commitment to solidaristic principles such as consensus, cohesion and inclusion. In the section following this one, I engage in a parallel discussion about how far awareness concerning the *causes* of child sexual abuse across Europe is similarly restricted by that commitment to solidaristic principles. So, let us now turn to issues about awareness regarding the extent of child sexual abuse.

Hetherington *et al.* (1997), and most other comparative commentators, have failed to recognize sufficiently that continental European countries might well benefit from drawing upon the English experience as far as understanding the extent of child sexual abuse is concerned. It should be clear from the tenor of previous chapters that I believe that English social policy-makers could usefully study some continental approaches to many child welfare issues, such as day-care provision, family financial support and juvenile justice. What I am suggesting now, however, is that such exchange is not a purely one-way street: the English welfare context may also have some positive experiences to offer the rest of Europe regarding the recognition of certain social problems, including child sexual abuse. For child sexual abuse may well not be the only welfare issue where English approaches are in some respects in advance of the rest of Europe. At the end of Chapter 7 I argued that Britain paid more attention both publicly and professionally to a range of social problems associated with forms of structural and personal oppression. Racism was identified as another such problem (Rex 1992; Mitchell and Russell 1994; Witte 1995).

In making this central point about the extent of anti-oppressive welfare practice in Britain I nevertheless need to add some important qualifications. First, I am by no means suggesting that in other European countries there is an absence of social activity designed to counter disadvantage and discrimination. For instance, let us briefly consider the central place of welfare strategies such as 'social pedagogy' in Germany and *'animation'* and *'education'* in France (Cannan *et al.* 1992: 73–4). Lorenz (1994: 87–104) correctly notes that these are complex concepts, hard to translate into British welfare practice and containing ideas of both social liberation and social control. However, there is no doubt that in certain of their aspects they imply broad social action designed to counter disadvantage. On the other hand, these continental approaches do not seem to address social problems as directly as outcomes of structural oppression, whereas mainstream British welfare perspectives often do make those connections explicit in practice (Thompson 1993). For instance, it is surely significant that despite a serious attack on social work education by the British Conservative government, mainstream training there continues to be centred to a considerable extent on overtly anti-discriminatory and anti-oppressive practice principles.

The second qualification which I want to add is that I fully acknowledge that the extent of social oppression in Britain is certainly no less than in other European countries. Moreover, the legal and procedural frameworks within which British welfare workers operate often limit their capacity to engage in the anti-oppressive practice for which they are trained and to which many adhere (Dominelli 1988; Dominelli and McLeod 1989; Ahmad 1990; Barnes 1991; Pringle 1995; Logan *et al.* 1996). Anti-oppressive welfare practice in Britain is always open to attack and retrenchment: its presence remains somewhat tenuous. Nevertheless, I still maintain that in the British welfare context awareness of structural oppressions and anti-oppressive action to counter them often exceed that which occurs in many other European countries.

My third qualification is to remind readers once again that after eighteen years of right-wing social policies there are many child welfare services in Western and Northern Europe that are far superior to those in the United Kingdom. As we have seen throughout this book, provision in Britain is often woefully limited despite the country's relative national wealth. So I am not seeking to engage in an anti-continental programme here: Britain could clearly seek to absorb creatively many useful experiences from continental welfare practices. My point in this chapter is simply to emphasize that in one very important respect the British welfare context also has something to offer the rest of Europe: the beginnings of a framework for a genuine anti-oppressive welfare practice which might effectively challenge major forms of social oppression that many continental welfare systems largely ignore.

Why does British anti-oppressive welfare practice seem to be relatively advanced despite the relative absence of a solidaristic welfare context in the United Kingdom? In fact I want to turn that question on its head and suggest that the development of an overtly anti-oppressive welfare framework may actually be in part the *result* of that lack of a solidaristic context. The social problems where British practice does seem to be more progressive, compared to continental Europe, are precisely those, such as child sexual abuse and racism, which most sharply reveal deep and extensive fissures in the social fabric. Is there, then, some reason why socially divisive issues may reach public and professional agendas in Britain more effectively than in other European countries?

I want to suggest that societies with marked conflictual features, such as Britain, may be more open about the extent of their social divisions than societies with a firmer commitment to ideals of social cohesion, consensus and inclusion. In such a conflictual social context as exists in Britain, problems associated with deep disadvantage may be both more obvious and more acknowledged than in societies where there is greater positive aspiration to the ideals of social inclusion and solidarity – and where there is also a greater belief that such aspirations have been partly achieved.

I am not suggesting that it is easy to place such divisive issues on public and professional agendas even in relatively conflictual social contexts. Quite the contrary. At the end of Chapter 7 we saw that the maintenance of anti-racist public and professional practices in Britain is a continual and draining struggle, largely dependent on the ongoing efforts of committed activists (Mitchell and Russell 1994). Similarly, it is clear that child sexual abuse (and sexual violence more generally) only accessed the highest public and professional agendas in Britain due to the struggles of survivors and their allies, often feminist or pro-feminist in their political perspectives (Nelson 1987; Dobash and Dobash 1992). The struggle by survivors and their allies continues to try to maintain child sexual abuse as a public and professional issue which still challenges those oppressive power relations that engender it (Pringle 1995: Chapters 8 and 9). Anti-oppressive welfare practice is never easy, wherever it takes place. However, there may be less resistance to it in Britain than in welfare contexts with a high commitment to principles of social solidarity.

Those welfare contexts – for instance, France – may more easily endorse broadly-based and generally supportive welfare measures aimed at binding the body politic than countries such as Britain. However, at the same time, the former may be highly disinclined to endorse welfare perspectives or initiatives which challenge the oppressive structures that continue to underpin and permeate that body politic.

In developing this analysis around social solidarity I acknowledge that a commitment to it may promote valuable and extensive welfare measures such as those relating to children and their carers in the Nordic states, France and Belgium. Nor do I deny that the relative historic and institutional absence of a solidaristic commitment from the British welfare scene has placed a regrettable limitation on the scope of social policy in the United Kingdom. What I am suggesting, however, is that a commitment to principles of social solidarity may often be a two-edged sword: it is naive and simplistic to regard that commitment, in itself, as being purely 'a good thing'. For oppressive social measures and a denial of structural oppression may sometimes be its outcome, as we saw in our discussion concerning RMI in Chapter 3. This form of analysis seems to be largely absent in much comparative social policy literature. For an example of this absence let us return to the specific focus of this chapter, child sexual abuse.

In contrasting the solidaristic contexts of Germany or France with the more conflictual English one, Hetherington *et al.* (1997) fail to recognize that the latter may indirectly contribute to a clearer view of the extent of child sexual abuse in England. Hetherington *et al.* (1997) view principles of social solidarity and the systems for protecting children on the continent which are associated with them as largely positive. From the point of view of child sexual abuse, I disagree with their analysis for reasons which we have discussed earlier.

However, it could be argued that this analysis is based on a false premise: perhaps lower levels of awareness about child sexual abuse in continental Europe simply reflect lower prevalence rates there compared to England. Is child sexual abuse only an English problem?

This question has already been partly answered earlier in the chapter, when I referred to Finkelhor's (1991) review of global prevalence data. As already noted, Finkelhor's review indicates that geographical location is probably not a major determinant of prevalence study levels. The idea that levels of child sexual abuse are not markedly different across Europe also gains support from the recent scandals in various European countries where the phenomenon has previously been denied or underestimated. Quite suddenly the populations of several countries are having to question previous assumptions not only about the levels of sexual violence towards children but also about the nature of their societies. Belgium and the Dutroux case is an obvious example (*The Guardian* 15 and 21 October 1996). In Ireland there have been a series of clerical scandals and the Kilkenny Investigation (Buckley 1996a, b, 1997). In Denmark, the 'Roum case' could be seen as a backlash against the rising awareness of child sexual abuse there (Harder 1997). In Eastern Europe too there are signs of a developing recognition of the issue: for instance, about the extent of paedophilic sex tourism by West Europeans (*The Guardian* 31 August 1996; *The European* 30 November to 6 December 1996).

Thus I discount the idea that child sexual abuse is a largely English problem. As far as the members of the European Union are concerned, denial about the extent of sexual abuse now seems to remain highest in some countries of Northern and Southern Europe (Harder and Pringle 1997; Chapters 4 and 5, this volume).

Summary

Child sexual abuse may well be a massive European social problem rather than being confined to the shores of Britain. Across Europe, awareness about the extent of sexual abuse is far higher in the United Kingdom than elsewhere, though a developing recognition seems to be occurring in some other countries. The greater level of awareness in Britain may partly arise from the fact that this country seems less institutionally and historically committed to a consensual and solidaristic ideal of social relations than its continental neighbours. That particular social context can also be linked to the more advanced development of an anti-oppressive social welfare perspective in Britain.

However, in discussing awareness about sexual abuse across Europe, I have so far tended to concentrate on the subject of its extent. I now want to consider another aspect of sexual abuse where differences in social context have created a similar contrast between England and much of continental Europe: explanations of why sexual abuse happens and of how it can be therapeutically addressed.

Social solidarity: a potential barrier to understanding child sexual abuse

Earlier in this chapter we noted that the dominant statutory welfare model for protecting children against sexual abuse in England has until now been one of child protection. Hetherington *et al.* (1997) and I (Pringle 1997a; Chapter 2, this volume) have identified a strong link between the features of that model and the individualistic social context which exists in England. We also agree that the child protection model is inadequate, though probably for different reasons. Finally both of us closely identify the family support model for the protection of children which exists in countries such as Belgium, France, the Netherlands and Germany with relatively solidaristic and consensual social contexts.

However, at this point I part company with Hetherington *et al.* (1997), since they then go on to imply that the family support model is a more effective way of protecting children from all forms of abuse. By contrast, I regard the model as being equally inadequate in terms of dealing with child sexual abuse. Earlier in this chapter I provided evidence for that view by surveying what has happened in those countries where a family support model predominates. We noted that the ineffectiveness of the model derived from its reliance on flawed family systems explanations for why child sexual abuse happens. In England, many social welfare commentators and practitioners are aware of the weaknesses of the family systems approach to child sexual abuse and are more likely to adopt at least in part some form of feminist anti-oppressive practice stance in relation to the problem. This represents another major cleavage between England and those continental countries. It is that cleavage I want to explore in this section.

We have already suggested that a link may exist between a high commitment to solidaristic principles such as cohesion, consensus and inclusion in the welfare context of a country and limitations on recognizing the extent of social problems which sharply reveal major fissures in the body politic: child sexual abuse being one example. I now want to note that such a welfare context is also likely to adopt a family systems explanation for sexual abuse. As we might expect, this is because the family systems approach challenges hegemonic social interests, particularly those relating to the gender order, far less than feminist and anti-oppressive explanations. Conversely, it is easy to see why feminist and anti-oppressive therapeutic strategies in relation to child sexual abuse might be more readily developed in a welfare context where principles of social solidarity are less entrenched: England being our case in point. Earlier in this chapter, I explained why feminist and anti-oppressive practice approaches (as opposed to family systems ones) are likely to offer more effective ways of dealing with child sexual abuse. This may then be another example of the way English practice can be a positive source of inspiration for its continental neighbours. Unfortunately, before we become too positive about English practice we need to recall once again that the procedural, legislative and economic frameworks within which English statutory social workers have to operate often restrict the actions of practitioners who may want to adopt some feminist and anti-oppressive approaches (Pringle 1997a).

I do not believe that the adoption in England of a continental-style family support model to replace in part the child protection model will produce a better outcome for children who have been sexually abused. Both models, for different reasons, are probaly disastrous as welfare responses to child sexual abuse. The child protection model misses most sexual abuse and drains resources away from preventative and therapeutic services towards investigations which often prove ineffective (Pringle 1997a). The family support model fails to address power dynamics which lie at the heart of most child sexual abuse and thereby potentially offers succour to abusers. Like the child protection model, it also misses the majority of sexual abuse cases. In addition, the family support model may lead to unwarranted blaming of non-abusing parents and encourage unsafe family reunifications (Pringle 1992, 1993).

Finally in this section I want to draw readers' attention to one central flaw which is shared by both the child protection and family support models: a flaw which further necessitates an alternative and radical welfare approach to child sexual abuse. For professional services in England and continental Europe probably deal with only a tiny proportion of the total number of child sexual abuse cases such as are revealed by general prevalence surveys in Britain (for instance, Kelly *et al*. 1991). If there was a demand for professional services from all those children who are subject to child sexual abuse then those services would be massively overwhelmed at once. Moreover, it is hard to see how professional services could ever be sufficiently funded to encompass that massive problem. For this reason any real attempt to provide help to those who have been abused cannot be based *primarily* on professional services. In order to meet effectively the needs of the mass of children who are sexually abused, we require in all European countries a helping approach which is based on radically different foundations from those which underpin either of the professional models, child protection or family support: an approach which encompasses the principles of anti-oppressive practice that we have explored in this chapter. In short, we need a third way (Pringle 1996b; Gray *et al.* 1997).

PROTECTING CHILDREN IN EUROPE: A THIRD WAY?

Drawing upon feminist, pro-feminist and anti-oppressive approaches, I want to suggest an alternative third model for the provision of assistance to children who have been sexually abused. This seeks to link professional workers with services primarily provided by community-based networks. Research into professional and non-professional service provision for survivors of sexual abuse (Gray *et al.* 1996, 1997) has also suggested that statutory social work agencies must develop complementary ways of working with survivor-focused and/or survivor-led non-statutory groups who can themselves provide the majority of services required.

This is indeed radically different from anything which currently exists on a large scale anywhere in Europe, including Britain. In outlining this third way, I will draw heavily upon feminist and anti-oppressive research and practice experience, largely drawn from within the United Kingdom, where some important, though relatively small-scale, initiatives have already taken place. However, I am aware that similar mainly small-scale initiatives are occurring in other countries (see Chapters 3 and 4). Furthermore, Harder (Harder 1997; Pringle and Harder 1997) has formulated a not dissimilar approach based on Danish experience and research.

Partnership between service users and service providers is an increasingly important concept in the field of British social care (HMSO 1990), even though the reality of such partnership is often open to doubt (Langan 1993: 150–3). Within the context of constant struggle, some highly creative and striking partnership initiatives have been developed in the field of adult care (Beresford and Croft 1993), particularly between statutory agencies and groups within the powerful disability movement (Silburn 1993). Such partnership in the context of child sexual abuse seems to be especially problematic but also potentially positive. As Beresford and Croft (1993: 170) note, child protection 'is the most contentious area of social work practice and raises wider issues of participation with particular intensity'. No doubt this largely arises from the fact that child abuse focuses our attention on, and crucially seeks us to challenge, dimensions of structural power in the way we have described earlier in this chapter (Pringle 1995: 175).

As we have seen, there is a desperate need for extensive preventative and therapeutic services in the area of child sexual abuse across Europe. To avoid the drawbacks which we have identified above in two professionally based approaches (child protection and family support), I am suggesting that many of these services should be both genuinely user-led and user-provided. However, this should not be an excuse for governmental cost-cutting, either in Britain or anywhere else. These services would have to be adequately supported by central and local government. By 'supported' I mean not simply money. I am also referring to non-cash facilities and, most importantly, to staff time. Welfare professionals would still have an important role within this model, albeit rather different from the one they fulfil at present regarding sexual abuse in the English context. The role of professionals in this 'third way' would be twofold. First, they would act as enablers for user-centred and user-led services via advice and consultancy. Second, they would provide the mechanism for legal mandates and criminal sanctions where required. In some respects such an approach would probably fit with greater ease into welfare systems where principles of subsidiarity are already more central than in England (Hetherington *et al.* 1997; Chapter 3, this volume).

The outlines of this community-oriented model obviously need further clarification. However, some major elements within it are relatively clear. First, in terms of energy, commitment and understanding, the key figures in this approach must be adult survivors, non-abusing parents of child survivors and their allies in both communities and professional agencies. Models for these kinds of local networks already exist both in theory (Pringle 1995: 204–19; Smith 1994, 1995) and in practice (Pringle 1995: 196–201).

In terms of theoretical analysis, the work of Gerrilyn Smith is particularly important. Her reworking of Finkelhor's 'four conditions model' for the process by which sexual abuse of children occurs (Finkelhor 1984) deserves far more attention among welfare academics and professionals than it has so far received (Smith 1996: 73–5). Her central idea is the devising of strategies by which a protective ring of adults within the community can in a sense 'insulate' a child from potential perpetrators, an idea which must play an important part in any community-oriented model for the safety of children (Smith 1994). Writing from within the English experience, she notes:

> we, as a community of adults, are reluctant to take responsibility for protecting other people's children. Hence, protectiveness has become increasingly professionalised and more removed from the natural networks that surround children where it would be most effective.
>
> (Smith 1996: 79)

She goes on to say:

> Instilling knowledge and skills into the community about the reality of
> sexual abuse and how to help reduce the risks must be an essential part of
> an overall child protection strategy . . . The importance of involving the com-
> munity is both a short-term necessity and a long-term goal . . . We need
> better communication between adults in the community to foster the view
> that the safety and protection of children is truly a shared responsibility.
>   (Smith 1996: 80–1)

As for the area of practice, Smith (1996: 80) notes that in Britain the
reality is that already 'a substantial proportion of child protection is
dealt with by the community'. There are numerous survivor-led and/or
survivor-centred community-based groups around the whole country
carrying out major work in their localities: determining the amount and
form of services required; putting pressure on local and/or central government to provide services to match those requirements or, indeed, to
provide resources so the local groups can deliver them directly; raising
awareness in their communities not only about the extent and dynamics
of sexual abuse but also about how positively to protect children; evaluating services already provided; and, most of all, providing invaluable
therapeutic help to survivors and non-abusing parents. We are suggesting a much more systematic, coordinated and supported development of
such initiatives where preventative, protective and therapeutic community networks are at the centre of children's protection rather than being
marginal to a system dominated by ineffective welfare bureaucracies.

A community-oriented response must be closely linked with challenges at every other level of society to those relations of structural
power which we have seen underpin sexual abuse, particularly those
relating to hegemonic forms of masculinity and heterosexuality (Pringle
1995: Chapter 8). This means action not only at individual and local
community levels but also at a societal level, entailing a range of initiatives. One such societal initiative that already exists in practice is the
Zero Tolerance Trust, which began in Edinburgh and has spread its
powerful campaigns to many other conurbations in Britain and, indeed,
around the world (Foley 1993; Salond 1994; Pringle 1995: 164–7). Moreover, it is essential that the response to sexual abuse at all these levels is
interlinked and coordinated. For instance, one highly successful sexual
abuse initiative in Newcastle upon Tyne, People Against Child Sexual
Abuse (PACSA), has been based on a service user-led group. It has coordinated efforts involving individual, local and community action, as well as
engaging with national media and the central political process (Pringle
1995: 196–8).

As we pointed out earlier, we need to bear in mind that recent prevalence studies suggest that child sexual abuse may be one of the most widespread problems faced by our societies. What lies behind the policy advocated here is a belief that a truly effective challenge to child sexual abuse can best (and perhaps only) be founded upon a community-oriented response. Such a response is, of course, not without major problems and needs more thought. After all, what precisely do we mean by a 'community'? And how is one to decide which members of that community are potentially protective and which potentially abusive? Nevertheless, I believe that the practice which already exists and the work of commentators such as Smith provide the basis for a fruitful development of this approach, not only in Britain but also across Europe.

CONCLUSIONS

This chapter has presented various opportunities to us in the context of our overall enterprise of surveying child sexual abuse across Europe. First, as a case study it has demonstrated how analyses presented in previous chapters on one particular issue can be brought together as a whole. Second, we have been able to take forward our analysis regarding the specific social problem of child sexual abuse and suggest a radically different way of dealing with it based on anti-oppressive practice principles. Third, we have been able to use the issue of child sexual abuse to explore broader transnational themes. In particular, we have been able to develop a wide-ranging analysis about the different levels of commitment to principles of social solidarity which exist in the welfare systems of Europe.

In developing this analysis we have hypothesized that a high national commitment to principles and ideals of social solidarity may have both positive and negative welfare outcomes. On the positive side, it may provide the necessary impetus for supportive welfare measures designed to meet the needs of sections of the population who are socially excluded. On the negative side, it may engender resistance to a full recognition and understanding of welfare problems which reveal deep social fissures. Moreover, welfare policies designed to promote social inclusion may promote social control and attempt to cover up sharp social divisions rather than challenging them.

Conversely, a society, such as that in Britain, where solidaristic principles seem to be less institutionally prominent may tend to implement narrower welfare measures which are less broadly supportive and sometimes socially divisive. That is the severe disadvantage of a relatively conflictual welfare context. However, I have also suggested that such an inhospitable social climate may at a more profound level also provide the conditions for a fuller recognition of social problems associated with major structural forms of oppression – and encourage the challenging of those structures by radical welfare approaches. In this and previous chapters we have used sexual violence and racism as examples of such social problems. In the next and final chapter of our study one of my aims is to expand upon this important theme.

CONCLUSION: CHILDREN AND EUROPE

INTRODUCTION

My aim here is to review some of the main themes which have run through previous chapters, to draw them together and to take them a stage further. Recalling Chapter 1, I would identify two interlinking themes as being central to this book:

1 To analyse the extent and nature of the various forms of oppression and discrimination which bear down on children and their carers both inside and outside families. In addition, to assess how far different welfare systems alleviate and/or intensify such forms of oppression. Finally, to outline models of practice aimed at effectively challenging those forms of oppression.
2 To consider whether there are any taxonomies or categorizations regarding those complex welfare responses which may help us to make sense of what is happening to children in Europe.

Let us then review each of these themes in turn.

CHILDREN AND OPPRESSION IN EUROPE

One overriding conclusion of our study is depressing. Across Europe massive numbers of children are subject to a complex interplay of a range of social oppressions. The manifestations of these oppressions in the form of social problems vary hugely between parts of Europe, different countries and a host of intranational variables. Ultimately, of course, each child's precise experience of oppression remains individual. However, we can be relatively specific about the most important vectors of oppression which shape the context for children's individual lives across Europe. In no hierarchical order, these vectors of oppression are racism, sexism, classism, disablism, heterosexism and ageism.

Europe presents a kaleidoscope of children's oppression. The previous chapters have attempted to portray some aspects of that complex and dynamic picture. Although generalization can be hazardous in this context, nevertheless we can make several overall observations about the process by which those vectors of oppression impinge on the lives of children and their carers.

Major forms of child oppression

First, although the specific forms of oppression experienced by children across Europe are manifold, some of them are particularly significant in terms of their breadth and impact. Here I will mention only three for the purposes of illustration.

One is poverty. Reflecting the complexity of power relations associated with forms of oppression, we need to recognize that poverty is both a difficult issue to define (Nolan and Whelan 1996) and one which takes different forms in different settings (Paugam 1996). Moreover, it is clear from our survey that poverty illustrates the way social disadvantage results from the dynamic interaction of a series of oppressive relations clustered around issues such as class, 'race' and gender. Previous chapters have demonstrated that family poverty is a major issue in all European countries (Ramprakash 1994; Nolan and Whelan 1996; Ruxton 1996, 1997) – with high unemployment levels, relative to the past, making it impossible for even the Nordic countries to feel complacent.

My second example of broad disadvantage is the impact of racism on the lives of children. Once again, the actual manifestations of this form of oppression are varied. For instance, in parts of the former Yugoslavia we might consider a very direct impact in terms of migration and war casualties (Ruxton 1996: Chapters 15 and 16; Chapter 6, this volume). In Sweden we recall the evidence about juvenile justice and migrant children (see Chapter 5). As regards Western Europe more generally, we saw acknowledgement of 'race' and culture issues in day-care services to varying degrees across Europe (Chapters 2 and 3). Some manifestations of racism traverse all Europe's geographical boundaries: for instance, the impact of racism on employment prospects and earning capacity, which in turn impacts on family poverty.

The final example of broadly based oppression against children in Europe is the one we focused upon in Chapter 8: child sexual abuse. If the actual prevalence levels in the rest of Europe are anywhere near the levels suggested for Britain by recent research studies (for instance, Kelly *et al.* 1991), then this is a huge social problem directly affecting a very significant proportion of European children. Moreover, in Chapter 8 we saw that the vectors of oppression underpinning the generation of child sexual abuse are precisely the same as those we outlined above.

Welfare systems and the oppression of children

Another overall comment we can make about the dynamics of oppression impacting on the lives of children and their carers across Europe relates to the welfare systems in different countries. I have noted in a previous study (Pringle 1995) that welfare systems may often reinforce social oppression rather than challenging it. This occurs because those same oppressive power dynamics structure welfare systems just as much as the societies in which welfare systems are situated. I believe our survey here has borne this out transnationally.

Of course, that is not to say that European welfare systems have purely negative outcomes. No doubt all of them positively alleviate some forms of social disadvantage regarding children to different extents. On the other hand, previous chapters have revealed many examples of welfare systems contributing either directly or indirectly to the oppression of children, and I provide a few examples now.

First, speaking as a researcher in the United Kingdom, it is particularly appropriate to highlight the interrelationship of British day-care services, welfare benefits, housing provision and labour market structures, and the massive negative impact of that relationship on family incomes relative to most other West European countries (see Chapter 2). This includes the impact on the incomes of many lone parents (European Observatory on National Family Policies 1996). Moreover, in Chapter 2 we saw that these policies were once again structured by the same range of oppressions.

Second, in Chapter 6 we reviewed the impact on children and their carers of social dislocation in the various countries of Eastern Europe. Within this analysis we noted that the developing welfare structures in those countries often made a negative contribution to the situation – partly as a result of pressures exerted by international agencies such as the IMF and the World Bank (Deacon and Hulse 1997).

Third, as we saw in Chapter 8, no system for the protection of children in any European country adequately addresses the huge dangers posed by child sexual abuse. This includes states with relatively well developed services based on a family support model and England's lumbering bureaucratic machine founded on the principles of child protection. One central reason for this failure is that both models are permeated, albeit in different ways, by oppressive assumptions relating to issues of gender, sexuality, class and age (Pringle 1995: Chapters 3 and 8; Harder

and Pringle 1997). That judgement is supported by our growing awareness, primarily in Britain but increasingly across Europe, of welfare
professionals who themselves directly abuse children.

Our analysis in Chapter 8 also underlined the way in which welfare
policies premised on the objectives of social consensus, social inclusion
and social cohesion can sometimes result in the extension of social
control or the denial of major forms of oppression. As regards the latter,
sexual violence and racism were the two main examples we used to
illustrate the point, though many other social problems would have
been equally relevant.

On the other hand, we must acknowledge that welfare systems in, for
instance, the Nordic countries and France *do* offer more supportive measures to children and their carers than is the case in the United Kingdom
(see Chapters 2, 3 and 5). Moreover, a commitment to principles of
social solidarity can clearly often be a source of positive welfare initiatives and of resistance to the kinds of welfare retrenchment now current
in the member states of the European Union prior to European Monetary
Union (*The European* 3–9 October 1996). The relative absence of such
a commitment in the United Kingdom during the dismantling of the
British 'welfare state' from 1979 until 1997 was surely a critical factor
(Clarke 1993; Hetherington *et al.* 1997; Pringle 1997a; Chapter 2, this
volume). Overall, perhaps we should conclude that the objectives of
social inclusion and social solidarity often have complex, contradictory
and sometimes negative welfare outcomes.

Challenging the oppression of children

Let us summarize so far. The major disadvantages suffered by children
across Europe may be regarded as the outcomes of interacting and oppressive power relations associated with racism, sexism, heterosexism,
disablism, classism and ageism. It seems that current welfare systems in
Europe frequently fail to challenge those relations of power which underpin social disadvantage and may often reinforce them due to the fact
that they too are reflections of the same oppressive power relations. In
this context, we are left with an important question: how can those
forms of oppression which cause damage to children be effectively challenged? Can a truly anti-oppressive framework for action be developed?
Moreover, it follows from our previous discussion that whatever the
answers, they must include the means by which the oppressive features
of welfare systems themselves are challenged – since they are clearly
part of the problem.

Elsewhere (Pringle 1995: Chapter 9) I developed an anti-oppressive
welfare framework as applied to the broad issue of men's practices in

social welfare. More recently I applied the same framework to the context of child abuse (Pringle 1997a). At the end of the previous chapter in this study I outlined a version of the framework in relation to challenging child sexual abuse. Because I have described fully the component parts of the framework in those references I do not intend to repeat them here. Suffice it to say that the framework is based on the following essentials (Pringle 1995: Chapter 9):

- a need to address the whole interacting range of social oppressions mentioned above, since they cannot be realistically isolated one from another;
- systemically to challenge social oppression within all relevant social domains, ranging from the personal and intrapsychic right through to societal initiatives;
- the forging of an essential, and genuine, partnership between welfare service users and welfare workers in implementing the framework.

A welfare perspective based on explicitly anti-oppressive principles seems to be more widely shared among professionals in the United Kingdom than elsewhere in Europe, even though the scope for British workers to implement such principles is often restricted by procedural regulation and resource limitation, both of them features of the British welfare system developed mainly in the period 1979–97. In Chapter 8 I offered a possible explanation of why anti-oppressive principles are relatively influential in Britain and why the awareness of structural forms of oppression bearing down on children and their carers seems so acute in that country compared to most other European states.

I believe that the kinds of anti-oppressive framework which I have discussed can be adapted by welfare professionals, policy-makers and academics across Europe so as to address those many other manifestations of social oppression impacting upon children and their carers surveyed in this study. For instance, I noted in Chapter 8 that a similar model to my community-oriented one had been suggested in Denmark by Margit Harder (1997) in relation to various forms of child abuse. I leave it to readers to extend this process of adaption for themselves.

CHILDREN AND WELFARE: PATTERNS OF SERVICE PROVISION ACROSS EUROPE

Introduction

Discussion of the differential development of anti-oppressive practice across Europe naturally leads to the second major theme which has run throughout this book: how far are there clear patterns of child welfare service provision across Europe? Is it possible to develop a framework of welfare systems in Europe similar to Esping-Andersen's (1990) but at the same time including the much wider range of welfare provisions surveyed by this study?

In Chapter 1 I reviewed the various critiques of Esping-Andersen's framework, noting that many of them fell into two overlapping categories: one category focused on the extent to which his analysis had overlooked issues of gender and sexism in welfare regime formation; the other category sought to widen the range of welfare provisions to be surveyed from the relatively narrow limits adopted by Esping-Andersen.

This study has attempted to consider Esping-Andersen's framework utilizing both forms of critique. First, I have sought to assess welfare systems in terms of how far they address not only gender but also the full range of anti-oppressive issues. Second, welfare systems have been evaluated by surveying a much wider range of social provision than most previous studies have attempted, including benefits support to families, parental leave arrangements, day-care services and a broad spectrum of social care initiatives. I now outline my judgement regarding Esping-Andersen's framework by addressing these two categories of critique in turn. I will refer to the first as the anti-oppressive critique and the second as the data range critique.

Again, instead of simply replicating the overall analysis presented in previous chapters about patterns of provision, I shall here choose a few examples to illustrate my main conclusions on this score.

The anti-oppressive critique

First, in assesing the effectiveness of welfare systems, one of my main criteria has been a consideration of how far they address that range of social oppressions which I have frequently alluded to here (Thompson 1993; Dalrymple and Burke 1995; Lavalette and Pratt 1996: Part 2). The picture is in fact complex. Previous feminist and pro-feminist critiques had already indicated the oversimplifications to which Esping-Andersen's framework could lead (Duncan 1995). Our analysis confirmed and expanded the validity of that critique.

Contrasts and complexities: the Nordic states and the United Kingdom

The Nordic states and the United Kingdom provide an illustration of this complex picture. The former are often regarded by commentators as the closest to the ideal of 'social democratic' welfare harmony in Europe. The latter is usually portrayed as having developed marked 'neo-liberal' tendencies since 1979 (Esping-Andersen 1996b). In Chapter 5 we surveyed data indicating who precisely provides childcare in the Nordic countries and also who is employed within the welfare sector. This survey revealed fissures along gender lines in the 'social democratic' fabric and also confirmed a degree of heterogeneity among those countries which has often been neglected (Leira 1994). Those complexities which were revealed within patterns of Nordic provision were echoed when we considered attitudes towards issues of racism there. Once again, the social democratic ideal appeared to be somewhat tarnished. We should acknowledge that the Nordic states have instituted, to greater or lesser extents, some of the most progressive child and family measures in Europe. However, our analysis still indicates that the usual picture presented of uniform social democratic cohesion is far too simplistic.

We can then contrast this with the situation in Britain. Let us admit first of all that our study of welfare in relation to children and their carers suggests that Britain's reputation as the most neo-liberal welfare system in Europe is unfortunately well justified in many respects (Byrne 1997: 32). However, this welfare profile does not apply to all aspects of the British welfare context as we can see when we address complex issues of gender and 'race'.

In relation to gender, let us consider the example of men and childcare practice. As we have seen in various chapters, this issue has been addressed in quite a wide range of countries on the continent of Europe, not least Italy (Chapter 4) and the Nordic states (Chapter 5), as well as by the European Commission itself (Chapter 7). The perspective adopted in those countries towards a greater potential role for men in child welfare work has been both highly positive and perhaps rather uncritical.

In Britain, there has also been a great deal of interest in the subject, often from perspectives similar to those on the continent (Chapters 2, 7 and 8). However, our survey also revealed an important critique of these perspectives, a critique developed largely in the United Kingdom. This critique acknowledges the potentially valuable role of more men working in professional childcare but only with the proviso that such men should adopt a broader anti-oppressive perspective on men's practices, not least the isue of men's violences to children and women (Hearn 1990; Pringle 1990, 1995, 1997b, e). It is therefore no accident that some of the most creative practice debates (Catty 1996) and policies (Meleady 1997) in Europe about involving more men safely in childcare are occurring in the United Kingdom. This anti-oppressive perspective clearly bears little relation to the neo-liberalism which characterizes some other areas of the welfare scene in Britain.

Similarly, in Chapters 7 and 8 we noted that although racism is widespread in Britain and measures taken to counter it leave an immense amount to be desired, nevertheless there are grounds for arguing that public and professional welfare awareness of that issue is probably greater in the United Kingdom than in the remainder of Europe. Moreover, we have seen that this relative welfare sensitivity to issues of racism in the United Kingdom extends to the childcare field (Children in Scotland 1994). We did acknowledge in Chapter 8 that the anti-oppressive progress made in this area was always under severe pressure of being turned back and that in this sense it was tenuous. Nevertheless, some progress has been made. Therefore, once again, this specific aspect of the welfare context in Britain does not sit easily with Britain's neo-liberal characterization.

While there is no doubt that the welfare context in the United Kingdom is generally characterized by neo-liberal features, there are clearly some important anti-oppressive exceptions to that rule. Thus both Britain and the Nordic states, in opposite ways, fail fully to conform to Esping-Andersen-style categorizations. On the one hand, oppressive subtexts seem to disturb the apparent social cohesion of the Nordic states to greater or lesser extents. On the other hand, the largely neo-liberal portrait of Britain may have overall validity but it disregards some important respects in which the United Kingdom has developed anti-oppressive welfare approaches more effectively, albeit tenuously, than much of the remainder of Europe.

What adds extra significance to this comparison between the Nordic states and Britain is that, as we have previously discussed, our explanation of Britain's greater welfare awareness around some issues of oppression centres partly on the relative absence of a commitment to principles of social solidarity there. Conversely, I am arguing that a relative denial of some forms of social oppression in the Nordic states can be partly attributed to their strong commitment to those very same principles. Yet, within many comparative analyses, such as that of Esping-Andersen (1990, 1996b), commitment to social solidarity is often identified, uncritically, as a primary hallmark of a 'progressive' welfare system. As we have seen throughout this final chapter, while in very many cases that may be a valid judgement, there are grounds for believing that the situation is often more complex as well.

The data range critique

In Chapter 1 I reviewed some of those studies which had sought to reclassify welfare systems in Western Europe by comparing wider forms of social provision than were included in Esping-Andersen's (1990) original framework: in particular those studies which had reviewed services such as day-care in their analysis. I also noted the more complex comparative survey provided by Hantrais and Letablier (1996), which largely eschewed simplistic taxonomies in favour of multidimensionality. In the present study I have sought to review an even wider range of provision than Hantrais and Letablier, and therefore have discovered a considerable degree of complexity in the resulting picture. I will now provide a few examples of that complexity.

Financial support, day-care and leave arrangements
As far as provision in the form of financial support, day-care and parental leave arrangements is concerned, our analysis largely replicates that of Hantrais and Letablier (1996): a series of multidimensional constellations of states around issues such as family and employment policies (pp. 124–35), national conceptualizations of family policy (pp. 143–4) and family models (pp. 178–81). Although these constellations are not identical, there is considerable overlap between them. In reviewing recent research, Ruxton has provided a useful summary of the main contours of that overlap:

> it appears that France, Belgium and Luxembourg have consistently given a high level of financial support to the family through the tax and benefit system. Denmark, Finland and Sweden have been leaders in terms of provision of childcare and leave arrangements, and have placed considerable emphasis on the needs of children and gendeer equality. Over the last 15 years at least, the UK has prioritised the reduction of the role of the state by emphasising family responsibilities for caring. Meanwhile in Germany, although there is a commitment in the Constitution to supporting the family, the approach has remained relatively conservative, tending to prioritise married families over less traditional arrangements.
>
> (Ruxton 1997: 18)

To this summary we need to add our conclusions about the countries of Southern Europe, which are again similar to those of Hantrais and Letablier (1996). In their multidimensional classifications, Hantrais and Letablier do cluster these countries together. For instance, in terms of the family responsibilities/employment issue, we have seen that they define Portugal, Spain and Greece as adopting a non-interventionist stance arising from financial constraints, while characterizing the United Kingdom (and to some extent Ireland) as non-interventionist on ideological grounds (Hantrais and Letablier 1996: 132–4).

Of course, once again, Hantrais and Letablier acknowledge complexity within and between these classifications. They note the ambivalent position of Italy, which in some cases is aligned with Germany and Austria and at other times with the other Mediterranean countries. Similarly, they correctly emphasize the distinctive position of Portugal among

Mediterranean countries as regards the high full-time economic activity there of mothers with young children.

The ambivalent position of Italy, which is asssociated with sharp regional north–south differences, recalls the importance of regional variations which are often underplayed in comparative studies (Duncan 1995) – and we saw in Chapter 4 that such variations were especially pertinent to the situation in the Mediterranean countries. All these issues are involved in the debate about the disputed legitimacy of a discrete Mediterranean or Catholic corporatist model, which was addressed in Chapter 4. I will not rehearse the debate again here, nor the even more anomolous position of Ireland within that debate. However, we may note that this debate reinforces the overall picture of complexity in relation to European family policies. And that once again underscores the oversimplification created by broad taxonomic analyses such as Esping-Andersen's.

One of the most glaring discrepancies between Esping-Andersen's analysis and the more complex patterns which have emerged in the work of feminist scholars (Sainsbury 1994; Duncan 1995) and in Hantrais and Letablier (1996) is the position of France and Germany (see Chapter 3). When social provisions such as financial family support, day-care and parental leave arrangements are scrutinized, the mismatch between the family policies of these two allegedly 'conservative corporatist' countries is considerable.

The inadequacy of Esping-Andersen's categorizations in sufficiently embracing levels of complexity is also illustrated by attempts to apply his framework to the 'new democracies' of Eastern Europe. As we saw in Chapter 6, such attempts have sometimes led to confusion and contradiction, partly because so many trends change there with such rapidity at this time. However, those confusions also arise out of the social and cultural heterogeneity of these countries and out of their social and cultural differences, to greater or lesser extents, from Western Europe.

Social care services

The analysis of Hantrais and Letablier (1996) is limited by the fact that they fail to address a wide range of social care provisions for children. In this study I have attempted to embrace several of these forms of social care: services addressed included out-of-home placement, juvenile justice and the protection of children. Comparison of these areas created an even more complex picture than that provided by Hantrais and Letablier (1996), thereby increasing my doubts about the value of all-encompassing taxonomies.

On the other hand, some of our social care comparisons produced country groupings less divergent from Esping-Andersen's formulation than those resulting from the analysis of day-care and financial support.

For instance, we saw that current patterns of supportive juvenile justice provision in much of Western and Northern Europe tend to be consistent with the commitment to solidaristic principles pertaining there. On the other hand, English juvenile justice provision in the 1990s has possessed distinct neo-liberal features. However, there was still a degree of complexity within this picture which made taxonomic generalization less convincing. We discovered that many of the relatively supportive policies now utilized in West and North Europe were in fact previously developed during the 1980s in Britain (Downes 1994; Pitts 1994). The divergence between Britain and the continent along this dimension is thus a relatively recent phenomenon and may have some specific, rather than structural, causes such as the policies of particular Home Secretaries in the Conservative government of 1979–97.

The survey in previous chapters of systems for the protection of children across Europe also seems at first sight to produce a picture not wholly unrelated to some of the categorizations suggested by Esping-Andersen. For instance, Cooper *et al.* (1995) and Hetherington *et al.* (1997) make a clear and convincing connection between those protective systems in, say, France, Germany and Belgium and the wider welfare contexts in these countries, which are informed by principles of subsidiarity and solidarity. Pringle (1997a) makes a similarly clear link between the child protection model of England and broader Thatcherite neo-liberal welfare policies. Bini and Toselli (1997), as well as Hetherington *et al.* (1997), make reference to regional variations, resource restrictions and the influence of Catholic family ideologies in their analysis of the Italian child protection picture – all of which are reminiscent of discussions about a Mediterranean welfare regime. Pringle and Harder (1997) note the relatively universalist and socially supportive nature of Nordic child protective services and their connection with a social democratic welfare approach.

However, a closer inspection of European protective services once again opens up major complexities which can be missed when using an overgeneralized framework. One element of that complexity relates to the situation in specific countries. For example, despite some similarities in the protective systems of Denmark and Finland, Pringle and Harder (1997) point out the degree of heterogeneity existing between the two. Moreover, the analyses of Buckley (1997) and of Pringle and Harder (1997) suggest that the shape of protective services in Ireland defies simple categorization.

Another element of complexity relating to the protection of children suggests a more fundamental problem with a broad analysis such as Esping-Andersen's. This discrepancy is best illustrated by the detailed analysis of child sexual abuse in Chapter 8. It was acknowledged that

service provision relating to child sexual abuse across the Euro-
nion did bear some connection to Esping-Andersen's categoriza-
On the other hand, a central theme in Chapter 8 was that levels of
professional and public awareness towards child sexual abuse in the
states of Western and Northern continental Europe are considerably
lower than those in England, partly as a result of the relatively greater
commitment to principles of social solidarity which pertain in the former
countries. Moreover, it was argued that this same commitment was
partially responsible for the practice failings of the family support model
which dominates responses to child sexual abuse in those countries.

In England the service situation was more complex. On the one hand,
most statutory responses to child sexual abuse in England were inadequate because of problems associated with the neo-liberal child protection model and the procedures derived from it. All of those unhelpful
features were largely outcomes of the Thatcherite influence on social
policy post-1979. On the other hand, a considerable number of welfare
professionals have been positively influenced in their practice by the
greater awareness of abuse which exists in Britain and by feminist/anti-
oppressive perspectives on how to deal with the issue which are particularly prevalent in Britain. Thus once again the characterization of the
welfare context in the United Kingdom as being neo-liberal has to be
qualified, even though as a generalization it retains some validity.

SOCIAL SOLIDARITY AND ANTI-OPPRESSIVE PRACTICE

Whereas many analyses of welfare systems indicate that a societal commitment to principles of solidarity often contributes to the development of more supportive and/or extensive welfare services, my analysis
of child sexual abuse suggests that *sometimes* such a commitment can
hamper recognition of social problems and produce responses to them
which fail to address crucial issues of structural social oppression. By
contrast, greater levels of awareness and more radical anti-oppressive
practice responses might be possible in welfare contexts (like Britain)
which are based on less consensual and solidaristic principles. I extended
this analysis beyond child sexual abuse by positing that such a state of
affairs may also exist in relation to many other social problems associated with child welfare – such as racism.

It was argued that a broad anti-oppressive approach to child and family welfare issues was required, with service users and ex-service users
at its heart as both policy-makers and providers of services. Only such
a response offered any real hope if social problems relating to children

were to be effectively tackled. In Chapter 8 I provided an example of such a framework using child sexual abuse as an example and drawing on English research and practice.

This central issue concerning the hypothesized, potentially inverse, relationship between anti-oppressive practice and a commitment to solidaristic principles extends my critique of Esping-Andersen and those who draw upon his analysis. Moreover, the resulting call for a thorough-going anti-oppressive practice perspective on child welfare matters clearly connects with my earlier critique of his approach and with the strategy for effectively challenging the oppression of children outlined in the first section of this chapter.

Of course, in principle it is conceivable that a sufficiently powerful welfare commitment to social solidarity could in itself actually promote a thoroughgoing anti-oppressive welfare programme. However, this would only occur *if* such a commitment led to a radical and thoroughgoing critique of social institutions and structures. In other words, it is not the idea of social solidarity itself which is the problem: the difficulty lies in the way it has been interpreted and constructed in the countries of Europe. The point I am making is that there is no sign anywhere in continental Europe of solidaristic principles being interpreted and acted upon in ways which encourage the kind of profoundly radical anti-oppressive transformation that is essential if the social problems bearing down on children and their carers are to be really challenged. I want briefly to explore this further.

Some recent contributions to the debate about social solidarity offer insights into this phenomenon. Writing from a more predominantly class-based perspective than my own, both Levitas (1996) and Byrne (1997) provide a critique of solidaristic approaches to welfare as they have in practice been manifested. Byrne argues that such approaches have not been directed at sufficiently structural targets:

> Levitas (1996) was absolutely right to say that the starting point for an understanding of what is called 'social exclusion' is the nature of capital-ism itself . . . What is so profoundly depressing is that almost nowhere can we identify coherent political forces which are prepared to attack, even in a reformist fashion, capitalism itself.
>
> (Byrne 1997: 44)

Levitas herself broadens out this argument regarding solidaristic dis-courses to embrace other forms of oppression:

> The core of my objection to this discourse is that it obscures the fact that the positions into which people are 'integrated' through paid work are funda-mentally unequal . . . the term 'social exclusion' presumes that 'inclusion'

is beneficial. It is salutary to remember that even if women, ethnic minorities and disabled people achieve equal opportunities within the labour market, it will still be the case that what 'integration' means is participation in a capitalist economy driven by profit and based upon exploitation. The dichotomous model of exclusion and integration obscures this fact.

(Levitas 1996: 18)

In the anti-oppressive analysis which runs throughout this book I have not privileged the ground of class and capitalism as much as Byrne or Levitas, preferring a broader approach involving all major forms of social oppression (Pringle 1995; Chapter 1, this volume). Nevertheless, I believe that the central point made by Levitas and Byrne is correct: real world policies aimed at social inclusion, social exclusion and the promotion of social solidarity have not sought to transform the underlying structural sources of social oppression and so in practice the effect has been one of collusion rather than challenge. A transformatory politics is surely inimical to the rather consensual welfare contexts of Western, Northern and Southern continental Europe. Despite severe economic pressures, these contexts are still largely based on various forms of corporatism (see Chapters 3–5).

As for the countries of Eastern Europe, we saw in Chapter 6 that any judgement about their welfare trajectories is hazardous, partly because of their heterogeneity. We can, however, make two relevant observations. First, in their pre-1989 histories these counties all experienced a particularly oppressive and socially controlling form of solidarity which graphically illustrates why I am so ambivalent about that concept. Second, since the disintegration of the Eastern bloc, most of these countries have embraced a market-based approach to welfare with various degrees of enthusiasm, while at the same time the oppressions to which children are subject seem to mount daily. A critical transformatory welfare approach to sources of social oppression seems even less likely there than in Western Europe.

It is the overarching theme and conclusion of this book that a broad anti-oppressive welfare approach, challenging the sources of oppressive power relations which structure children's lives, needs to be developed across Europe. As readers might already guess, I am not confident that this can be achieved for a variety of reasons, two of which I mention now.

First, as we have seen, the social contexts in many European countries are resistant to welfare approaches which seek to challenge structural forms of oppression in a concerted way. Furthermore, in Chapter 7 we observed that there seems little prospect that the European Union or any other pan-European institution can, or wants to, effectively change this state of affairs. Certainly the social and economic tensions between Union member states, as well as the potential exacerbation of these tensions by the imminent inclusion of some Eastern European countries, suggests that the European Union is unlikely to become a concerted and major force for progressive social change in Europe (Leibfried 1994).

As far as children are concerned, this situation can be linked to my second reason for doubting the emergence of a broad anti-oppressive welfare strategy across Europe. Children lack economic, social and political power (Ruxton 1996) – and the parents of many of the most disadvantaged children are likewise relatively powerless. As we saw in Chapter 7, The European Union has so far presented a useful example of the lack of value attached to the interests of children by politicians. Moreover, it is estimated that by 2025 the proportion of younger people in many European countries will fall, while the proportion of older people rises. In a context of ongoing resource constraints, Ruxton (1997) is therefore surely right to question what political importance, relatively speaking, may be attached to the welfare needs of children for the future.

One country in Europe where there has been some sign of a tentative shift in the direction of an anti-oppressive welfare practice, the United Kingdom, has now elected a social democratic party into government after almost twenty years of right-wing rule. Such a political change might be assumed to accelerate the shift towards anti-oppressive welfare practice which from 1979 until 1997 struggled in a most hostile political climate. However, the new government is heavily committed to the concepts of social inclusion (Levitas 1996; Byrne 1997) and of a 'stakeholder society' (Burkitt and Ashton 1996). In the light of what we have said about the ambiguous, even sometimes inverse, relationship between a commitment to principles of social solidarity and a transformatory anti-oppressive welfare practice in Europe, we should perhaps not expect much from the new Labour administration either for children or for adults. Early signs in relation to policies aimed at lone parents suggest that this pessimism is well justified. We may once again find the rallying cries of social inclusion and solidarity used as apparently benign justifications for considerably less benign welfare policies.

Finally, in conclusion, I want to turn away from detailed policy speculations and refocus on what is the fundamental concern of this book: the welfare of children. We have seen that almost nothing about the issue of children and social welfare in Europe is simple: complexity and paradox have constantly presented themselves to us. Yet the pain of children in distress is simple as far as the emotional response which it demands is concerned. If we forget that central fact amid all the complexities and paradoxes then we shall never have any chance of overcoming those massive barriers to the relief of children which we have surveyed in this volume.

REFERENCES

Acosta, E. (1990) Spain, in A. Sale and M. Davies (eds) *Child Protection Policies and Practice in Europe*. London: NSPCC.

Ahmad, B. (1990) *Black Perspectives in Social Work*. Birmingham: Venture Press.

Alber, J. (1995) A framework for the comparative study of social services, *Journal of European Social Policy*, 5(2), 131–49.

Allen, N. (1992) *Making Sense of the Children Act*, 2nd edn. Harlow: Longman.

Allen, S. and Macey, M. (1994) Some issues of race, ethnicity and nationalism, in P. Brown and R. Crompton (eds) *Economic Restructuring and Social Exclusion*. London: UCL Press.

Aluffi-Pentini, A. and Lorenz, W. (eds) (1996) *Anti-racist Work with Young People: European Experiences and Approaches*. Lyme Regis: Russell House Publishing.

Alund, A. and Schierup, C.-U. (1993) The thorny road to Europe: Swedish immigrant policy in transition, in J. Solomos and J. Wrench (eds) *Racism and Migration in Western Europe*. Oxford: Berg.

Anttonen, A. and Sipila, J. (1996) European social care services: is it possible to identify models?, *Journal of European Social Policy*, 6, 87–100.

Armstrong, H. and Hollows, A. (1991) Responses to child abuse in the EC, in M. Hill (ed.) *Social Work and the European Community*. London: Jessica Kingsley Publications.

Armstrong, L. (1991) Surviving the incest industry, *Trouble and Strife*, 21, 29–32.

Aslanbeigu, N., Pressman, S. and Summerfield, G. (1994) *Women in the Age of Economic Transformation: Gender Impact of Reform in Post-socialist and Developing Countries*. London: Routledge.

Assiter, A. (1996) *Enlightened Women: Modernist Feminism in a Postmodern Age*. London: Routledge.

Ayala, L. (1994) Social needs, inequality and the welfare state in Spain: trends and prospects, *Journal of European Social Policy*, 4(3), 159–79.

Back-Wicklund, M. (1996) Parenting and childhood in modern family cultures. Paper delivered at University of Sunderland, October.

Back-Wicklund, M. (1997) Personal communication.

Bacon, W.M. Jr and Pol, L.G. (1994) The economic status of women in romania, in N. Aslanbeigu, S. Pressman and G. Summerfield (eds) *Women in the Age of Economic Transformation: Gender Impact of Reform in Post-socialist and Developing Countries*. London: Routledge.

Barberan, J.M. (1996) Mediation in Spanish youth justice, *Social Work in Europe*, 3(3), 36–8.

Barker, R.W. (1994) *Lone Fathers and Masculinities*. Aldershot: Avebury.

Barn, R. (1993) *Black Children in the Public Care System.* London: Batsford.

Barnes, C. (1991) *Disabled People in Britain and Discrimination.* London: Hurst.

Begg, I. and Nectoux, F. (1995) Social protection and economic union, *Journal of European Social Policy*, 5(4), 285–302.

Benson, C. and Clay, E. (1992) *Eastern Europe and the Former Soviet Union: Economic Change, Social Welfare and Aid.* London: Overseas Development Institute.

Beresford, P. and Croft, S. (1993) *Citizen Involvement.* London: Macmillan.

Berridge, D. (1994) Foster and residential care reassessed: a research perspective, *Chidren and Society*, 8, 132–50.

Bielawska-Batorowicz, E. (1992) Personal communication.

Bini, L. and Toselli, M. (1997) Child protection in Italy, in M. Harder and K. Pringle (eds) *Protecting Children in Europe: Towards a New Millennium.* Aalborg: Aalborg University Press.

Birks, C. (ed) (1995) *Child Abuse in Europe (Volume 1).* Nurnberg: Emwe-Verlag.

Biskup, P. (1990) Czechoslovakia, in A. Sale and M. Davies (eds) *Child Protection Policies and Practice in Europe.* London: NSPCC.

Bodzansky, H. (1990) Hungary, in A. Sale and M. Davies (eds) *Child Protection Policies and Practice in Europe.* London: NSPCC.

Brindle, D. (1997) *The Guardian*, 20 November 1997, 2.

Brown, P. and Crompton, R. (1994) *Economic Restructuring and Social Exclusion.* London: UCL Press.

Buckley, H. (1996a) Child abuse guidelines in Ireland: for whose protection?, *Administration*, 44(2), 37–56.

Buckley, H. (1996b) Beyond the rhetoric: a qualitative study of child protection in Ireland, conference paper, ISPCAN Congress, Dublin, August.

Buckley, H. (1997) Child protection in Ireland, in M. Harder and K. Pringle (eds) *Protecting Children in Europe: Towards a New Millennium.* Aalborg: Aalborg University Press.

Bullock, R. (1993) The United Kingdom, in M. Colton and W. Hellinckx (eds) *Child Care in the EC: a Country-specific Guide to Foster Care and Residential Care.* Aldershot: Arena.

Burkitt, B. and Ashton, F. (1996) The birth of the stakeholder society, *Critical Social Policy*, 16(4), 3–16.

Byrne, D. (1997) Social exclusion and capitalism, *Critical Social Policy*, 17(1), 27–51.

Campbell, B. (1995) A question of priorities, *Community Care*, 24–30 August.

Cannan, C. (1992) *Changing Families, Changing Welfare: Family Centres and the Welfare State.* Hemel Hempstead: Harvester Wheatsheaf.

Cannan, C. (1996) The impact of social development and anti-exclusion policies on the French social work professions, *Social Work in Europe*, 3(2), 1–4.

Cannan, C., Berry, L. and Lyons, K. (1992) *Social Work and Europe.* London: Macmillan.

Carabine, J. (1996) A straight playing field or queering the pitch: centring sexuality in social policy, *Feminist Review*, 54, 31–64.

Carlen, P. and Wardhaugh, J. (1991) Locking up our daughters, in P. Carter, T. Jeffs and M.K. Smith (eds) *Social Work and Social Welfare Year Book 3.* Buckingham: Open University Press.

Casas, F. (1993) Spain, in M. Colton and W. Hellinckx (eds) *Child Care in the EC: a Country-specific Guide to Foster Care and Residential Care.* Aldershot: Arena.

Catty, J. (ed.) (1996) *Men in Family Centres.* Newcastle upon Tyne: Save the Children Fund.

CCETSW (1995) *Paper 30: Rules and Requirements in Assuring Quality in the Diploma in Social Work – 1,* revised edition. London: CCETSW.

Chandler, T. (1993) Working with fathers in a family centre, *Working With Men,* 4, 11–13.

Children in Scotland (1994) *Challenging Racism in the Early Years.* Edinburgh: HMSO.

Clarke, J. (ed.) (1993) *A Crisis in Care.* London: Sage.

Clarke, J. and Langan, M. (1993) Restructuring welfare: the British welfare regime in the 1980s, in A. Cochrane and J. Clarke (eds) *Comparing Welfare States.* London: Sage.

Clemente, R.M. (1990) Portugal, in A. Sale and M. Davies (eds) *Child Protection Policies and Practice in Europe.* London: NSPCC.

Cochrane, A. (1993a) The problem of poverty, in R. Dallos and E. Mclaughlin (eds) *Social Problems and the Family.* London: Sage Publications.

Cochrane, A. (1993b) Challenges from the centre, in A. Clarke (ed.) *A Crisis in Care.* London: Sage.

Cochrane, A. and Clarke, J. (eds) (1993) *Comparing Welfare States.* London: Sage.

Colla-Muller, H. (1993) Germany, in M. Colton and W. Hellinckx (eds) *Child Care in the EC: a Country-specific Guide to Foster Care and Residential Care.* Aldershot: Arena.

Colton, M. and Hellinckx, W. (eds) (1993) *Child Care in the EC: a Country-specific Guide to Foster Care and Residential Care.* Aldershot: Arena.

Connell, R.W. (1987) *Gender and Power: Society, the Person and Sexual Politics.* Cambridge: Polity Press.

Connell, R.W. (1995) *Masculinities.* Cambridge: Polity Press.

Cooper, A. (1994a) In care or en famille?, *Social Work in Europe,* 1(1), 59–67.

Cooper, A. (1994b) A tale of two cultures – race, ideology and child protection work in France and England, *Social Work in Europe,* 1(3), 53–60.

Cooper, A., Hetherington, R., Baistow, K., Pitts, J. and Spriggs, A. (1995) *Positive Child Protection: a View from Abroad.* Lyme Regis: Russell House Publishing.

Cornia, G.A. (1991) Economic reforms and child welfare: in pursuit of adequate safety nets for children, in G.A. Cornia and S. Sipos (eds) *Children and the Transition to the Market Economy.* Aldershot: Avebury.

Cornia, G.A. and Sipos, S. (eds) (1991) *Children and the Transition to the Market Economy.* Aldershot: Avebury.

Corrin, C. (1992) Gendered identities: women's experience of change in Hungary, in S. Rai, H. Pilkington and A. Phizaclea (eds) *Women in the Face of Change: the Soviet Union, Eastern Europe and China.* London: Routledge.

Council of Europe (1990) *Proceedings of the Colloquy on Violence within the Family: Measures in the Social Field.* Strasbourg: Council of Europe.

Council of Europe (1996a) *Children's Rights and Childhood Policies in Europe: New Approaches? Closing Conference of the Childhood Policies Project, Leipzig, 30 May – 1 June 1996.* Strasbourg: Council of Europe.

Council of Europe (1996b) *The Interests of the Child: Child Day Care and Family Policies.* Position Paper Prepared By Working Group II of the Childhood Policies Project. Strasbourg: The Council of Europe.

Cousins, C. (1995) Women and social policy in Spain: the development of a gendered welfare regime, *Journal of European Social Policy*, 5(3), 175–97.

Dalrymple, J. and Burke, B. (1995) *Anti-oppressive Practice: Social Care and the Law.* Buckingham: Open University Press.

Daly, M. (1994) Comparing welfare states: towards a gender friendly approach, in D. Sainsbury (ed.) *Gendering Welfare States.* London: Sage.

Davies, C. and Davies, M. (1997) Child abuse prevention in Europe: extracts from the NSPCC report, *Social Work in Europe*, 4(1), 31–5.

Davies, G., Wilson, C., Mitchell, R. and Milsom, J. (1994) *Videotaping Children's Evidence: an Evaluation.* London: HMSO.

Davies, M. and Sale, A. (1989) *Child Protection in Europe.* London: NSPCC.

Davis, E., Kidd, L. and Pringle, K. (1987) *Child Sexual Abuse Training Programme for Foster Parents with Teenage Placements.* Newcastle upon Tyne: Barnardos.

de Ruyter, M.H. (1990) The Netherlands, in A. Sale and M. Davies (eds) *Child Protection Policies and Practices in Europe.* London: NSPCC.

Deacon, B. (1992) Social welfare developments in Eastern Europe and the future for socialist welfare, in P. Carter, T. Jeffs and M.K. Smith (eds) *Changing Social Work and Welfare.* Buckingham: Open University Press.

Deacon, B. (1993) Developments in East European social policy, in C. Jones (ed.) *New Perspectives on the Welfare State in Europe.* London: Routledge.

Deacon, B. and Hulse, M. (1997) the making of post-communist social policy: the role of international agencies, *Journal of Social Policy*, 28, 43–61.

Department of Health (1988) *Protecting Children: a Guide for Social Workers Undertaking a Comprehensive Assessment.* London: HMSO.

Department of Health (1989) *Working Together under the Children Act.* London: HMSO.

Department of Health (1995) *Child Protection: Messages from Research.* London: HMSO.

Dobash, R.E. and Dobash, R.P. (1992) *Women, Violence and Social Change.* London: Routledge.

Dobson, R. (1997) Dealing with the devil, *The Guardian*, 8 January, 2–3.

Dominelli, L. (1988) *Anti-racist Social Work.* London: Macmillan.

Dominelli, L. (1991) *Women Across Continents: Feminist Comparative Social Policy.* Hemel Hempstead: Harvester Wheatsheaf.

Dominelli, L. and McLeod, E. (1989) *Feminist Social Work.* London: Macmillan.

Downes, D. (1994) Serious diversions: juvenile crime and justice in Europe and the lessons for Britain, *Social Work in Europe*, 1(2), 4–12.

Duncan, S. (1995) Theorizing European gender systems, *Journal of European Social Policy*, 5(4), 263–84.

Einhorn, B. (1994) *Cinderella Goes to Market.* London: Verso.

Eklund, L. (1993) The Swedish debate on sexual offences against children, *Current Sweden*, 396, 4.

Elliott, M. (ed.) (1993) *Female Sexual Abuse of Children: the Ultimate Taboo.* Harlow: Longman.

Ely, P. and Stanley, C. (1990) *Delinquency Prevention and Child Protection in France*. London: NACRO.

Esping-Andersen, G. (1990) *The Three Worlds of Welfare Capitalism*. Cambridge: Polity Press.

Esping-Andersen, G. (ed.) (1996a) *Welfare States in Transition*. London: Sage.

Esping-Andersen, G. (1996b) After the Golden Age? Welfare state dilemmas in a global economy, in G. Esping-Andersen (ed.) *Welfare States in Transition*. London: Sage.

European Commission (1990) *Childcare in the European Communities 1985–1990*. Brussels: European Commission.

European Commission (1992) *Council Recommendation on Child Care* (92/241/ EEC). Brussels: European Commission.

European Commission (1993) *Men as Carers*. Brussels: European Commission.

European Commission (1994) *European Social Policy: a Way Forward for The Union*, COM(94) 333, White Paper. Brussels: European Commission.

European Commission (1996a) *A Review of Services for Young Children in the European Union 1990–1995*. Brussels: European Commission.

European Commission (1996b) *Men as Workers in Childcare Services*. Brussels: European Commission.

European Commission (1996c) *School-age Childcare in the European Union*. Brussels: European Commission.

European Commission (undated) *Fathers, Nurseries and Childcare*. Brussels: European Commission.

European Observatory on National Family Policies (1996) *A Synthesis of National Family Policies*. York: University of York.

Falkner, G. (1996) The Maastricht Protocol on Social Policy: theory and practice, *Journal of European Social Policy*, 6(1), 1–16.

Ferge, Z. (1991) Social security systems in the new democracies of Central and Eastern Europe: past legacies and possible futures, in G.A. Cornia and S. Sipos (eds) *Children and the Transition to the Market Economy*. Aldershot: Avebury.

Ferge, Z. (1993) Social change in Eastern Europe: the prospects for children and families in Hungary, in H. Ferguson, R. Gilligan and R. Torode (eds) *Surviving Childhood Adversity*. Dublin: Social Studies Press.

Ferguson, H. (1996) The protection of children in time: child protection and the lives and deaths of children in child abuse cases in sociohistorical perspective, *Child and Family Social Work*, 1(4), 205–17.

Ferguson, H., Gilligan, R. and Torode, R. (eds) (1993) *Surviving Childhood Adversity*. Dublin: Social Studies Press.

Ferrara, M. (1996) The 'Southern model' of welfare in social Europe, *Journal of European Social Policy*, 6(1), 17–37.

Finkelhor, D. (1991) The scope of the problem, in K. Murray and D.A. Gough (eds) *Intervening in Child Sexual Abuse*. Edinburgh: Scottish Academic Press.

Finklelhor, D., Araji, S., Baron, L., Browne, A., Peters, S.D. and Wyatt, G.E. (1986) *A Sourcebook on Child Sexual Abuse*. Newbury Park, CA: Sage Publications.

Finkelhor, D., Hotaling, G., Lewis, I. and Smith, C. (1990) Sexual abuse in a national survey of adult men and women, *Child Abuse And Neglect*, 14, 19–28.

Finkelhor, D., Williams, L.M. and Burns, N. (1988) *Nursery Crimes: Sexual Abuse in Day Care*. Newbury Park, CA: Sage.

Fisher, D. (1994) Adult sex offenders: who are they? Why and how do they do it?, in T. Morrison, M. Erooga and R.C. Beckett (eds) *Sexual Offending Against Children: Assessment and Treatment of Male Abusers*. London: Routledge.

Flissing, B. (1997) Men as carers in Sweden, paper delivered at International Seminar on Men as Workers in Services for Young Children: Issues of a Mixed Gender Workforce, Thomas Coram Research Unit, Henley on Thames, 31 May.

Foley, R. (1993) Zero tolerance, *Trouble and Strife*, 27, 16–20.

Franklin, B. and Parton, N. (eds) (1991) *Social Work, the Media and Public Relations*. London: Routledge.

Frost, N. and Stein, M. (1989) *The Politics of Child Welfare*. Hemel Hempstead, England: Harvester Wheatsheaf.

Game, A. (1991) *Undoing the Social: towards a Deconstructive Sociology*. Buckingham: Open University Press.

George, M. (1996) On the agenda, *Community Care*, 18–24 April, 25.

George, V. (1996) The demand for welfare, in V. George and P. Taylor-Gooby (eds) *European Welfare Policy: Squaring the Welfare Circle*. London: Macmillan.

Giddens, A. (1990) *The Consequences of Modernity*. Stanford: Stanford University Press.

Gilligan, R. (1993) Ireland, in M. Colton and W. Hellinckx (eds) *Child Care in the EC: a Country-specific Guide to Foster Care and Residential Care*. Aldershot: Arena.

Gilroy, P. (1993) *The Black Atlantic*. London: Verso.

Ginsburg, N. (1992) *Divisions of Welfare*. London: Sage.

Ginsburg, N. (1993) Sweden: the social democratic case, in A. Cochrane and J. Clarke (eds) *Comparing Welfare States*. London: Sage.

Girodet, D. (1990) France, in A. Sale and M. Davies (eds) *Child Protection Policies and Practice in Europe*. London: NSPCC.

Golombok, S., Spencer, A. and Rutter, M. (1983) Children in lesbian and single parent households: psychosexual and psychiatric appraisal, *Journal of Child Psychology and Psychiatry*, 24, 551–72.

Gotting, U. (1994) Destruction, adjustment and innovation: social policy transformation in Eastern and Central Europe, *Journal of European Social Policy*, 4(3), 181–200.

Gould, A. (1988) *Conflict and Control in Welfare Policy*. London: Longman.

Gould, A. (1993) *Capitalist Welfare Systems: a Comparison of Japan, Britain and Sweden*. Harlow: Longman.

Gould, A. (1996) Sweden: the last bastion of welfare democracy, in V. George and P. Taylor-Gooby (eds) *European Welfare Policy: Squaring the Welfare Circle*. London: Macmillan.

Gray, S., Higgs, M. and Pringle, K. (1996) Services for people who have been sexually abused, in L. Mckie (ed.) *Researching Women's Health: Methods and Process*. London: Mark Allen Publishing.

Gray, S., Higgs, M. and Pringle, K. (1997) User-centred responses to child sexual abuse: the way forward, *Child and Family Social Work*, 2(1), 49–57.

Green, P. (1995) How the Czechs won OECD race, *The European*, 23–29 November, 19.

Grevot, A. (1996a) Welfare reform winter storm: social work on a knife edge, *Social Work in Europe*, 3(1), 53–4.

Grevot, A. (1996b) The changing role of associations in French social welfare, *Social Work in Europe*, 3(2), 5–7.

Gustafsson, S. (1994) Childcare and types of welfare states, in D. Sainsbury (ed.) *Gendering Welfare States*. London: Sage.

Hallett, C. (1995) Child abuse: an academic overview, in P. Kingston and B. Penhale (eds) *Family Violence and the Caring Professions*. London: Macmillan.

Hanks, H., Kreutzer, N. and Bielawska-Batorowicz, E. (1991) Child protection in Europe, *Community Paediatric Group Newsletter*, Autumn.

Hanks, H. and Saradjian, J. (1991) Women who abuse children sexually: characteristics of sexual abuse of children by women. *Human Systems: the Journal of Systemic Consultation and Management*, 2, 247–62.

Hantrais, L. (1995) Social policy in the European Union. London: Macmillan.

Hantrais, L. and Letablier, M.-T. (1996) Families and family policies in Europe. Harlow: Addison Wesley Longman.

Harder, M. (1997) Child protection in Denmark, in M. Harder and K. Pringle (eds) *Protecting Children in Europe: towards a New Millennium*. Aalborg: Aalborg University Press.

Harder, M. and Pringle, K. (eds) (1997) *Protecting Children in Europe: towards a New Millennium*. Aalborg: Aalborg University Press.

Hart de Ruyter, M. (1990) The Netherlands, in A. Sale and M. Davies (eds) *Child Protection Policies and Practice in Europe*. London: NSPCC.

Haughlund, E. (1997) Men as carers in Norway, paper delivered at International Seminar on Men as Workers in Services for Young Children: Issues of a Mixed Gender Workforce, Thomas Coram Research Unit, Henley on Thames, 31 May.

Hauser, R., Frick, J., Mueller, K. and Wagner, G.G. (1994) Inequality in income: a comparison of East and West Germans before reunification and during transition, *Journal of European Social Policy*, 4(4), 277–95.

Heap, K.K. (1990) Norway, in A. Sale and M. Davies (eds) *Child Protection Policies and Practice in Europe*. London: NSPCC.

Hearn, J. (1990) 'Child abuse' and men's violence, in Violence Against Children Study Group (eds), *Taking Child Abuse Seriously*. London: Unwin Hyman.

Helm, M., Pringle, K. and Taylor, R. (eds) (1993) *Surviving Sexual Abuse*. Barkingside: Barnardos.

Hetherington, R. (1996) Prevention and Education in work with children and families, in D. Batty and D. Cullen (eds) *Child Protection: the Therapeutic Option*. London: British Agencies for Adoption and Fostering.

Hetherington, R., Cooper, A., Smith, P. and Wilford, G. (1997) *Protecting Children: Messages from Europe*. Lyme Regis: Russell House Publishing.

Heward, C. (1996) Masculinities and families, in M. Mac an Ghaill (ed.) *Understanding Masculinities*. Buckingham: Open University Press.

Hill, M. (ed.) (1991) *Social Work and the European Community*. London: Jessica Kingsley Publishers.

Hill, M. and Cairns-Smith, D.A. (1995) Developing a childcare management training course for Romania, *Social Work in Europe*, 2(1), 20–7.

HMSO (1989) *Children Act 1989*. London: HMSO.

HMSO (1990) *National Health Service and Community Care Act*. London: HMSO.

Home Office (1992) *Memorandum of Good Practice on Video Recorded Interviews with Child Witnesses for Criminal Proceedings*. London: HMSO.

Hooper, C. (1992) *Mothers Surviving Child Sexual Abuse*. London: Routledge.

Hudson, A. (1992) The child sexual abuse industry and gender relations in social work, in M. Langan and L. Day (eds) *Women, Oppression and Social Work: Issues in Anti-discriminatory Practice*. London: Routledge.

Hutton, W. (1996) *The State We're In*. London: Jonathan Cape.

Hutz, P. (1990) West Germany, in A. Sale and M. Davies (eds) *Child Protection Policies and Practice in Europe*. London: NSPCC.

Jackson, V. (1996) *Racism and Child Protection*. London: Cassell.

Jonsson, E. (1997) *Intervention bei sexuellem Missbrauch*. Frankfurt am Main: Peter Lang.

Jones, L., Pringle, K. and Zaccheo, M.A. (1988) Can young people change the care system?, *Social Work Today*, 19(51), 14–15.

Junger-Tas, J. (1992) Stategies for dealing with delinquents: a European perpective, in R. Bullock (ed.) *Problem Adolescents: an International View*. London: Whiting and Birch.

Kangas, O. (1994) The merging of welfare state models? Past and present trends in Finnish and Swedish social policy, *Journal of European Social Policy*, 4(2), 79–94.

Katrougalos, G.S. (1996) The South European welfare model: the Greek welfare state, in search of an identity, *Journal of European Social Policy*, 6(1), 39–60.

Kelly, L. (1991) Unspeakable acts: women who abuse, *Trouble And Strife*, 21, 13–20.

Kelly, L. (1996) When does the speaking profit us? Reflections on the challenges of developing feminist perspectives on abuse and violence by women, in M. Hester, L. Kelly and J. Radford (eds) *Women, Violence and Male Power*. Buckingham: Open University Press.

Kelly, L., Regan, L. and Burton, S. (1991) *An Exploratory Study of the Prevalence of Sexual Abuse in a Sample of 16–21 Year-Olds*. London: Polytechnic of North London.

Kemecsei, E. (1995) The family under the impact of change in Hungary, *Social Work in Europe*, 2(1), 30–5.

Kemppainen, M. (1994) Finland: trends in Finnish child welfare, in M. Gottesman (ed.) *Recent Changes and New Trends in Extrafamilial Child Care: an International Perspective*. London: Whiting and Birch.

Kennedy, M. and Kelly, L. (eds) (1992) Special issue on abuse and children with disabilities, *Child Abuse Review*, 1(3).

Kidd, L. and Pringle, K. (1988) The politics of child sexual abuse, *Social Work Today*, 20(3), 14–15.

Kurczewski, J. (1994) Privatizing the Polish family, in M. McLean and J. Kurczewski (eds) *Families, Politics and the Law*. Oxford: Clarendon Press.

Kwak, A. (1994) Children's rights and adoption, in M. McLean and J. Kurczewski (eds) *Families, Politics and the Law*. Oxford: Clarendon Press.

Lane, J.-E. and Ersson, S.O. (1996) *European Politics: an Introduction*. London: Sage.

Langan, M. (1993) New directions in social work, in J. Clarke (ed.) *A Crisis in Care*. London: Sage.

Langan, M. and Ostner, I. (1991) Gender and welfare: towards a comparative framework, in G. Room (ed.) *Towards a European Welfare State*. Bath: SAUS.

Lavalette, M. and Pratt, A. (eds) (1996) *Social Policy: a Conceptual and Theoretical Introduction*. London: Sage.

Laws, S. (1994) Un-valued families, *Trouble and Strife*, 28, 5–11.

Leibfried, S. (1993) Towards a European welfare state, in C. Jones (ed.) *New Perspectives on the Welfare State in Europe*. London: Routledge.

Leibfried, S. (1994) The social dimension of the European Union: en route to positively joint sovereignty?, *Journal of European Social Policy*, 4(4), 239–62.

Leira, A. (1994) Combining work and family: working mothers in Scandinavia and the European Community, in P. Brown and R. Crompton (eds) *Economic Restructuring and Social Exclusion*. London: UCL Press.

Leven, B. (1994) The status of women and Poland's transition to a market economy, in N. Aslanbeigu, S. Pressman and G. Summerfield (eds) *Women in the Age of Economic Transformation: Gender Impact of Reform in Post-socialist and Developing Countries*. London: Routledge.

Levitas, R. (1996) The concept of social exclusion and the new Durkheimian hegemony, *Critical Social Policy*, 16(1), 5–20.

Lewis, J. (ed.) (1993) *Women and Social Policies in Europe: Work, Family and the State*. Aldershot: Edward Elgar Publishing.

Lewis, B. and Schnapper, D. (eds) (1994) *Muslims in Europe*. London: Pinter Publishers.

Lister, P.G. (1995) Child protection work in Scotland, in C. Birks (ed.) *Child Abuse in Europe (Volume 1)*. Nurnberg: Emwe-Verlag.

Logan, J., Kershaw, S., Karban, K., Mills, S., Trotter, J. and Sinclair, M. (1996) *Confronting Prejudice: Lesbian and Gay Issues in Social Work Education*. Aldershot: Arena.

Lorenz, W. (1994) *Social Work in a Changing Europe*. London: Routledge.

Lorenz, W. (1995) What ways forward for welfare agencies? European trends in youth services, *Social Work in Europe*, 2(2), 3–7.

Lupton, C. and Gillespie, T. (eds) (1994) *Working with Violence*. London: Macmillan.

McCollum, H., Kelly, L. and Radford, J. (1994) Wars against women, *Trouble and Strife*, 28, 12–18.

McLaughlin, E. (1993) Ireland: Catholic corporatism, in A. Cochrane and J. Clarke (eds) *Comparing Welfare States*. London: Sage.

McLean, M. and Kurczewski, J. (eds) (1994a) *Families, Politics and the Law*. Oxford: Clarendon Press.

McLean, M. and Kurczewski, J. (1994b) The issues in context, in M. McLean and J. Kurczewski (eds) *Families, Politics and the Law*. Oxford: Clarendon Press.

MacLeod, M. and Saraga, E. (1988) Challenging the orthodoxy: towards a feminist theory and practice, *Feminist Review*, 28, 16–55.

MacLeod, M. and Saraga, E. (1991) Clearing a path through the undergrowth: a feminist reading of recent literature on child sexual abuse, in P. Carter, T. Jeffs and M.K. Smith (eds) *Social Work and Social Welfare Yearbook: 3.* Buckingham: Open University Press.

Macey, M. and Moxon, E. (1996) An examination of anti-racist and anti-oppressive theory and practice in social work education, *British Journal of Social Work*, 26, 297–314.

Madge, N. (1994) *Children and Residential Care in Europe.* London: National Children's Bureau.

Madge, N. and Attridge, K. (1996) Children and families, in B. Mundy and P. Ely (eds) *Social Care in Europe.* Hemel Hempstead: Prentice Hall Europe.

Makkai, T. (1994) Social policy and gender in Eastern Europe, in D. Sainsbury (ed.) *Gendering Welfare States.* London: Sage.

Mansson, S.-A., Back-Wicklund, M. and Plantin, L. (1996) Report of Joint Research Project on Fatherhood, Universities of Goteborg and Sunderland, unpublished. University of Goteborg.

Marneffe, C., Boemans, E. and Lampoo, A. (1990) Belgium, in A. Sale and M. Davies (eds) *Child Protection Policies and Practice in Europe.* London: NSPCC.

Marshall, B.L. (1994) *Engendering Modernity: Feminism, Social Theory and Social Change.* Cambridge: Polity.

Marsiglio, W. (1995) *Fatherhood: Contemporary Theory, Research, and Social Policy.* Thousand Oaks, CA: Sage.

Masters, C. (1997) *The European*, 25 September–1 October 1997, 7.

Meleady, C. (1997) Men as carers: Sheffield Children's Centre, paper delivered at International Seminar on Men as Workers in Services for Young Children: Issues of a Mixed Gender Workforce, Thomas Coram Research Unit, Henley on Thames, 31 May.

Melhbye, J. (1993) Denmark, in M. Colton and W. Hellinckx (eds) *Child Care in the EC: a Country-specific Guide to Foster Care and Residential Care.* Aldershot: Arena.

Merrick, J. (1990) Denmark, in A. Sale and M. Davies (eds) *Child Protection Policies and Practice in Europe.* London: NSPCC.

Millar, J. (1994) State, family and personal responsibility: the changing balance for lone mothers in the United Kingdom, *Feminist Review*, 48, 24–39.

Millard, P. (1997) The influence of the Catholic hierarchy in Poland, 1989–96, *Journal of European Social Policy*, 7(2), 83–100.

Mitchell, M. and Russell, D. (1994) Race, citizenship and 'Fortress Europe', in P. Brown and R. Crompton (eds) *Economic Restructuring and Social Exclusion.* London: UCL Press.

Modrzejewska, P. (1990) Poland, in A. Sale and M. Davies (eds) *Child Protection Policies and Practice in Europe.* London: NSPCC.

Mullender, A. and Morley, R. (eds) (1994) *Children Living with Domestic Violence: Putting Men's Abuse of Women on the Child Care Agenda.* London: Whiting and Birch.

Munday, B. (1996a) Introduction: definitions and comparisons in Europe, in B. Mundy and P. Ely (eds) *Social Care in Europe.* Hemel Hempstead: Prentice Hall Europe.

Munday, B. (1996b) Social care in the member states of the European Union: contexts and overview, in B. Mundy and P. Ely (eds) *Social Care in Europe.* Hemel Hempstead: Prentice Hall Europe.

Mundy, B. and Ely, P. (eds) (1996) *Social Care in Europe.* Hemel Hempstead: Prentice Hall Europe.

Naudin, T. and Clarke, H. (1996) Bending rules in race to EMU, *The European,* 7–13 November, 19.

Nelson, S. (1987) *Incest: Fact or Myth.* Edinburgh: Strathmullion.

Nolan, B. and Whelan, C.T. (1996) Measuring poverty using income and deprivation indicators: alternative approaches, *Journal of European Social Policy,* 6(3), 225–40.

Novak, T. (1997) Hounding delinquents: the introduction of the Jobseeker's Allowance, *Critical Social Policy,* 17(1), 99–109.

O'Higgins, K. (1993) Surviving separation: traveller children in substitute care, in H. Ferguson, R. Gilligan and R. Torode (eds) *Surviving Childhood Adversity.* Dublin: Social Studies Press.

O'Riley, D. (1997) *The European,* 27 March–2 April, 10.

Otithearnaith, C. (1990) The Republic of Ireland, in A. Sale and M. Davies (eds) *Child Protection Policies and Practice in Europe.* London: NSPCC.

Parton, N. (1991) *Governing the Family: Child Care, Child Protection and the State.* London: Macmillan.

Parton, N. (ed.) (1996a) *Social Theory, Social Change and Social Work.* London: Routledge.

Parton, N. (1996b) Social work, risk and the blaming system, in N. Parton (ed.) *Social Theory, Social Change and Social Work.* London: Routledge.

Parton, N. (1996c) Child protection, family support and social work, *Child and Family Social Work,* 1(1), 3–11.

Parton, N. (ed.) (1997) *Child Protection and Family Support.* London: Routledge.

Parton, N., Thorpe, O. and Wattam, C. (1997) *Child Protection: Risk and the Moral Order.* London: Macmillan.

Patterson, C.J. (1992) Children of lesbian and gay parents, *Child Development,* 63, 1025–42.

Paugam, S. (1996) Poverty and social disqualification: a comparative analysis of cumulative social disadvantage in Europe, *Journal of European Social Policy,* 6(4), 287–303.

Paulischin, H. (1990) Austria, in A. Sale and M. Davies (eds) *Child Protection Policies and Practice in Europe.* London: NSPCC.

Penna, S. and O'Brien, M. (1996) Postmodernism and social policy: a small step forwards?, *Journal of Social Policy,* 25(1), 39–61.

Pestoff, V. (ed.) (1995) *Reforming Social Services in Central and Eastern Europe – an Eleven Nation Overview.* Warsaw and Krakow: Friedrich Ebert Stiftung and Krakow Academy of Economics.

Pitts, J. (1990) *Working with Young Offenders.* London: Macmillan.

Pitts, J. (1994) European juvenile justice 1994: Britain goes into reverse, *Social Work in Europe,* 1(1), 33–5.

Pitts, J. (1995) Public issues and private troubles: a tale of two cities, *Social Work in Europe,* 2(1), 3–11.

Planicka, H. (1995) Child abuse in Austria, in C. Birks (ed.) *Child Abuse in Europe (Volume 1)*. Nurnberg: Emwe-Verlag.

Plantin, L. and Mansson, S.-A. (1997) Fatherhood and masculinities, unpublished report of the Joint Fatherhood Research Project, Universities of Goteborg and Sunderland.

Pochet, P., Antoons, J., Barbier, C. and Moro, E. (1996a) European briefing, *Journal of European Social Policy*, 6(1), 61–8.

Pochet, P., Barbier, C., Moro, E., Raulier, A., Turloot, L. and Vernay, C. (1996b) European briefing, *Journal of European Social Policy*, 6(2), 163–8.

Pringle, K. (1990) *Managing to Survive*. Barkingside: Barnardos.

Pringle, K. (1992) Child sexual abuse perpetrated by welfare personnel and the problem of men, *Critical Social Policy*, 36, 4–19.

Pringle, K. (1993) Gender issues in child sexual abuse committed by foster carers: a case study for the welfare services?, in H. Ferguson, R. Gilligan and R. Torode (eds) *Surviving Childhood Adversity*. Dublin: Social Studies Press.

Pringle, K. (1994) The problem of men revisited, *Working With Men*, 2, 5–8.

Pringle, K. (1995) *Men, Masculinities and Social Welfare*. London: UCL Press.

Pringle, K. (1996a) Challenging oppressions, reconstructing masculinities, in T. Lloyd and T. Wood (eds) *What Next for Men?* London: Working With Men.

Pringle, K. (1996b) Protecting children against sexual abuse: a third way?, paper presented at conference on Human Services In Crisis: National and International Issues, Fitzwilliam College, University of Cambridge, September.

Pringle, K. (1996c) Summary of findings of University of Sunderland/University of Goteborg Joint Fatherhood Research Project, Unpublished, Centre for Social Research and Practice, University of Sunderland.

Pringle, K. (1997a) Protecting children in England and Wales, in M. Harder and K. Pringle (eds) *Protecting Children in Europe: towards a New Millennium*. Aalborg: Aalborg University Press.

Pringle, K. (1997b) Men in childcare, in J. Popay, J. Hearn and J. Edwards (eds) *Men, Gender Divisions and Welfare*. London: Routledge.

Pringle, K. (1997c) Men in social work: the double-edge, in A. Christie (ed.) *Men, Masculinities and Social Work*. London: Macmillan.

Pringle, K. (1997d) Report on Joint Fatherhood Research Project, Universities of Goteborg and Sunderland, unpublished, University of Sunderland.

Pringle, K. (1997e) Men as workers in professional childcare settings: an anti-oppressive practice framework, paper delivered at International Seminar on Men as Workers in Services for Young Children: Issues of a Mixed Gender Workforce, Thomas Coram Research Unit, Henley on Thames, 31 May.

Pringle, K. and Harder, M. (1997) Conclusion: transnational comparisons and future trajectories, in M. Harder and K. Pringle (eds) *Protecting Children in Europe: towards a New Millennium*. Aaalborg: Aalborg University Press.

Pronay, C., Paulischin, H. and Gruber, C. (1995) Child abuse in Austria, in C. Birks (ed.) *Child Abuse in Europe (Volume 1)*. Nurnberg: Emwe-Verlag.

Qvortrup, J. (1994) Childhood matters: an introduction, in J. Qvortrup, M. Bardy, G. Sgritta and H. Wintersberger (eds) *Childhood Matters: Social Theory, Practice and Politics*. Aldershot: Avebury.

Qvortrup, J., Bardy, M., Sgritta, G. and Wintersberger, H. (eds) *Childhood Matters: Social Theory, Practice and Politics*. Aldershot: Avebury.

Rai, S., Pilkington, H. and Phizaclea, A. (eds) (1992) *Women in the Face of Change: the Soviet Union, Eastern Europe and China*. London: Routledge.

Ramprakash, D. (1994) Poverty in the countries of the European Union: a synthesis of Eurostat's statistical research on poverty, *Journal of European Social Policy*, 4(2), 117–28.

Ray, L. (1994) The collapse of Soviet socialism: legitimation, regulation, and the new class, in P. Brown and R. Crompton (eds) *Economic Restructuring and Social Exclusion*. London: UCL Press.

Reder, P., Duncan, S. and Gray, M. (1993) *Beyond Blame: Child Abuse Tragedies Revisited*. London: Routledge.

Rex, J. (1992) Race and ethnicity in Europe, in J. Bailey (ed.) *Social Europe*. Harlow: Longman.

Rootes, C. and Davis, H. (1994) *Social Change and Political Transformation*. London: UCL Press.

Ruxton, S. (1991) What's he doing at the family centre? The dilemmas of men who care for children, MA Dissertation, Polytechnic of North London.

Ruxton, S. (1996) *Children in Europe*. London: NCH Action For Children.

Ruxton, S. (1997) Children in Europe – policies and prospects, *Social Work in Europe*, 4(1), 17–23.

Sainsbury, D. (ed.) (1994) *Gendering Welfare States*. London: Sage.

Sale, A. and Davies, M. (eds) (1990) *Child Protection Policies and Practice in Europe*. London: NSPCC.

Salond, I. (1994) The zero tolerance campaign, *Working with Men*, 1, 8–9.

Saraceno, C. and Negri, N. (1994) The changing Italian welfare state, *Journal of European Social Policy*, 4(1), 19–34.

Saraga, E. (1993) The abuse of children, in R. Dallos and E. Mclaughlin (eds) *Social Problems and the Family*. London: Sage Publications.

Sarnecki, J. (1989) *Juvenile Delinquency in Sweden: an Overview*. Stockholm: National Council for Crime Prevention.

Schweie, K. (1994) Labour market, welfare state and family institutions: the links to mothers' poverty risks, *Journal of European Social Policy*, 4(3), 201–24.

Seifert, R. (1996) The second front: the logic of sexual violence in wars, *Women's Studies International Forum*, 19(1/2), 35–43.

Siaroff, A. (1994) Work, welfare and gender equality: a new typology, in D. Sainsbury (ed.) *Gendering Welfare States*. London: Sage.

Silburn, L. (1994) A social model in a medical world, in J. Swain, V. Finkelstein, S. French and M. Oliver (eds) *Disabling Barriers – Enabling Environments*. London: Sage.

Sipos, S. (1991) Current and structural problems affecting children in Central and Eastern Europe, in G.A. Cornia and S. Sipos (eds) *Children and the Transition to the Market Economy*. Aldershot: Avebury.

Smart, V. (1996) *The European*, 22–28 August, 7.

Smith, G. (1994) Parent, partner, protector: conflicting role demands for mothers of sexually abused children, in T. Morrison, M. Erooga and R. Beckett (eds) *Sexual Offending Against Children: Assessment and Treatment of Male Abusers*. London: Routledge.

Smith, G. (1995) *The Protector's Handbook*. London: The Women's Press.

Smith, G. (1996) Reassessing protectiveness, in D. Batty and D. Cullen (eds) *Child Protection: The Therapeutic Option*. London: British Agencies for Adoption and Fostering.

Sobiech, R. (1994) The social problem of child abuse in Poland: the conflict between privacy and control, in M. McLean and J. Kurczewski (eds) *Families, Politics and the Law*. Oxford: Clarendon Press.

Solomon, R. (1994) East meets West: developing a community fostering service in Warsaw, *Social Work in Europe*, 1(1), 11–20.

Spano, A. (1996) The economic and cultural dimensions of poverty in Italy: the implications for social policy, *Social Work in Europe*, 3(2), 18–24.

Speiss, G. (1994) Diverting away from custody, diverting away from trial – how far can we go? The German experience, *Social Work in Europe*, 1(2), 28–38.

Sperling, L. and Bretherton, C. (1996) Women's policy networks and the European Union, *Women's Studies International Forum*, 19(3), 303–14.

Spicker, P. (1991) Solidarity, in G. Room (ed.) *Towards a European Welfare State*. Bath: SAUS.

Spicker, P. (1995) Inserting the excluded: the impact of the Revenu Minimum d'Insertion on poverty in France, *Social Work in Europe*, 2(2), 8–14.

Standing, G. (1996) Social protection in Central and Eastern Europe: a tale of slipping anchors and torn safety nets, in G. Esping-Andersen (ed.) *Welfare States in Transition*. London: Sage.

Stelmaszuck, Z.W. (1994) Fostering in Poland, *Social Work in Europe*, 1(2), 39–41.

Stephens, J.D. (1996) The Scandinavian welfare states: achievements, crisis and prospects, in G. Esping-Andersen (ed.) *Welfare States in Transition*. London: Sage.

Swithinbank, A. (1996) The European Union and social care, in B. Mundy and P. Ely (eds) *Social Care in Europe*. Hemel Hempstead: Prentice Hall Europe.

Szlezak, A. (1994) Allocating resources at times of crisis: divorce and separation in Poland, in M. McLean and J. Kurczewski (eds) *Families, Politics and the Law*. Oxford: Clarendon Press.

Thompson, N. (1993) *Anti-discrimimatory Practice*. London: Macmillan.

Thorpe, D. (1994) *Evaluating Child Protection*. Buckingham: Open University Press.

Tuomisto, R. and Vuori-Karvia, E. (1997) Child protection in Finland, in M. Harder and K. Pringle (eds) *Protecting Children in Europe: towards a New Millennium*. Aalborg: Aalborg University Press.

Vassalli, A. (1990) Italy, in A. Sale and M. Davies (eds) *Child Protection Policies and Practice in Europe*. London: NSPCC.

Van Montfoort, A. (1993) The protection of children in the Netherlands: between justice and welfare, in H. Ferguson, R. Gilligan and R. Torode (eds) *Surviving Childhood Adversity*. Dublin: Social Studies Press.

Vecchiato, T. (1993) Italy, in M. Colton and W. Hellinckx (eds) *Child Care in the EC: a Country-specific Guide to Foster Care and Residential Care.* Aldershot: Arena.

Vecernik, J. (1996) Incomes in Central Europe: distributions, patterns and perceptions, *Journal of European Social Policy*, 6(2), 101–22.

Vedder, P., Bonwer, E. and Pels, T. (1996) *Multicultural Child Care.* Clevedon: Multicultural Matters Ltd.

Vedel-Petersen, J. (1991) Families with young children – the situation in Denmark, in M. Hill (ed.) *Social Work and the European Community*, London: Jessica Kingsley Publications.

Von Strandmann, H.P. (1994) The new social work in East Germany, *Social Work in Europe*, 1(3), 4–9.

Walker, A. and Guillemand, A. (eds) (1993) *Older People in Europe: Social and Economic Policies – the 1993 Report of the European Observatory.* Brussels: European Commission.

Walker, M.A. (1988) The court disposal of young males, by race in London in 1983, *British Journal of Criminology*, 28, 441–51.

Wallace, C. (1995) Young people and families in Poland: changing times, changing dependencies?, *Journal of European Social Policy*, 5(2), 97–109.

Wattam, C. (1997) Can filtering processes be rationalised? In N. Parton (ed.) *Child Protection and Family Support.* London: Routledge.

Weclawowicz, G. (1996) *Contemporary Poland: Space and Society.* London: UCL Press.

Will, D. (1989) Feminism, child sexual abuse, and the (long overdue) demise of systems mysticism, *Context*, 9, 12–15.

Williams, F. (1993) Gender, 'race' and class in British welfare policy, in A. Cochrane and J. Clarke (eds) *Comparing Welfare States.* London: Sage.

Wilson, M. (1993) The German welfare state: a conservative regime in crisis, in A. Cochrane and J. Clarke (eds) *Comparing Welfare States.* London: Sage.

Wilson, V. (1996) People with disabilities, in B. Mundy and P. Ely (eds) *Social Care in Europe.* Hemel Hempstead: Prentice Hall Europe.

Windebank, J. (1996) To what extent can social policy challenge the dominant ideology of mothering? A cross-national comparison of Sweden, France and Britain, *Journal of European Social Policy*, 6(2), 147–61.

Wise, M. and Gibb, R. (1993) *Single Market to Social Europe: the European Community in the 1990s.* London: Longman.

Witte, R. (1995) Racist violence in Western Europe, *New Community*, 21(4), 489–500.

Wustendorfer, W. (1995) Violence against children in Germany, in C. Birks (ed.) *Child Abuse in Europe (Volume 1).* Nurnberg: Emwe-Verlag.

Zorc, D. (1994) Slovene youth in a period of transition from the socialist system to a modern European state, *Social Work in Europe*, 1(3), 14–17.

INDEX